49 Years

in the 49th State

A wildlife biologist reflects on nearly
50 years of adventure and exploration in Alaska

Patrick Valkenburg

PUBLICATION
CONSULTANT
Je Believe In The Power Of Author

PO Box 221974 Anchorage, Alaska 99522-1974
books@publicationconsultants.com www.publicationconsultants.com

ISBN Number Soft Cover: 978-1-63747-061-9
ISBN Number Hard Cover: 978-1-63747-082-4
eBook ISBN Number: 9978-1-63747-062-6

Library of Congress Catalog Card Number: 2021921217

Manufactured in the United States of America

Foreword

I've known Pat Valkenburg for most of the 49 years he writes about in this book. We both worked for the Wildlife Division within the Alaska Department of Fish & Game during much of that time. Looking back, those were the "Golden Years" at ADF&G. We had some of the best wildlife biologists in the world on our staff. It was almost like being on an All-Star team. Pat fit right in.

Pat came to Alaska in his early twenties, already a licensed pilot. That license and his adventurous spirit would come to define Pat over the next 49 years. He was seemingly always flying. If he wasn't in the air, he had either just returned from a trip or was planning the next one. Pat got more use out of his pilot's license than anyone I know. It was the best investment he ever made.

Pat has an upbeat personality and is always on the go; looking for the next adventure, whether that be on an ADF&G project or on his own time. I was lucky enough to share a few of those trips. He never hides from his own foibles. In fact, he often regales groups of friends with his own mistakes. Pat doesn't think small. He has always been willing to tackle big projects, even without any guarantee of success. You will read about several of them in the following pages.

When Pat is hot on the trail of a new adventure, he gives little thought to creature comforts. Unlike many of his peers, Pat is not discouraged by bad weather, failed equipment, hunger, or fatigue. He's willing to eat leaves and sleep on a rock if it means he will have fun and/or learn something new.

I've always been impressed by Pat's innate curiosity. He wants to know how things work, whether it be the engine in his plane or some complex biological system. His mind is that of a true scientist. As we both enter our 70s, Pat is still seeking those answers. Combined with

Foreword

his natural curiosity are a great depth of knowledge on a wide range of subjects and the ability to clearly recall arcane facts first learned decades ago. This combination of mental assets has made for some stimulating conversations over a beer or two around the evening fire. Pat's book contains the best of personal adventure, including some hunting, trapping, wildlife biology, aviation, and a curious mind. The pacing is fast. There is a new adventure every few pages, and you will come to the end before you are ready to be done.

- Randy Zarnke

Introduction

After decades of writing technical scientific articles and reports on caribou and other species, I have gradually come to the conclusion that, although technical writing is important, much of the effort wildlife biologists put into it is wasted. Technical scientific articles about wildlife management issues are read by a minuscule number of people and many of the articles are irrelevant to conservation or practical wildlife management. Wildlife management is generally not rocket-science (although there are some highly sophisticated technical aspects to it) and it is much more enjoyable than the vast majority of the boring technical articles make it out to be.

This book is really my first attempt to try to blend the fun of wildlife management with some of the biological discoveries and exciting projects I have been involved in over my 49 years in Alaska. I also tried to retell some of the things I heard from experienced people that I met in Alaska and northern Canada who have lived close to the land. Most of the experiences I had and people I met were while I was working directly for, or as a contractor with, the Alaska Department of Fish and Game (ADF&G). Some were while I worked as a private contractor for the Wildlife Conservation Society (WCS) in Alaska and Canada. I have also added some unique experiences I had on some hunting trips where they fit the context of individual chapters. Hunting, caribou research, and flying have been a big part of my life in Alaska, but if I had included chapters on those topics, they would have become much too long and overwhelmed the book. I'll consider writing up those subjects separately in the future.

Many of the ideas and discoveries I mention are not mine, but I have included them mostly because: a) they have influenced my thinking, b) are important but weren't adequately written up, or c) they haven't received enough attention, in my opinion. I have tried to give credit where credit is due. If I have neglected to give adequate credit, I apologize because any omissions were not intentional.

When I graduated with a Master's degree in Wildlife Management, I left the university with a decided bias. I had some outstanding and creative professors and I believed that universities were the center of the universe of knowledge that is needed for wildlife conservation and management. Fortunately, my first supervisor at ADF&G, Jim Davis, was a very good researcher, an excellent hand in the field, and a practical wildlife manager. More than anyone else, Jim made me realize a university education is just a start. After a few years, it also dawned on me most of the professors who taught wildlife management and conservation had never practiced it. This was reinforced by Dr. Samuel Harbo, who was one of my mentors at the University of Alaska. He had the opinion that university professors who taught Wildlife Management should not be hired until they spent many years working for a management agency.

After a career of actively working in the field in Alaska, Canada, and the Pacific Northwest, I now realize most of the knowledge needed for wildlife conservation and management resides with the state and provincial wildlife management agencies and to some extent with the federal agencies, especially those that have clear responsibilities for managing migratory birds and marine mammals. Little of this vast agency-held knowledge is adequately written up, either in technical articles or for public consumption. Neither is it adequately taught to students. Management biologists generally work hard on urgent everyday issues. Few have the time to write up what they know. Many are not good writers, most can't make writing a priority because they are too busy, and the demands of technical writing in the arcane language of scientific journals often seem absurd to practical biologists.

Unfortunately, over time, government agencies are becoming more and more bureaucratic, which makes it increasingly difficult to attract motivated goal-oriented achievers. Unless something is done to counteract the tendency for bureaucracies to grow, our wildlife resources will be managed by less and less competent people. Some competent people (those who are tolerant of bureaucracy or who have figured out how to survive and ignore it) will remain, but they will be too few. There needs to be a major and conscious effort to reduce the bureaucracy, including unnecessary administration and training, overblown concerns about safety, risk management, and liability, and less emphasis on time accounting, hazard pay, overtime, and the 8:00-5:00 mentality.

It also took me many years to discover that much of the valuable knowledge about wildlife also resides with keen observers who are interested in wildlife and animals but have no academic training as biologists. Many of these people, especially Native people, are often reticent to share their knowledge because they are sometimes embarrassed by their lack of formal education. I also include in this group many of the wildlife survey pilots I have had the opportunity to work with, as well as some trappers, guides, and birders. There is always the problem of sorting the reliable information from speculation and mythology, but ignoring the observations and opinions of untrained people results in dismissing a great deal of valuable knowledge. With patience and consideration, there is a lot to be learned by listening. That is the reason why former Alaskan Governor Jay Hammond strongly and successfully advocated for setting up the Board of Fish and Game (now the Board of Fish and the Board of Game) and the local state Advisory Committees that provide input to the boards. Alaska is an unusually good repository of popular knowledge about wildlife because of its abundance and variety of wildlife. Wild country attracts people with a strong interest in wildlife, and it takes interest to generate knowledge.

I feel lucky to have come to Alaska when I did. If I had not been offered a summer job by Audrey Magoun (my girlfriend and future wife) in 1972, I probably would not have come when I did. The timing of my arrival in Alaska was fortuitous. Although it was a period of rapid change for the state, it was also a period of great opportunity for an aspiring wildlife biologist. Very little was known about the ecological relationships of most animals, but the technology of using radio-collars had just arrived when I went to work for ADF&G. The fact that I also knew how to fly provided me with many opportunities to work frequently and economically in the most remote portions of the state. During the 1990s, partly because of luck, I essentially became the statewide caribou research biologist for ADF&G. I worked on all the caribou herds in Alaska except for the Kenai, Adak, and Denali herds. I also worked on several of the state's predator control programs from the 1980s through 2013, so I got to see firsthand how these, often controversial, programs worked or didn't work. I retired from ADF&G in 2003 to work on wolverine projects in Canada and to start my own flying business, specializing in wildlife surveys. I continued to work throughout Alaska, including Southeast Alaska, where I hadn't spent much time previously. In all, it was a phenomenal opportunity to see most of the state of Alaska and its diversity of wildlife.

Many of the stories and experiences I talk about in the book are not directly related to wildlife biology or management, but involve travel. Alaska and northern Canada are huge areas and extensive travel is necessary to get anything done. Most of this travel involves flying, and anytime one is flying, weather is a major concern. So, many of my stories are about weather and its influence on wildlife. Together, wildlife and weather make Alaska a very exciting place to live.

I tried to be true to the facts in the stories in this book and have checked many of them with my colleagues, my notes, diaries, and flight logs, and in unpublished and published documents. I kept a diary for about the first six years in Alaska and then sporadically thereafter. However, many of the stories I am relating from memory, and human memory is fallible. Some of the precise details might not be correct but the stories are true.

The course of one's life is determined to a large degree by random events and opportunities. I was born in South Africa and moved to the

U.S. with my parents when I was 10. If my parents had decided not to leave South Africa in 1960, I'm sure my life would have turned out quite differently. If my father had not been a well-educated engineer who was able to afford to send me to a university, things might have turned out differently as well. Then, if I had not been invited to come to Alaska by Audrey to work as her field assistant, my arrival in Alaska would certainly have been delayed. After that, I can point to just two critical choices I made to end up with my career in Alaska. My advice to young people is to be prepared for opportunities and be brave about making choices. If you are interested in wildlife and the outdoors, Alaska is full of opportunities, especially for people who are interested in learning to fly. Alaska still gives me a feeling of wonder and freedom that I just don't find anywhere else. The state is also full of interesting, eccentric, self-reliant, exceptionally competent, and often under-appreciated people. These individuals are often reclusive and can be found anywhere one travels in the state. They also make Alaska a very exciting place to be. The state has changed a lot in the 49 years I have known it, but it is still "The Last Best Place."

- The Author

Acknowledgments

I'd like to thank my wife Audrey most of all. She encouraged me to write this book. We have been friends, colleagues, companions in many adventures, and lovers for about 50 years. She is a better and more creative wildlife biologist than I will ever be. I'd also like to thank my son Toby and daughter-in-law Michelle, who are both now also professionals in aviation. Their counsel and advice are always valuable to me.

I'd like to thank all of the many colleagues I worked with at the Alaska Department of Fish and Game, U.S. Fish and Wildlife Service, U.S. Bureau of Land Management, National Park Service, University of Alaska, Yukon Wildlife Branch, Manitoba Department of Conservation, Newfoundland and Labrador Department of Environment and Conservation, Alaska Wildlife Troopers, Oregon Department of Fish and Wildlife, and Russian Academy of Sciences. These people and organizations are all part of a large community of professionals who are, above all, dedicated to wildlife management and conservation. Their cooperation on many different projects was invaluable. I'm sure I have used many of their ideas without giving adequate credit, but it is only because I liked the ideas.

I'd like to also thank the many pilots, flight instructors, and mechanics I worked with over the years. They not only made most of the field work possible, but also shared freely their vast knowledge of aircraft, safe flying practices, and wildlife. I'd like to thank a diverse group of people who contributed much to my general knowledge about Alaska, flying, boating, methods of getting things done in the arctic, geology, and wildlife in Alaska. These people particularly include Bob Ahgook, Anne and Jess Bachner, Gary Bamford, Dave Benitz, Tony Bernhardt, Michio Hoshino, Sydney Huntington, Don Kirk, Tina Laird, Guy Moyer, Simon Paneak, Earl Pilgrim, Jim Smith, Bill Waugaman, Lucky Egrass, O.J. Smith, and Wade Washke. I'm sure there are many others who deserve to be mentioned.

Acknowledgments

I am particularly indebted to Randy Zarnke who encouraged me to write a book, provided an example by writing several of his own books, and gave me all the help I needed to get this one done. Randy has also made a singular contribution to preserving the history of Alaska by working through the Alaska Trappers Association History Project to conduct interviews with exceptional Alaskans of all kinds. Justin Maple, editor of the Alaska Trapper, donated much of his valuable time to the Alaska Trappers Association and its history project. He prepared the maps for this book.

Tim Osborne edited a first draft of the book, provided some pictures taken during our trips and our work together, and reminded me of several things I should have included. Tim's boundless enthusiasm and scientific curiosity were always an inspiration.

William Brophy donated his professional editing skills to the final draft and greatly improved the book's readability. He also made me realize that a career of technical writing leads to bad habits in popular writing.

Ryan Ragan designed this book and the other books supported by the Alaska Trappers Association. His talent in creative book design is greatly appreciated.

Chapter 1

North Slope and Brooks Range Adventures

North to Alaska

I arrived in Alaska on May 25th, 1972 at age 21 to take a summer job as a field assistant on a study of the scavenging activities of arctic carnivores. The job was offered to me by Audrey Magoun who I met in Maine during 1969. Audrey was a year ahead of me in the Wildlife Management program at the University of Maine and she was only the third female student in the School of Forestry and Wildlife. We had been friends for several years and then fell in love just before she left to go to Alaska.

The summer job in Alaska was supposed to start on May 20th, but I still had some finals to take at the University of Maine, where I was completing my Bachelor's degree. I had taken a couple of the finals early so I could get away as soon as possible, but I was so excited about the trip to Alaska and the prospect of spending the summer in the Brooks Range with Audrey that my remaining final exams had become a low priority. I'm sure my final grades suffered as a result. The trip from Bangor, Maine to the Brooks Range was an adventure in itself, especially when viewed from a historical perspective. In the early 1970s, before there were any mileage programs with airlines, most airlines offered "Student Standby" fares that were less than half price. I flew from Bangor to JFK on Eastern Airlines for about $50 and then transferred to Pan-American for the direct flight from JFK to Fairbanks for $125. Pan-Am had recently started direct flights from New York to Tokyo in Boeing 707s but the planes didn't quite have enough fuel to fly non-stop, so they landed in Fairbanks to refuel.

There were just a few seats left on the Pan-Am flight and the connection was tight, so I heaved a big sigh of relief when I finally boarded. I do remember a first-class passenger who got on right after I did. He was carrying a rifle in a soft case and nonchalantly walked down the aisle and put the rifle into the coat closet in front of me. Since it was May, I assumed he was a bear hunter headed for Alaska. After about seven hours, we landed in Fairbanks and a half dozen people got off, including the guy with the rifle.

That flight from New York to Tokyo continued for several more years and was very handy for the few Fairbanks residents and occasional tourists who wanted to fly directly from Fairbanks to Tokyo or New York. The thought of going to Tokyo from Fairbanks was such a novelty that a student, who later became a fisheries biologist for ADF&G, got together with a couple of his friends and stowed away in the aircraft baggage compartment and flew over to have a look around Japan. They all worked as baggage handlers for Pan-Am, but only two of them were able to go because the third one had to close the baggage door from the outside. They were apprehended in Tokyo and sent right back, so they never did get to look around.

I ended up spending two nights and one full day in Fairbanks. There was public transportation then. It consisted of one, privately-owned bus driven by Walt Conant, who looked like Santa Claus. He drove back and forth between the University and downtown seven days a week. I rode the bus into town to buy some things, including a fishing license, at Frontier Sporting Goods, which was the main sporting goods store in town. A friend of Audrey's later took me out to the Malemute Saloon in Ester, where the draw was listening to Robert Service poetry, watching funny skits, eating peanuts, and drinking beer. It was a Gold Rush era building and the floor of the place was about three inches deep in peanut shells.

On my second day in Alaska, I was driven to the U.S. Fish and Wildlife Service hangar on the west side of Fairbanks International airport next to the control tower. There I met Don Fricke, Assistant

Manager for the Arctic National Wildlife Range (after 1980, the name was changed to the Arctic National Wildlife Refuge and the protected area was greatly expanded) and we flew in the Service's Beaver on amphibious floats to Fort Yukon, where we stopped for fuel.

At Fort Yukon I went inside the terminal building to use the facilities. A sign over the door on the inside said, "Fly Fort Yukon Air Service, we don't eat the passengers." Fort Yukon Air Service was owned by Cliff Fairchild, a real character and one of Interior Alaska's second generation of aviation pioneers. By putting up the sign, Cliff was demonstrating his rather eccentric and morbid sense of humor. The previous year, a medevac flight had taken off from Yellowknife in the Northwest Territories and flown to Coppermine (now officially called Kugluktuk) to pick up a pregnant woman, a nurse, and a young boy. On the way back, for some reason, the plane strayed about 60 degrees off course and crash-landed out of fuel in the central barrens. The pilot and young boy survived, but the pilot had eaten parts of the pregnant woman and the nurse before they were rescued over a month later. That was just before Emergency Locator Transmitters were required on aircraft.

From Fort Yukon, we continued on to Arctic Village, where the whole village came out to meet the plane. I had lunch there in a newly built lodge which was being rented by Renewable Resources Consulting Services, a private company working on a biological impact assessment for the proposed gas pipeline coming from Prudhoe Bay. The pipeline was going either along the Canning River, at that time the western boundary of the Arctic National Wildlife Range, into the Yukon and then down the Alaska Highway to link up with existing pipelines in northern Alberta, or along the arctic coast to the proposed new gas fields in the Mackenzie River Delta.

The Renewable Resources crew discussed three main topics over lunch. One was about a plane crash at Arctic Village the previous week, where a bear hunter from the Kenai had taken off from the village with 20 five-gallon cans of fuel in his Super Cub. The engine failed shortly after take-off and he tried to turn back to the runway. As often happens in situations like that, part way through the turn, the plane stalled and spun in. The resulting fire sent flames over 100 feet in the air and left a big burned spot on the side of the runway and a big impression on me. I had just received my pilot's license about two months before, so it was a lesson I never forgot. In the event of an engine failure on take-off, don't try to turn back to the runway unless you have lots of extra altitude.

The second subject was about a theft at the lodge the week before. While everyone had been sleeping, a couple of local men jimmied the door open and stole a bunch of personal gear, firearms, and food. The Renewable Resources crew contacted the State Trooper in Fort Yukon by high frequency (HF) radio and he came to investigate. It turned out the crime was rather easily solved and the perpetrators apprehended because one of them carried away, upside down, a #10 can of Tang that had been opened with a "church key" can opener. So, all the trooper had to do was follow the orange trail of Tang from the lodge a few hundred yards through town, to the house of one of the thieves, where almost all of the missing items were found. Alcohol may have been involved.

The third topic concerned the ongoing project to build new houses for everyone in Arctic Village. It was a federal program involving several agencies, including Bureau of Housing and Urban Development and the Bureau of Land Management. The idea was rather innovative. The federal government would hire local people to build their own houses for union-scale wages. Lumber, nails, and materials for floors and roofs would be provided for free and crews would be hired to go upriver and cut logs for the walls. The logs would be floated down to the village and one person was hired to sit on the river bank and catch the logs as they floated down. Everything had gone according to plan in the beginning, but then the key man who was supposed to be waiting for the logs had gone AWOL and missed most of the logs that floated past. When the cutting crew came back down, expecting to see all the logs, there were very few. So, they had to go back upriver and spend another week cutting more logs. The forest above Arctic Village on the East Fork of the Chandalar is pretty thin, so cutting the second set of logs for the whole village was a lot more difficult than cutting the first set. Because of delays, including the missing logs, the federal agency said they had run out of money for salaries. They were still going to provide all the materials for floors, roofs, and windows for free but people would not be paid to build their own houses. Everyone had immediately gone on strike and the project was stalled. Later that summer, more money was found for salaries and I heard the project was eventually completed.

From Arctic Village, I was taken by helicopter through Carter Pass in the Brooks Range and down the Canning River to Eagle Creek, where Audrey had her base camp. Although it was late May and early summer south of the Brooks Range, on the north side of the mountain range it was still winter with over four feet of snow on the ground and light all night long. It was sunny and warm during the day but as the sun sank toward the horizon, the temperature rapidly dropped below freezing. From about midnight until nine o'clock in the morning, we could walk around anywhere on snowshoes but as the sun rose in the sky and the temperature climbed, the snow turned to mush and any travel became impossible.

Audrey's graduate advisor, Dr. Fred Dean, was there and the three of us began collecting data for Audrey's project. At first, I addressed Fred as "Dr. Dean." He quickly corrected me and said, "my name is Fred and in Alaska we don't use formalities." It was a major change from Maine and I got to really appreciate that about Alaska and Alaskans.

Audrey had a permit from ADF&G to shoot a moose, five caribou, and a Dall sheep. Two caribou carcasses were also delivered by helicopter by Dr. Ken Neiland who was conducting disease studies on caribou in the area. The idea was to shoot an animal, then camp on a vantage point and watch all the scavengers that came to eat the carcass. The project was supported by the Arctic National Wildlife Range staff, including Range Manager Ave Thayer, who provided

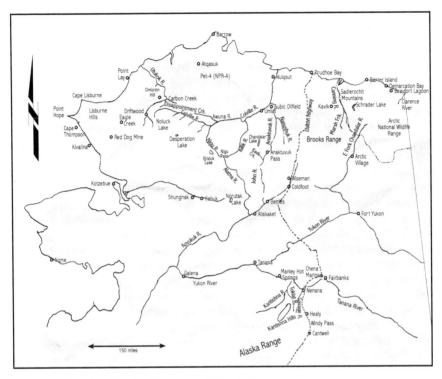

Northern Alaska, Brooks Range, and North Slope.

air support by dropping food when we needed more. With all the sitting around observing, we had lots of time to talk. Fred had been in Alaska for about 20 years, which seemed like a long time to me, and he was a very good naturalist. He knew all the birds and most of the wildflowers. I must have asked him at least 10,000 questions in the few days he was there with us. In hindsight, I was really impressed with his patience. I was thrilled to be in Alaska, and I wanted to know everything he knew about the state.

The day after I arrived, Fred shot a cow moose at the junction of Eagle Creek and the Canning River and we started watching it. It turned out to be one of the best carcasses we watched all summer. At first, there were just gulls and ravens, but they couldn't open the carcass. After five days, we watched a medium-brown grizzly bear traveling south along the Canning. He passed about a mile downwind from the carcass and suddenly stopped. He lifted his

17

head up, sniffed, and then started running straight for the carcass. It took him about five minutes on a dead run through deep snow. As soon as the bear arrived, he started tearing into the carcass with his teeth and claws. The moose had been dead long enough that the hair was slipping, and he was pulling out great gobs of it with his claws. He fed for about an hour and then started raking up vegetation to cover it. Pretty soon, he had a huge mound of vegetation and brush covering the carcass. Then he climbed on top and went to sleep. Over the next six days, he camped on the carcass, uncovering it and feeding, chasing ravens, and then covering it back up. On the sixth day after he found it, a blonde sow and a dark boar arrived. At first, there was a standoff, and then the two boars approached each other and stood up with open mouths. We expected to see a big fight. Instead, they made a trade. The dark boar went up to the carcass, uncovered it and started feeding on the remains of the 10-day old moose. The medium-brown boar, who had owned the carcass, went over to the blonde sow. They wandered off a couple of hundred yards and then he mounted her and they stayed locked together for 17 minutes. When they were done, the boar went over to a rushing stream and sat in it up to his neck to cool off. We named the stream "17-Minute Stream." The sow then went over to the carcass and fed. A short while later, the swap complete, the medium-brown boar and the blonde sow moved off out of sight. The dark boar remained in possession of the carcass for another few days. Five wolves came by next, but the dark boar was so aggressive in defending the putrid scraps the wolves decided it wasn't worth it, and left.

The evening before we were going to take down our spike camp and return to the base camp about three miles up Eagle Creek, we watched a grizzly (probably the one that had first found the carcass) head up the creek towards the camp and disappear in the fog. If he continued on that line of travel, we were afraid the bear would find the base camp, so the next morning I approached the camp cautiously with rifle at ready. The bear wasn't there, but it had done some marauding. It had torn up one of the tents and eaten some of our food. It also punched holes in a three-pound canned ham. The first night in the base camp was rather nerve wracking because we were afraid the bear would return. One of us tried to stay awake and on guard, while the other person slept. I was apparently more tired than afraid, so whenever it was my turn to be on guard, I promptly fell asleep. After the second time that happened, Audrey just decided to stay awake all night and sleep during the day. The bear must have been pretty full of moose and not all that interested in our food because it never returned.

Before we could depart the base camp and try to procure another carcass to watch, a ten-day snowstorm descended on the Brooks Range. During the storm, we spent most of the time in our four-man tent, sleeping and reading. I remember waking up once and looking at my watch and not knowing whether it was 2:00 am or 2:00 pm. The light level outside never seemed to change. Even though we were keeping a diary, we lost a day somewhere because of that storm and didn't figure it out until early September.

Fred returned in late June, and we went on a long hike north to Cache (Ikiakpuruk) Creek and then up Cache Creek to the Sadlerochit River and then over to Schrader Lake. During that hike, there was a 30-day period during which we saw no signs of humans, except for an old lichen-covered rock crib that was probably a cache built by prospector S.J. Marsh seventy years earlier. Marsh wrote about building the rock cache there to protect his supplies before continuing up the Canning River and then up the fork of the Canning that now bears his name. The summer of 1972 was before the over-the-pole flights to Europe began and there were not even any commercial jets or contrails in the sky.

We planned just enough food to get us to Schrader Lake where we expected to catch fish. However, it took us a few days longer to get there than originally planned because we watched one extra caribou carcass. We were also carrying heavy packs when we were hiking, so we needed considerably more food than we had consumed when staying near our base camp. Another problem was we only had one

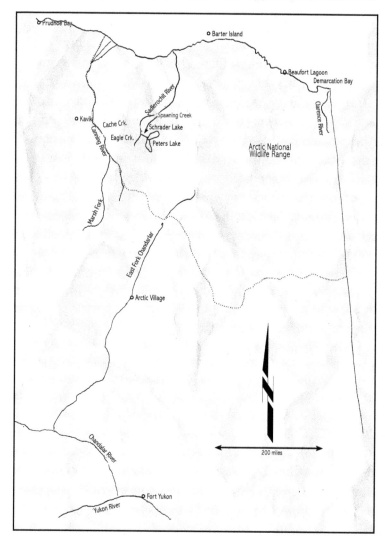

Northeastern Alaska and the Arctic National Wildlife Range as it was in the early 1970s.

cooking pot and Audrey and I filled it up at dinner time and shared it. With Fred there, we divided the contents of the pot three ways instead of two, so I was actually getting considerably less food at the evening meal. I was so hungry by the end of the hike all I could think about was food. Rather than complain, I just suffered and lost weight. After dinner, my thoughts turned to breakfast, and after breakfast, all I could think about was lunch. I'm sure I lost at least ten pounds by the time we got to Schrader Lake and I hadn't had much extra weight to start with. When we finally got there, I walked to the lake, caught an eight-pound lake trout, and then cooked and ate the whole thing. I was so full after that meal I could hardly move.

In 1972, there were two cabins at the mouth of Spawning Creek on the west side of the lake. They were built by Jim Magoffin in 1959, just before the Arctic National Wildlife Range had been created. Magoffin had founded Interior Airways and run a fleet of Hercules and C-46 aircraft to service the new oil developments at Prudhoe Bay. We stayed at the cabins for a few days to rest and recuperate and then Fred left by helicopter to go to Kavik and on to Fairbanks.

A couple of days before Fred left, Audrey and I were hiking from our observation camp down to the lake and one of my boot laces broke. I stopped and took the boot off and started rethreading the lace when it got dark. It was a very strange feeling, because the sky was clear. When I looked at the sun, it was completely hidden by the moon. Neither of us had heard that a total eclipse was predicted for early July in 1972.

The day after the eclipse, the ice started going out in Schrader Lake. It finally cleared on July 4th and the two days leading up to it were quite dramatic. The ice was still about four feet thick but the edges were rotting into "candle" ice, long shards or "candles" four feet long vertically with nothing bonding them together. The ice candles made a tinkling sound along the edge of the lake and the big ice sheets started moving with the wind and bulldozing gravel up on the shore in slow motion. By the time it was over, there were berm piles of gravel two feet high in some places around the lake. I doubt that ice ever makes it to the 4th of July at Schrader Lake anymore.

Although I thought it to be normal at the time, starting about the 25th of June, the mosquitoes became incredibly bad. By early July, it was impossible to be outside the tent without a head net. It was not so much the annoyance of having mosquitoes flying around or biting, it was more that you couldn't breathe without breathing in mosquitoes and coughing constantly. Fortunately, we had a butterfly net with us so when we climbed into the tent, we could use the net to catch the mosquitoes that had come inside. We cooked outside with our head nets on, but we couldn't entirely prevent the mosquitoes from diving into the food. Even lifting the lid for a few seconds resulted in lots of mosquitoes diving headfirst into the dinner. After a month of living that way, I developed an unconscious series of twitches and shakes that continued for a few days after the mosquitoes abruptly declined during the first few days of August. It turned out 1972 was an exceptional year in many ways. It was a very cold and snowy winter on the North Slope and the mosquitoes that summer were the worst that people could remember. In the Interior, the summer had been hot and dry and there were many forest fires. South winds had blown forest fire smoke onto the North Slope. The middle part of July had been smoky with extremely bad mosquitoes as well. We were very relieved when the wind changed in early August and the first frosts of the fall occurred. Within a few days of the first frosts, the mosquitoes died away almost completely and the fall colors came out.

At the time, the Arctic National Wildlife Range was very remote and had received little attention from biologists, tourists or anyone else, except along the coast where the Distant Early Warning (DEW) Line sites were constructed during the late 1950s and early 1960s. The Wildlife Range had not even had a staff until 1967. There had never been an attempt to count the Porcupine Caribou herd before 1972 and no information collected on the distribution of fish. When I asked Assistant Range Manager Don Fricke what kind of fish I could expect to catch in the Canning River, he told me there were probably just grayling there. You can imagine my surprise and delight one day in early August when I cast my size 0 Mepps grayling lure a little too far into the current of the Canning River and hooked onto a 30-inch arctic char.

We were picked up by helicopter in early September and taken to Kavik Airstrip where we waited several days in the fog for the Air

North Beech 18. That was my first of several rides to come on the Air North Twin Beech. I also got to know the owner, Tommy Olson, who was another of Alaska's second generation of pioneer aviators. Eight years later, when I took the FAA examination ride for my float rating, Tommy was my examiner. After the examination ride was over, he made me land in the Tanana River because he said it was important, for safety, to know how to land in Alaska's glacial, fast-flowing rivers. I doubt many instructors are willing to do that anymore. Tommy reached the end of a long and colorful career and retired shortly after that.

Because of the fog at Kavik on the North Slope, I missed my brother's wedding and I was supposed to be the best man. Kavik was an interesting place though, and there were quite a few moose in the willows nearby to keep us entertained. We also tried to find the recently introduced muskoxen as well.

Kavik airstrip had been constructed in 1968 to provide support for a well that was drilled on a ridge to the east. The well had been an oil prospect, but in 1969 the drill rig struck a huge quantity of natural gas instead. The unexpected quantity of gas resulted in an explosion that killed several drillers, or at least, that was the rumor three years later. Two more wells were drilled, but then no further work was done.

It was expected that the vast quantity of underlying natural gas would be developed, but that turned out to be vain hope and the airstrip was abandoned. Later, the ramp at the airstrip was leased by the state to a company that provided logistical support for geology crews and hunters and it has been a reliable place to get fuel and lodging on the North Slope for many years.

The following year, we continued collecting information for Audrey's Master's degree project by hiking up the Marsh Fork to its headwaters to observe scavengers. Although that area is now a well-known and popular sheep hunting area, it was only hunted by a single guide, Joe Hendriks, in the early 1970s and he was based at X-Ray Lake. While we were hiking the Marsh Fork, the skulls and horns of sheep that died during the harsh winters of 1970-71 and 1971-72 were everywhere. Sheep were still reasonably abundant and we kept track of the numbers of sheep we saw, but they obviously had been more abundant during the late 1960s.

During the following two years (1974-75), I worked on my Master's thesis project north of Denali National Park, trying to determine how important the proposed new extensions to the park were to the area's grizzly bears. Audrey and I reversed roles, I was now the Master's degree student and she was my field assistant. At the end of the summer of 1975, I calculated that during my first four years in Alaska I had walked about 4,000 miles and spent about 25% of my time living in a tent. It was a good introduction to the outdoor life in Alaska. Even after the first summer, I decided I was never leaving Alaska again. It was just too exciting and entirely different than anything I had experienced in the Lower 48 states.

Umiat

In the fall of 1975, I had the chance to visit Umiat on the Colville River. Umiat (meaning "boats" in the Inupiat language) was named in the early 1940s when an emergency airstrip was built there. The Colville had always been a major transportation corridor and Umiat was a traditional place to cache kayaks and larger skin boats. In 1945, because of the existing airstrip, it was also chosen as the eastern inland base camp for the exploration of Naval Petroleum Reserve No. 4, or Pet-4, as it was generally called. The Umiat area had a history of high-quality, amber-colored oil coming from small seeps along the bluffs of the river and several wells were drilled just to the west during the first phase of drilling. Small quantities of oil were discovered (most recently estimated at 250 million barrels) and a large quantity of gas was also discovered about 15 miles to the east at what became known as the Gubic gas field. Because the oil and gas discoveries were too small to be developed independently, industry interest in Umiat waned after the early 1960s. Umiat was essentially abandoned by the U.S. Navy and it was an incredible mess, with around 85,000 empty drums and tons and tons of batteries, transformers, and scrap metal left behind.

Then, in 1968, after oil was discovered at Prudhoe Bay and the Hickel Highway ice road was built through Anaktuvuk Pass in 1968-69, interest in Umiat picked up again. In 1973, because of the attention focused on the previously messy and irresponsible oil exploration, the U.S. Navy came back to Umiat to bury much of the debris they left behind and to conduct a final exploration for oil. Most of the debris was buried about a half mile northeast of Umiat in the floodplain of the Colville River. Unfortunately, that burial project was completed just before people really started paying attention to ground water pollution and the problems with burying hazardous waste. Umiat may be the most contaminated site on the whole North Slope. Exactly what was buried and where is not well-documented.

Because of the increasing attention being paid to the central Brooks Range and the North Slope, ADF&G had a house constructed in Bettles and an orange ATCO trailer (a modular steel building, generally 40 feet long by about 10 feet wide and 8 feet high with a flat roof) flown to Umiat in the early 1970s. An Area Game Biologist was planned to be based in Bettles, with an Assistant Area Biologist at Umiat. The expectation was that the Prudhoe Bay oil field would continue to expand to the south and west and the oil and gas discoveries near Umiat would be developed for production. In 1975, betting on the continued development of the Umiat area, two Fairbanks entrepreneurs, Bill Bubbel and O. J. Smith formed Umiat Enterprises. They built a base camp out of ATCO trailers on sleds pulled in by Nodwell tracked vehicles and bulldozers, started a flight service with a turbine engine powered Beaver, and were ready to provide a range of services and accommodations for government employees and contractors at Umiat. O.J.'s wife, Eleanor (Elly) and their son Ray and nephew Jay were also at Umiat much of the time, and Umiat Enterprises was also awarded a contract with the state to maintain the runway.

In 1975, ADF&G supported two graduate students to begin studies of moose and arctic foxes on the North Slope, and their field work was based out of the ATCO trailer in Umiat. I shared an office in Fairbanks with Eric Mould, the student assigned to the moose project, and he found out I was a pilot and could provide cheap transportation for him to get to Umiat. I had become a member of the Arctic Flying Club and could rent their airplanes for very reasonable rates. I was interested in "building hours" and I let my fellow students know I would fly them anywhere in flying club airplanes if they helped pay for the fuel. I made several trips for Eric in fall, winter, and spring in Cessna 172s and a Cessna 182 when I wasn't busy with my own field work on my Master's thesis project.

As a relative newcomer to Alaska and the arctic, I found Umiat to be a fascinating place in the mid-1970s, and I have been back there many times in the 45 years since I first saw it. There have been many changes, but it still retains much of its charm as a lonely outpost in a vast area of wild land. In the mid-1970s, the buildings at Umiat, except for the Umiat Enterprises trailer camp and the ADF&G orange ATCO trailer, were all abandoned and some were just skeletons. Some of them contained abandoned canned food and equipment. I hauled some of the old canned food back to Fairbanks, including #10 cans of Tang, and it was a welcome supplement to our usual fare of snowshoe hare and government surplus dried milk, oatmeal, and dried potatoes.

The ADF&G ATCO trailer was all electric and everything was powered by a 7.5 kW Onan diesel generator set up in an abandoned Quonset hut next door. It was a good set up, but the problem was no one at ADF&G who came to Umiat or the two graduate students knew anything about running equipment in the extreme cold. The generator failed several times when the temperature dropped below -40F because it got too cold, even while running. It needed to be in an insulated generator shed. Fortunately, O. J. was always willing to help. He was around 60 at the time and an experienced old hand at arctic operations.

Before one of my trips to Umiat with Eric, I asked John Coady (an ADF&G supervisor) if I could hunt a moose out of the orange trailer, partly in compensation for giving Eric free rides up there. Moose numbers were low around Fairbanks because of two extreme winters in the early 1970s, high wolf numbers, and overhunting of cow moose. I hadn't been able to get a moose that fall and I knew moose were abundant on the North Slope and the season was open all winter. John agreed to the idea, so I borrowed a Browning .270 rifle from a fellow student and brought it along on my next trip with Eric. The only rifle I owned at the time was a Model 94 Winchester .30-30 with a peep sight and I thought that would be marginal for a big bull moose. Audrey agreed to go with me and when we arrived at Umiat in early November, the temperature was around -30F.

The next morning, with the temperature about -40F, we headed out on snowshoes to the east, crossed the river, and climbed a bluff. We were only on the bluff for about five minutes when I spotted a big bull following a cow coming up the river. I made a long shot (for me) of about 200 yards and then ran down off the bluff to get closer to the wounded moose. I thought I made a pretty good shot but the moose quickly walked into a thick patch of willow where I couldn't see it. I searched around for a while and finally noticed a small cloud of ice fog hanging over the willows. The moose was obviously breathing hard and its breath was forming the ice fog. I walked in as quietly as I could and suddenly saw the moose looking at me from about 30 feet. One shot in the neck and the moose was down.

Up to that point, I had shot and butchered two moose in Alaska, but I never tried to cut one up at minus forty. I was worried that my hands were going to get frostbitten or my gloves were going to get wet with blood. It turned out not to be a problem. I just took my gloves off and whenever my hands started to get cold, I'd just put them under the moose's skin in contact with the warm meat. We worked on the moose for a couple of hours, skinning one side, removing a front and hind leg and gutting it. We then folded the skin back over the carcass and buried the legs under an insulating blanket of snow. We hoped it wouldn't freeze solid by the next morning. Eric had a little wooden L.L. Bean sled we brought with us and loaded some loose meat on it and headed for Umiat.

The next morning, I went over to find O. J. to see if he had a sled we could borrow. Eric's little wooden sled was a bit too small for the job and I was hoping that O. J. had an old military Ahkio (fiberglass toboggan-style sled) or a toboggan of some kind that would run better in the deep snow. I found O. J. working around the camp and told him that I shot a moose and it was about a mile down the river. I then asked him if he had a sled. He just laughed and said, "Oh hell, I've got something way better than that. We'll just take the Weasel." Weasels were small tracked vehicles designed during World War II and they were among the first all-terrain vehicles used in Alaska. Getting the Weasel going involved a typical arctic ordeal in frigid weather. First, we had to warm up and fuel up a Herman Nelson space heater and get it started, and then we had to warm up the Weasel and get it started. By the time we had burned two hours of precious daylight trying to get the Weasel going, I was beginning to wonder if the sled idea wasn't better. O. J. wouldn't hear of it—he obviously enjoyed using the Weasel.

After about 45 minutes of preheating, the Weasel started and O. J. had the satisfied grin of someone who had taken on a challenge, and won. The Weasel had seen better days and it had no muffler, so it was very loud. We went northeast along the trail to the Colville, crossed the river, and picked up our snowshoe tracks. The willows were thick and some were about 10 feet tall, so I offered to walk ahead of the Weasel and find a route to the moose that had the least willows. O. J. wouldn't hear of that either, and said, "You just sit right there, this old Weasel will go right over those little willows!" We started crashing through the willows making an incredible racket while not being able to see anything except willows folding and breaking off in front of us. I had no idea if we were even going in the right direction, but when we were in the thickest part of the willows and still at least a couple hundred yards from the moose carcass, the engine of the Weasel started vibrating really badly and banging against the side of the engine compartment. O. J. stopped the Weasel, shut off the engine, and then opened the cowling in the cab of the machine. Fortunately, he had a flashlight. After looking around a bit, he said, "OK, I see the problem, one of the engine mounts has come loose."

He tried to reach in and retrieve the nut and washers that were in the bottom on the engine compartment but the space was too small. He looked at Audrey and said, "You got the smallest hands. See if you can't reach down in there and gather up all those loose parts." Audrey took her coat off, rolled up her sleeve, and reached down and came up with a nut and a lock washer—the kind that is spring loaded and split. Not being very mechanically inclined at the time, she took a close look at the lock washer and exclaimed, "Oh, that's the problem, the washer's broken." Well, O. J. acted like that was the funniest thing he had ever heard in his life and started laughing in his high, squeaky laugh. He just couldn't stop laughing. His laughing got me laughing and both of us had the giggles pretty badly. Finally, we got it under control and we asked Audrey, who wasn't getting the same enjoyment out of the situation as we were, to put the washer and nut back on the engine mount and tighten it as best she could. We then proceeded on, mowing down the willows until we got to the moose, with O. J. occasionally chuckling and shaking his head. He remembered Audrey's comment about the "broken" washer for years.

I was pleasantly surprised we had found the moose so easily and it wasn't completely frozen, despite the -40F temperature. The moose hide thrown over the carcass with some snow piled on it was very effective insulation. The three of us made short work of loading the moose onto the back of the Weasel and O. J. drove us all back to Umiat. The next problem with the moose meat at Umiat was getting it to Fairbanks. The plane I had brought up was a maroon and white Cessna 172 (N35752).

Fortunately, the next morning the temperature was about 15 degrees warmer, and I was optimistic about getting the meat to Bettles. The Arctic Flying Club had a policy of not allowing members to fly its aircraft in temperatures colder than -30F and it had warmed up to about -25F. I had left a catalytic heater that burned Blazo (white gasoline) in the cowling of the plane overnight, but when I tried to start the plane in the morning it wouldn't go. That's when I learned about frosted spark plugs. O. J. heard me unsuccessfully cranking over the engine and came over to see if he could help. He said the combination of the catalytic heater putting out moisture, but not getting the engine above freezing, and the failed starting attempt had probably resulted in frosted plugs.

He said the only solution now was some serious heat with the Herman Nelson. About 30 minutes of pouring 250,000 BTUs per hour of heat into the Cessna, with one trunk of the heater in the engine and the other one in the cabin, we had the Cessna read to go.

This was my first trip to the North Slope in serious cold weather, but I was pretty confident I could get to Bettles with the moose and then get back to Umiat, even with the short daylight. When I loaded the frozen legs and meat of the moose, the tail of the airplane sagged to the ground, with the nosewheel dangling in the air, completely off the ground. I was concerned the load was too heavy (it was 695 pounds when weighed at Bettles) and consulted with O. J. He said, "Oh no, that's perfectly normal with a heavy load. It's not possible to overload a single-engine aircraft. A single engine aircraft will fly with whatever you can get into it. When you get in and start the engine, the nose will come down." He was right, at least about the nose coming down. The rest I wasn't so sure about, but after I had about 20 years flying in Alaska with lots of heavy loads in small, single engine aircraft, I more or less had to agree with him.

I took off and headed for Bettles, but I had to fly down the Colville to the Anaktuvuk River and then up the Anaktuvuk towards Anaktuvuk Pass. I was flying under a low ceiling with about two miles visibility, following the willows of the Anaktuvuk River south, when the river appeared to fork. The right fork seemed to be a narrow tributary, so I picked what appeared to be the biggest fork and continued on. After about 20 minutes, the clouds started lifting but all I saw ahead of me was mountains and there was no sign of a pass. That got me totally confused, but at least I could climb, so I gave the engine full throttle and started climbing towards the mountains. Despite the heavy load, I managed to get up to 6,000 feet and continued south over the mountains, just having to dodge the highest peaks and wondering how I could possibly have missed Anaktuvuk Pass. Finally, I got close enough to Bettles that I picked up their non-directional beacon on the plane's automatic direction finder. The rest of the flight was uneventful and I dropped off the moose at the Bettles Lodge and asked Jerry Kocer to freight it to Fairbanks for me. I then refueled and headed back to Umiat. The visibility was down to a mile in light snow on the north side of Anaktuvuk Pass and the clouds were lowering. If it hadn't been for the willows along the Anaktuvuk River and the Colville, it would have been a complete whiteout. I arrived right at dark and Audrey, O. J., and Eric were glad to see me, especially Audrey. As it had started to get dark, O. J. said to Audrey, "I hope that man of yours knows his way around out there, it's starting to look pretty white." The only thing that comment accomplished was to make Audrey even more worried than she already was.

When I got on the ground, I mentioned to O. J. about getting lost going up the Anaktuvuk River on the way to Bettles. He said, "Oh yeah, I forgot to warn you about that, when you get to the mouth of the Nanushuk, you have to be careful and keep to the right, otherwise you end up going up the Nanushuk into the mountains." Apparently, it was a common mistake.

Despite all the work involved in getting the moose at Umiat and getting it back to Fairbanks, we felt like it was all worth it, until we tasted the meat. For some reason, it ended up being the worst tasting moose meat we ever had. I left it frozen outside our cabin in Fairbanks all winter, and brought it inside one leg at a time, whenever we needed more meat. As soon as it thawed inside the cabin, it developed a petroleum-like smell. Like most bulls shot at that time of year, it had used up almost all its fat during the rut, but we never did figure out what caused the petroleum-like smell. Was it hormones from the rut, or had it come in contact with fuel on the back of the Weasel? It probably had also frozen too quickly, which would have made it tough, but that didn't explain the petroleum-like smell.

I made more trips to Umiat over the next several years and got to know O. J. pretty well. He was a real Alaskan, self-educated, very capable, and very helpful. He loved Umiat and he had a great sense of humor. He occasionally helped himself to the ADF&G fuel drums but always claimed he was going to replace the fuel. Even if he occasionally forgot, I always thought that was a small price to pay for all the help he provided to graduate students and ADF&G staff over the years. Just before he died in 1999, O. J. had become something of a celebrity, and the few tourists and river floaters that came through Umiat went out of their way to talk to him. I'm not sure if anyone officially interviewed him, but he was full of very entertaining and funny old Alaskan adventure tales, many about himself and his brother Hardy and their flying adventures in the 1950s and 1960s, including hunting polar bears out on the sea ice north of Alaska.

In 1978, the ADF&G Division of Sport Fish remodeled the old Quonset hut that the Game Division had used as a generator shed. The Quonset was insulated, painted, and divided into four bedrooms, a living/cooking area, and a workshop. The Sport Fish crews, led by Terry Bendock, Mike Doxey, and John Burr, then embarked on a remarkable five-year effort to inventory the fish resources on the central and western North Slope. They used two little John Deere Spitfire snowmachines in winter, and aircraft, helicopters, and a big riverboat in summer. The boat was named the "D-2 Maru," and with it they ran more than 100 miles up the Colville River. The thoroughness, efficiency, and volume of valuable information produced by that relatively inexpensive effort will likely never be duplicated.

Besides all the changes with oil exploration and development around Umiat, there were also major changes with wildlife in the Colville River valley over the years. The Colville River is a major, navigable river, and its valley is the largest on the North Slope. It is also the most biologically productive because of the extensive willows and alders present along it.

Some of the biggest biological changes have involved the abundance of moose along the Colville and other rivers on the North Slope. ADF&G biologist John Coady reviewed the historical changes in moose abundance up to 1970, when the first formal moose count was completed. Since 1974, the ADF&G has conducted annual moose surveys, several of which I flew from the late 1970s to the early 1990s. Although moose were present on the eastern North Slope after the 1880s, breeding populations of moose did not get established along the Colville until after 1950.

During the 1950s, there was an extensive federal wolf control program, called "Operation Umiat", and hundreds of wolves were killed to hasten the recovery of the Western Arctic Caribou herd. Jay Hammond, who later became governor of Alaska in the 1970s, participated in that wolf control program. Moose undoubtedly benefitted from the program too, and by 1970, they were abundant. The severe winters of 1970-71 and 1971-72 probably reduced moose numbers and certainly slowed their increase, but moose then continued to increase until the early 1990s, when the population crashed. When I first visited Umiat in 1976, moose were abundant, groups of moose occupied every major willow patch, and large bulls could be seen everywhere along the Colville between the Anaktuvuk River and the Killik River. Interest in hunting moose had just begun to increase, and Fairbanks Flight Service, one of the large air services in Fairbanks, maintained a seasonal moose hunting camp for its employees on a large gravel bar near the mouth of the Killik River, called "Killik Bend." The Colville River, mostly from the Killik River down to Umiat, the Chandler River, and several other North Slope rivers became popular destinations for Fairbanks moose hunters. About 60 moose were taken on the Colville and the Chandler each year for many years. Native people on the North Slope did not hunt moose on the Colville above Umiat or on the Chandler in winter or in summer during those years. There were plenty of moose and caribou downriver from Umiat for the small number of people that lived in Nuiqsut, a village that was reestablished on the lower Colville River in 1973.

Despite considerable effort and studies by ADF&G and the North Slope Borough to determine the reasons for the crash in moose numbers in the mid-1990s, the causes of the crash were never clear, except that few calves were produced, fewer survived, and many adults died. Moose recovered after a few years but were never again as abundant as they had been at their peak

ADF&G field camp at Umiat (2017). Mark Keech rides one of the old John Deere Spitfire snowmachines that were used by ADF&G Sport Fish biologists to inventory fisheries resources on the western North Slope during the late 1970s.

during 1985-1990. Then, there was another mysterious crash around 2009-2011. The cause of that decline has not really been determined either, but a big increase in wolf numbers was suspected, or at least associated with it.

In contrast to Interior Alaska, where snowshoe hares were super-abundant in the early 1970s, they were unknown in the Colville River valley until around 1990. I saw a set of hare tracks near Umiat in 1978, but they did not become established along the Colville until the early 1990s, when they suddenly erupted. After the early 1990s, hares increased steadily and probably reached a peak around 2019. Lynx also became abundant and lynx tracks have now been commonly seen along the lower Colville River for about 20 years. Another change since the 1970s was the arrival of muskrats on the North Slope. Sometime during the early 1980s, I saw what I thought was a muskrat when I was hunting caribou along the Colville River. I had never heard of muskrats on the North Slope and never talked to anyone who had seen a muskrat or muskrat "pushup." Pushups are places where muskrats stuff aquatic vegetation in holes in the ice so they can surface, rest, and breathe while swimming under the ice. In 2016, while we were doing wolverine surveys, I saw a muskrat pushup on a lake near the confluence of the Anaktuvuk and Colville rivers and I landed to investigate it. Since then, I have heard that muskrats are now commonly seen. I haven't seen any beaver yet, but I wouldn't be surprised if beaver eventually make it to the Colville River too.

Willows girdled by snowshoe hares along the Colville River in 2018. Hares were virtually unknown on the North Slope until they erupted in the early 1990s.

Driftwood
Building the ADF&G Field Camp

ADF&G needed a good base camp for greatly expanded studies on wildlife in northwest Alaska during the late 1970s. The Western Arctic Caribou Herd crashed from 242,000 in 1970 to about 75,000 in 1976 and the crash caused a social and political crisis. There was also increasing interest in northwestern Alaska because of the transfer of Pet-4 from the U.S. Navy to BLM in 1976, and proposed Congressional legislation to withdraw "National Interest Lands" for special purposes.

When doing spring and summer field work on the Western Arctic Caribou Herd during the 1960s, ADF&G historically used an old airstrip at Brady on the upper Colville River. The Brady airstrip washed out in the late 1960s and then ADF&G biologists operated from the Naval Arctic Research Lab (NARL) cabin at Noluck Lake by landing on the ice. After the ice became too soft at Noluck Lake during early June in 1975 and 1976, ADF&G biologists tried to operate out of the abandoned Project Chariot site at Cape Thompson on the coast south of Point Hope. Project Chariot had been a crazy scheme to blow an unneeded harbor into the rocky coastline of northwestern Alaska in the early 1960s using nuclear weapons, just to prove it could be done. The runways and buildings that had been built there and then abandoned were nice, but the weather at Cape Thompson was atrocious. When the wind was calm, the area fogged in, and when the fog lifted, it was usually too windy to fly. Because of the impossible weather, in July 1976, the ADF&G caribou census crew moved to the Driftwood airstrip and lived there in tents.

Driftwood was an airstrip about one mile north of the confluence of Driftwood Creek and the Utukok River in the far northwest of Alaska. The name "Utukok" is an Inupiat word meaning old, or ancient, and referred to an older civilization of people who once lived along the coast near the mouth of the river. The airstrip on the upper river was built during the late 1940s to provide access to the southwestern portion of Pet-4. Driftwood was originally constructed to be about 3,500 feet long and about 150 feet wide so that it could accommodate C-46 (Curtiss Commando) and C-47 (DC-3 Dakota) aircraft and smaller Bush aircraft that were commonly in use at the time, like the Noorduyn Norseman. During the late 1940s and early 1950s these aircraft hauled in loads of fuel in drums (40 in the C-46, 20 in the C-47, and 7 at a time in the Norseman). They also hauled in the equipment and the people needed to operate the "Cat" trains and explore the geology of the area. Cat trains are a series of large sledges pulled usually by a large bulldozer. The sledges include sleeping and cooking trailers, workshops, and seismic equipment. There were never any permanent buildings at Driftwood so the camps there were made of Cat trains. Geologists also left their tracked Weasels there when they were not using them.

I had just been hired as a Game Biologist I by ADF&G in February 1977 and one of my first assignments was to design, prefabricate, and build a large tent frame at Driftwood which was to become ADF&Gs permanent base camp on the western North Slope. It turned out to be quite an adventure. Another newly hired employee, Ron Ball, and I built the tent frame, disassembled it and packaged the pieces so they would fit into the ADF&G de Havilland Beaver in two loads. About the first week of May, Bill Griffin, a muskox biologist and pilot for ADF&G, was going to fly us up to Driftwood with the first load and then come back two days later with the remaining load. Then, after two more days, he was supposed to come back with a third load of gear and equipment and give us a ride back to Fairbanks.

In the first load, we had 2-foot x 4-foot pieces of 5/8 plywood, 2x4s for the floor, and all the gear we needed to survive in the sub-zero temperatures that were still prevailing there at night. Bill removed the wheel-skis to give us an extra 500-pound payload. He had a report from Buck Maxon at Kotzebue that the strip was good for wheels. Since Ron had never seen the Brooks Range before, he rode in the right front seat and I was in the back, sitting on the lumber, surrounded by baggage with a large rope for a seat belt. I could only see out the left rear window. Bill was a safe and experienced pilot and a well-known flight instructor and FAA examiner. But he was also a rather nervous flier and an eccentric character, and he had little experience flying in the western Brooks Range. I didn't know it when we took off, but by the end of the next few days, I would have a pretty good introduction to his eccentricities. The flight from Fairbanks to Bettles was uncomfortable for me, but otherwise uneventful. We refueled in Bettles, and the Beaver held just enough fuel to get from Bettles to Driftwood and back. From Bettles, we flew over to the Alatna River and up that river to Nigu Pass. From Nigu Pass, we flew down the Nigu River. When we were just past Etivluk Lake and clear of the highest mountains of the Brooks Range, Bill turned the plane on a westerly heading and made an announcement.

"We'll be at Noluck Lake in one hour and five minutes" he said. I wasn't sure why he mentioned Noluck Lake but I assumed that was a navigation landmark he was familiar with because ADF&G had used the lake in the past. In the era before GPS, pilots navigated by map and compass and used geographic landmarks to know where they were. Getting lost was a common phenomenon and always something to be concerned about.

For the next one hour and five minutes Bill didn't even look at a map or really look outside the plane, other than to glance ahead and to the mountains to the left of us. I just assumed that he knew the area so well, and his time estimate was so precise, that looking at a map wasn't necessary. We didn't have an intercom or even wear hearing protection in those days, so there was not much communication inside the plane because of the loud rumble of the big Pratt and Whitney radial engine.

I didn't own a watch at the time, but after what seemed like a long time, all of a sudden, Bill looked at his watch and announced in a loud voice, "OK, we should be at Noluck Lake" and then he started looking around outside the plane.

After craning his neck around to the left and to the right, he started flying around in circles and finally picked up the Cape Lisburne Sectional Aeronautical Chart. He turned the map around several times and I could tell by the look on his face he had become concerned. After a few more minutes of flying in circles and turning the map round and round, he made another rather loud and startling announcement. "If you don't know exactly where you are, you're lost. And we're lost!"

I didn't quite know what to say, and Ron, who had never flown anywhere in Alaska before, just stared at Bill in disbelief. I had some experience reading Sectional Aeronautical Charts and knew they were actually pretty good maps. I also concluded that I better start trying to figure out where we were…. fast. At least the weather was good and we had enough fuel to get back to Bettles or down to Kotzebue, but I wanted to get going on the wall tent and not have to repeat the rather uncomfortable flight.

I asked Bill for the map. He was understandably reluctant to give it to me. I was 26 at the time, I looked young for my age, and I had obviously never been there before. But I assured him I was also a pilot and I knew how to read Sectionals. Finally, he handed me the map and I tried to get oriented by figuring out which way the rivers were flowing. Noluck Lake is essentially at the head of the Colville River and the river flows east from there. The drainages west of the Colville all flow north and then northwest.

With the Beaver wandering around in circles, and me only being able to see out of the left rear window, it took me about ten minutes to finally get oriented. I yelled up to Bill, "Hey, I think we are still in the Colville drainage north of Noluck." Bill was very nervous and either couldn't hear me over the sound of the engine or was too preoccupied to listen, so I had to yell the same thing three times. After the third time, I also added, "If you go straight south, I think we'll be able to see Noluck Lake." He finally paid attention and turned the plane south, but I had to keep on him to prevent him from deviating and flying circles again. After flying for about ten minutes, we came over a low ridge and there ahead of us was Noluck Lake, with the old yellow (NARL) cabin on the south side. We had only been flying about 1,000 feet over the ground and if we had just been 1,000 feet higher, we probably could have seen the lake from where we started circling.

Bill was ecstatic and yelled, "There it is, there it is, that's Noluck Lake! We're not lost anymore!" He then whipped the plane around onto a northwesterly heading, scaring the daylights out of Ron, while at the same time yelling, "Don't take your eyes off that lake!" Which was impossible, of course, because we were now headed directly away from it.

Amazingly enough, given the snow-covered landscape and lack of recognizable landmarks, Bill brought us straight to Driftwood after about 20 minutes. I was just starting to feel a bit more relaxed as he made a high pass over the runway, which was not easy to see. He then made a gradual, circling turn, before lining up on the approach. With the nose of the plane angled down as it was descending toward the runway, when I raised myself up from my position in the back so that my head hit the cabin roof, I could just see ahead of the plane through the windshield. To my horror, I could see we were actually lined up on the river, not the runway, and when we were about 200 yards from touchdown, I yelled, "Hey Bill, the runway's over there!" and pointed ten degrees to the left. He realized his error immediately and turned toward the runway, touching down just as the plane leveled out again.

Ron and I were very glad to be on the ground and felt like our immediate troubles were over. Bill's troubles would continue, however. He had used up so much fuel wandering around in circles north of Noluck that he didn't think he could make Bettles, so he flew to Kotzebue and spent the night there instead. The next morning, he got a late start after a night of relaxing in Rothman's hotel, and he ended up spending the next night at the Bettles Lodge. Because it was early May, and light all night, several people in the office were a bit skeptical of the need to spend two nights on the return. Bill was a confirmed penny pincher and he was notorious for doing whatever he could to get extra travel expenses.

Over the next several years, I heard lots of funny stories about Bill Griffin from biologists he had worked with, and from several people at Anaktuvuk Pass. They had once been sent to Chandler Lake to help get the ADF&G Beaver on floats back into the lake after it had somehow ended up high and dry in the tundra. Bill had come in to land with a fisheries biologist and a graduate student. He had flown low down most of the length of the seven-mile-long lake, touched down at the last moment, bounced into the air and ended up in the tundra 50 feet from the shore. He then got out and started frantically digging with his hands in the tundra behind the plane. His passengers just watched in amazement, not understanding why he landed so long, and also why he started digging in the tundra with his hands. Bill finally realized the futility of his digging and got back in the plane and called Bettles Lodge on the HF radio. In a few hours, Paul Shanahan arrived with a number of people from Anaktuvuk Pass with picks and shovels. A famous comment made by one of the older men from Anaktuvuk who helped was, "Big lake, too!" obviously also amazed at why Bill hadn't touched down a little sooner.

By digging, shoveling, and pushing they got the plane back into the water after several hours. However, the floats leaked badly, so Bill had taken off and left the people from Anaktuvuk behind. He then hadn't remembered to call Shanahan for a couple of days, so the Anaktuvuk guys got an unexpected two-day fishing vacation at Chandler Lake with no tents, sleeping bags, or bug dope.

One of the other famous stories about Bill was about how he successfully took off with three people and a full load of gear in a Cessna 180 at the Nuiqsut village airstrip with the parking brake fully engaged. The runway had just recently been built and it was muddy and slippery. Bill had not realized anything was wrong until the plane used up a couple of thousand feet getting off. He glanced down after getting airborne and noticed the brake was on and exclaimed, "This 180 is a really strong airplane. It just got off the ground with the parking brake on!"

Bill certainly was an eccentric character and an occasional klutz. But he was also a good instructor, if you could overlook his eccentricities. I obtained my Instrument rating with him in 1982. By the time his flying career was over, he had participated, one way or another, in helping over 1,700 people learn to fly, a record exceeded by only one other flight instructor in the U.S.

It took Ron and I one day to build the floor of the tent frame and we then made a Visqueen tent on top of the floor, which heated up nicely in the sun. The sun was already just going around in circles, with 24 hours of daylight. When it was relatively high in the sky from about 10:00 am until about 8:00 pm it was warm inside our Visqueen tent, but when it was low on the northern horizon, the temperature was still getting down to -20F at night. We waited for two more days and finally Bill showed up with the second load. We finished constructing the tent frame, put the tent over it, and installed the oil stove. We now had a relatively luxurious camp and with nothing more to do we occupied our time catching ground squirrels and tying little collars of surveyor's tape around their necks.

After three more days of waiting and playing with the local ground squirrels, there was still no sign of Bill. On the fourth day, Buck Maxon showed up in his turbine-powered Twin Beechcraft (Hamilton Westwind II) with a load of fuel drums. He said he had received word from the ADF&G office in Fairbanks that we were to get a ride back with him to Kotzebue and then go back to Fairbanks, via Anchorage, on Wien Air Alaska.

After a couple of weeks in Fairbanks, we returned to Driftwood at the end of May to begin the caribou and grizzly bear work that would be based from there for the next six years. However, after the fourth year, it was clear that the airstrip was on borrowed time. Unfortunately, it was built in the valley bottom along the east side of the Utukok River and it was subject to flooding. By the time we built the ADF&G field camp there in May 1977, the runway had been

ADF&G technician Ron Ball waiting for the second Beaver load of building materials during construction of the ADF&G field camp at Driftwood in 1977. The temperature was still getting down to - 20F at night in early May.

cut almost in half by the changing channel of the river. The south end was already growing up to willows about four to six feet high. We maintained the north 2,000 feet of the runway so that we could bring in aviation fuel, jet fuel, and stove oil, and so that we could base our de Havilland Beaver there for photographing aggregations of caribou. The 2,000 feet runway was plenty long enough for the Beaver and just long enough for Buck Maxon to bring in his Twin Beech, or single-engine Otter, with 7 drums of avgas (80/87 and 100/130 octane) or Jet-B in each load.

While we were living in the camp at Driftwood, working on Audrey's Ph. D. project on wolverines, we endured several floods. Some of the floods we were able to divert, but others caused damage to the runway that was difficult to repair. In 1980, Audrey and I were alone there in late May. We had just closed down her spike camps after making one last snowmachine trip up the river and we were doing some camp chores. I had waited as long as possible to switch my

Cub from skis to wheels and I had been landing and parking the plane on a slough of the river because the runway was bare. Finally, I decided to switch over on the afternoon of the 25th of May. I was getting a little sleepy at about 1:00 pm and decided to take a short nap in my sun-warmed tent and then switch over to wheels after my nap. I looked over at the plane sitting on the snow-filled slough of the river, and it looked fine, but I decided to move it to the runway so it would be ready to work on after my nap. I started it up and flew it off the slough and landed on some remaining melting snow on the edge of the runway and then went and lay down. About 30 minutes later, I woke up to the sound of running water and went out of my tent and looked at the slough where the plane had been parked. I couldn't believe my eyes. The slough was now a torrent of raging, brown water. If I had not moved it, the plane would have been gone, washed away by the break-up. It was a valuable lesson I never forgot; break-up on North Slope rivers can be sudden and unexpected because the mountains warm up first and water starts flowing on top of the ice and snow of the rivers. Fortunately, that year was a relatively mild break-up and the Utukok stayed mostly within its existing channels.

Audrey and I were again alone at Driftwood in 1981 when break-up came. We had been anticipating it and hoping the river would stay in its banks, but the snow was deep, May had been cold, and the weather warmed up fast at the end of the month. The first gush of brown water stayed in the river channels, but the water kept rising. I built a small berm across the south end of the runway to prevent minor flooding but it was soon clear that the water would overwhelm it. Just before the runway flooded, we got in the Cub and flew over to Noluck Lake and landed on the ice in front of the old NARL cabin. We stayed there for two days while waiting for the flooding to end at Driftwood. ADF&G caribou researchers had used the NARL cabin for calving ground work in early June before we built the Driftwood field camp. The ice was good for landing on wheels there until around the 10th of June through the early 1980s. The lake had also been used occasionally by exploration crews. A relic of that era is an Interior Airways C-46 that punched through the ice while taxing

ADF&G field camp at Driftwood. Driftwood was an airstrip constructed on the Utukok River by the Navy in the 1940s. It was originally about 3,500 feet long but was rendered unusable for large aircraft by 1983 and completely destroyed by river flooding around 2015.

during June 1968. Attempts to salvage the plane were unsuccessful and it was abandoned. We used some of the seats of the plane as furniture in the Driftwood field camp. Noluck Lake eventually drained and the NARL cabin shifted and became unusable because of melting permafrost. The lake has since refilled but the NARL cabin remains unusable. Another casualty of the warming arctic.

The Rolligon

In 1980, we shared the use of the Driftwood airstrip with a U.S. Geological Survey exploration crew that was exploring NPR-A for coal. The crew leader was Irving Tailleur, a well-known geologist who had a reputation for pioneering mineral discoveries, including the large lead, zinc, and silver deposits that he found in the late 1960s in northwestern Alaska after talking to pilot John Baker in Kotzebue. These deposits were developed into the Red Dog mine in the early 1980s.

Tailleur had also worked extensively at exploring coal deposits in northwestern Alaska and had the reputation of being able to get a lot done with very little money, a remarkable thing even in the 1970s. He borrowed a small Rolligon ATV from Husky Oil and had driven it about 70 miles to Driftwood from the Akulik exploration strip near the coast. This particular model of Rolligon was about the size of a large pickup truck. It had four sausage-shaped tires, each about five feet in diameter and six feet long. These low-pressure tires could roll over the tundra and not leave a mark. It was an amazing machine.

Tailleur mounted a small auger drill on the back of the Rolligon and spent the summer of 1980 driving around mapping the extensive shallow coal deposits within about 50 miles of Driftwood. Western NPR-A and the area between NPR-A and the coast are underlain by huge quantities of fairly high quality, low-sulfur coal. The coal deposits are so shallow in many places the spoil mounds in front of ground squirrel holes are mostly black with fine coal. The existence of the coal deposits had been known to Europeans since the late 1800s, but the logistics of getting the coal out and the long distance to markets had precluded commercial development. There had always been some local use of coal and some interest in developing it as a source of locally-produced energy and there was also renewed interest in the resources of the National Petroleum Reserve, so Tailleur received a limited budget to do more coal recon work with the borrowed Rolligon.

Towards the end of the summer, the clutch went out on the Rolligon while the crew was starting down a long slope about ten miles north of Driftwood. Since the engine provided the main braking for the machine, it gradually gathered speed on a largely out of control trip to the bottom of the slope where it stopped just short of a deep gully. The crew thought about jumping out, but were lurching and bouncing so much that all they could do was hold on tight. Surprisingly, none of the crew were injured and the Rolligon was not damaged. The US Geologic Survey (USGS) camp had a helicopter at Driftwood and went to rescue the Rolligon crew and figure out what parts were needed for repairs. After about ten days, a new clutch arrived from the manufacturer in Texas, but it turned out to be the wrong part and had to be sent back. It was mid-August by that time and the project was slated to end. Tailleur was going to leave a skeleton crew of three college kids at Driftwood to fix the Rolligon when the new parts arrived. He asked me if I could fly the crew and parts out to the Rolligon in my 90 horsepower Cub when they arrived. He gave me $100 in cash and left.

Unfortunately, the day before the parts finally arrived I had tipped my Cub up on its nose and bent the propeller while picking up a wolverine live-trap. I was waiting for a new prop to be delivered. With the weather cooling down and winter approaching, the students were anxious to get the Rolligon fixed and back to Driftwood so they could leave. I straightened and filed my prop as best I could and was able to take two of the USGS crew and the new clutch down to a gravel bar about two miles from the Rolligon, although my Cub's engine vibrated considerably. I was impressed when I heard the Rolligon chugging into camp the next morning. Tailleur had given those youngsters a big responsibility and they met the challenge, an experience they would undoubtedly remember for the rest of their lives.

After the coal project was over, the Rolligon was left at Driftwood. While waiting for the caribou to aggregate in early July one year, we decided to try to get it going again. Fortunately, one of the ADF&G crew, Tim Smith, knew something about diesel engines and after replacing the dead battery with one of ours and getting the engine going, we were able to air up the tires with the engine-driven compressor. We soon had the Rolligon rolling again.

Since he had been the key man in getting it running, Tim got to drive it first. It was great fun and we all rode along, but because the tires were slick with no tread at all, going up steep slopes and cut banks was difficult. Tim made the mistake of driving it out into the Utukok River and quickly found out that it floated very well but was completely out of control in the water. We just went round and round down the river with all tires spinning and flinging water. It finally grounded in a shallow spot and Tim was able to drive it out of the river. Besides having some fun with the Rolligon, it proved to be quite useful. We drove it up to the big old Pet-4 barrel cache and loaded it with old diesel to use in the camp oil stove.

One day, we also got the bright idea to use the Rolligon to retrieve drop tanks that had been jettisoned from F-4 Phantom jets. We had seen several of those from the air within a few miles of Driftwood. From the 1960s, until they were replaced by F-15s in the late 1980s, there were two F-4s based at Galena. During the Cold War (until the base was closed in 1993) these aircraft were frequently used to intercept the Russian Bear bombers that tested U.S. air defenses around Alaska. As soon as the 370-gallon auxiliary drop tanks were emptied, they were jettisoned. We brought two of them into Driftwood with the Rolligon and hoped to use them for fuel storage, but they had developed leaks after their freefall from high altitude.

Visitors

We seldom had visitors at Driftwood but I remember three occasions when unexpected visitors interrupted the solitude at the camp. Audrey and I were alone in camp one day in late May 1980 when a young man walked into camp exhausted and out of food. After a cup of tea and some Pilot Bread and peanut butter he told us his story. He had decided to float the Colville River from its headwaters down to Umiat as soon as the ice went out. He arrived in Kotzebue in mid-May and heard from someone that the ice was already out on the upper Colville, so he chartered an aircraft and was dropped at

Noluck Lake. He then dragged the kayak about 3 miles west to the very head of the Colville and headed downstream. What he didn't realize was that the breakup on the Colville had been exceptionally early that year, with the first flush of water occurring about the 15th of May. Right after he arrived on the 17th, the weather turned cold once more and the remaining ice jams on the river started to solidify, with the river itself starting to refreeze. He made it about 15 miles down the river and then upset and damaged the kayak in an ice jam. He lost most of his food and had no way of contacting anyone. Fortunately, the pilot who dropped him off told him about ADF&G's field camp at Driftwood and he decided that his best chance of survival was to walk the 40 miles west to the camp. He stayed with us a couple of days and then caught a ride back to Kotzebue on a backhaul with Buck Maxon.

On another occasion, in June 1981, a large army green Bell UH-1 (Huey) helicopter approached Driftwood and landed. It turned out to be part of an effort to clean up the barrel caches that had been left lying around after the Pet-4 exploration. The crew was dressed in military fatigues, with canteens on their belts, and their leader asked if we knew of any barrel caches. We pointed out the large cache of about 150 empty drums and 50 full drums that was plainly visible from camp. They apparently hadn't noticed it on the way in. They fired up the Huey and flew up and looked it over and came back. We weren't sure what their plan was, but they were obviously not equipped to deal with a barrel cache of that size. Apparently, they just decided to map the cache and come back at some later time. The crew leader then came into the cook tent and asked if he could fill his canteen with drinking water. We pointed to our aluminum water container with a tap on it and he proceeded to fill his canteen, all the while telling us about how he just didn't trust the water in the local creeks and rivers. There was too much chance of catching something from it (no one talked about *Giardia* back then). After he left, we all just started laughing. No one had bothered to interrupt and tell the guy that when our water container was empty, we just carried it out to the river and filled it up again—it was not treated at all. And, the last time I checked in 2016, the drum cache was still there.

Audrey was alone at Driftwood in early April 1981 while I was in Fairbanks working on the Delta caribou project. I happened to be in the Fairbanks office around mid-day when one of the clerical staff came and told me that Audrey called in from Driftwood on the sideband high frequency (HF) radio. I went into the radio room and called back, "KTI 56 Driftwood, this is WJC 77 Fairbanks Fish and Game. Audrey, did you try to call, over?" She replied, "Yes, I did. The camp has just been robbed by people on snowmachines, and they stole my backpack with all my personal gear in it, over."

Apparently, while she had been away up the river, three men on snowmachines came into the camp and stole some food, a barrel of avgas, and some of her personal gear. I told Audrey I would head up in the state-owned Scout aircraft and that John Coady would also call Roland Young, the Fish and Wildlife Protection Officer in Kotzebue. A couple of hours later, Roland left Kotzebue about the same time I left Fairbanks. He had landed at Driftwood in his state Super Cub, talked to Audrey, and then headed north, following the snowmachine tracks of the thieves. He caught up with them at the Carbon Creek cabin about 50 miles north of Driftwood. The tracks indicated they had also just shot a moose out of season and made no attempt to salvage the meat. They were probably planning to use the carcass for luring in wolverines and wolves. Roland landed and talked to the three men. They were from the village of Wainwright and told him they thought Driftwood was abandoned so they just helped themselves to what they could conveniently haul away. They also said they had just found the moose dead. It was obviously a bogus story because the Driftwood camp was not "abandoned" and there were fresh tracks in the snow all around. The moose appeared to be freshly dead too, with nothing but snowmachine tracks around it. Roland told them they were going to be cited into court in Wainwright, and then he left. The men were eventually arraigned and admitted their guilt about the theft at Driftwood. They were required by the magistrate to write a letter of apology to Audrey, and send back Audrey's personal gear in the mail. They were also given a week of community service but nothing was done about the illegally taken moose because there apparently was not enough evidence that they had killed it and they wouldn't admit to it.

When I arrived at Driftwood in the ADF&G Bellanca Scout about seven hours after the theft occurred, I also followed the snowmachine tracks of the thieves. About ten miles north of Driftwood, I found the stolen barrel of fuel up on the top of a high ridge. The tracks leading to it indicated they were having trouble towing the full drum on their sled. In those days, people on the North Slope did not use hitches on their sleds. They just tied the heavy wooden sleds to their snowmachines with about a hundred feet of nylon rope. On the downhills, especially when pulling a heavy load, the sleds were largely out of control. The drum had been a real handful and I saw a couple places where it had almost overtaken the snowmachine. So, the thieves just decided to cache the drum for future use rather than drag it any further. I went back to the camp, picked up a barrel pump and eleven 5-gallon cans and returned to the drum. The top of the drum had been marked, "80/87, Property of ADF&G". One of the thieves used a screwdriver and scratched out the "ADF&G" and then scratched, "Freddy A" instead, as if to say, "Keep your hands off my stolen fuel." I got a pretty good chuckle out of that. I flew the cans back to Driftwood and then returned for the empty drum.

Our trips to and from Driftwood also resulted in several adventures, partly because it was a long way from Fairbanks and took four to six hours depending on the plane and the weather, and partly because the weather reporting and communications were poor. Once someone left Fairbanks headed for Driftwood, or vice versa, there was no way to communicate with them if the weather changed. On one occasion, Jim Davis left Fairbanks in late May with a very full load in the Scout, including eight white goslings that Audrey had wanted to raise that summer. After he was about two hours into the flight, a strong south wind started blowing at Driftwood but there was no way we could warn Jim. Strong south winds in the western Brooks Range result in bad turbulence on the north side of the mountains and ridges. As he was flying low across Noluck Lake, Jim ran into a severe mountain wave downdraft that nearly slammed him into the water. With full power, he just barely cleared the lakeshore on the far end of the lake. Just then, a voice came over the radio on 123.6 (the Bettles Flight Service and traffic frequency) and said, "Hey Jim, is that you down there?" He responded in a shaky voice several times but couldn't raise anyone. He then tried two air-to-air frequencies (122.9 and 122.8) and finally, the emergency frequency (121.5) and still got no response. He arrived in Driftwood pretty shaken up by the whole experience and with goose crap all around on the inside of the cabin. The little goslings didn't seem to have suffered, but Jim never did figure out who called on the radio. We just joked with him about it being the voice of God on 123.6, helping to deliver him out of a tight spot.

Another time, I was headed up to Driftwood in early November in my 90 horsepower Cub. Because of the short daylight and the slow speed of my Cub, I left Fairbanks in the dark at about 7:00 am. After refueling at Bettles, I headed northwest at 7,000 feet, high enough to go direct. I was optimistic about making it to Driftwood just before dark, but when I had about an hour and a half to go, I started seeing clouds and fog ahead. Looking to the south, I could see the Noatak Valley fogging in rapidly and I started worrying about arriving at Driftwood in the dusk and the fog. Instead, I diverted to Desperation Lake (the name seemed appropriate) instead and landed in about ten inches of snow on top of the lake ice. Within minutes, the lake fogged in and everything around was white. The only object I could see was the airplane, and when I looked away from it, I immediately became disoriented and had trouble standing upright. The human brain is not well-adapted to dealing with pure white conditions, at least mine wasn't.

I put the engine cover on, got out some Blazo, and got my catalytic heater going to keep the engine warm and then crawled into my tent. I awoke to a beautiful dawn, with no remaining fog, and clear skies. I had the airplane skis tied to my wing struts and would have changed over from wheels, but I didn't have a jack. Instead, I just taxied back and forth several times and beat a track in the snow. On about the fifth attempt, I got the plane airborne and then noticed I had the carburetor heat on. Carburetor heat robs about 10 percent of the power from the engine, so without it I probably could have got airborne on the second try, once I had a track beaten down in the snow! Anyway, I was glad to be back in the air and headed for Driftwood. I arrived there at 10:00 am and immediately asked what the weather had been like the previous evening. Audrey said it had been a beautiful clear evening with no fog at all!

One of the most bizarre things that happened to me on the way to Driftwood was on the Colville River. I had landed in my Cub to try to shoot a caribou for meat. I was on a nice big gravel bar near the mouth of the Awuna River and was just starting to unload the plane to set up camp, when a loud voice behind me said, "Hi, how ya doin?" I was so startled that I jerked upright and hit my head on the underside of the wing. I turned around and there stood a young man with a scraggly beard and a worried look on his face. I said, "Well hi, where'd you come from?" That got him going on a long and improbable story that took about five minutes to tell. He said he had once floated the Colville River with Dr. Tom Cade from Cornell University while doing surveys for birds of prey along the river. A couple of years had gone by and then he decided he liked the Colville so much that he wanted to go and live there. His plan had been to fly up with a load of gear, build a small house in the willows at the mouth of the Awuna, and then walk cross-country out to Umiat. The following year he was going to come back with his wife and live there permanently. Ron Costello had flown him in from Bettles to the Awuna in a Cessna 206 and he had been there for three weeks without seeing an airplane. During the three weeks, he had second thoughts about the whole plan and decided the idea of walking to Umiat wasn't feasible. So, he was now looking for a ride out. It certainly was a crazy story, especially the part about walking to Umiat. It would have been an easy 5-day float, but walking? No way! It was 150 miles of tussocks.

After he related the basics of the story, the man asked if I would fly him to Umiat. I said no, I wasn't going that way and I didn't have any extra fuel, nor any extra fuel in Umiat. He then said he'd pay me $500 to take him to Umiat. That was a lot of money then, but it would mean he'd have to leave all his junk behind and I didn't like that idea, either. And it didn't solve the fuel problem. I might have been able to get fuel from O. J. at Umiat, but I wasn't sure he had any. I countered that what I would do was call the Fairbanks office on the HF radio when I got to Driftwood and have them call Ron Costello and relay the message that he wanted to be picked up. That seemed to satisfy him, but I started having second thoughts about hunting on that side of the Colville. I was looking forward to a nice, relaxing hunt for a couple of days and didn't like the idea of being bothered by this crazy man. I told him I was going to take off and land and hunt on the other side of the river for a couple of days because there were more caribou over there, and then I'd go on to Driftwood and call the office to relay his story and request to be picked up. I assured him I was a responsible person and he needn't worry about being stranded on the Colville with winter coming. I then repacked the plane and flew over to the other side of the river. About an hour later, Jim Davis arrived in his Piper PA-12 Super Cruiser with Audrey. I knew Jim was about two hours behind me and I had told him to look for my plane somewhere around the mouth of the Awuna.

We all went caribou hunting the next day and each of us shot a caribou. Later in the afternoon, while we were packing the caribou meat back to the plane, I heard distant yelling coming from the other side of the Colville. It was the crazy man, and he was trying to get our attention. When I got done with my pack load, I went over to the river bank to see what he wanted. We started shouting back and forth to each other across about 100 yards of water. He was obviously desperate and didn't feel comfortable relying on me just getting a message to Ron Costello. He was really worried that he would end up dying there on the Colville. He yelled, "I'll pay you $1,000 to take me to Barrow!" I yelled back, "There is too much fog in Barrow this time of year." Then he yelled, "I'll pay you $1,000 to take me to Umiat." Well, rather than continue yelling back and forth, I decided to fly across the river and talk to him. I did that, and I managed to talk him down out of his panicked state of mind. I assured him once again we had an HF radio at Driftwood and both Audrey and Jim knew the situation and all three of us together were not likely going to forget about him. There were still about ten days or more before snow would come and there was plenty of time for Ron to get back to pick him up. He seemed to be satisfied with that so I flew back over to our camp. We left the next day and when I got to Driftwood, I called the office and passed on the message. I saw Ron the next time I was in Bettles about a month later and I asked him if he had picked up the guy at the mouth of the Awuna. Ron said he had, but when he landed on the gravel bar, the guy had come running out of the willows and Ron thought he was going to run into the propeller he was so eager to get to the plane. They loaded everything up and flew back to Bettles and the guy gave away most of his gear to people in Bettles and then headed back to the Lower 48. I could understand falling in love with the North Slope, it really is a fascinating place. But living in the willows on the upper Colville, permanently?

Driftwood Comes to an End

The 1981 flood did substantial damage to the runway at Driftwood, removing about 12 inches of the gravel surface from the north end. Subsequent floods continued to remove gravel, and we finally abandoned Driftwood in 1982 because flooding finally made the runway unsuitable for larger aircraft that were needed for fuel deliveries.

In 1986, four years after we had abandoned Driftwood and started using Eagle Creek strip instead, I flew the Beaver over to Driftwood with Bob Nelson, the Area Biologist from Nome, to look at the old camp and clean it up. It was a mess. People had been staying in the tent frame cabin (we had eventually enclosed it with plywood) and skinning foxes and wolverines there and leaving the carcasses, food, and garbage around. Grizzly bears had found it and torn apart the inside of the cabin. We spent a couple of hours picking up garbage, torn up pieces of table cloth, old cardboard boxes, and bear scats with garbage in them. One bear scat I found was pretty impressive. In it was a 24 x 4-inch long piece of cloth-backed, plastic table cloth and an old metal spice can. Both had gone right through the bear intact.

After we picked up all the garbage, we threw it inside the wrecked cabin, rolled a contaminated drum of fuel inside and tipped it over. It was a warm day and I could see the fumes of fuel shimmering around the cabin. I then made a Molotov cocktail, which I lit and threw into the cabin. It made a spectacular explosion and I had to run to get away from the flames, which grew to about 100 feet in height. Bob and I climbed into the Beaver and left, and that was the end of the Driftwood field camp.

The last time I landed at Driftwood was in 2013. What had been the old 3,500-foot strip looked just like a river channel. There were still a few drums at the old USGS camp, but the Rolligon was buried in the gravel in the middle of the Utukok River, with just a couple of feet of the top of the cab showing. People from Barrow or Wainwright had taken an old pile of plywood from the former USGS camp and built a new cabin about 300 yards to the east, up above the flood plain. That cabin is now listed as a North Slope Borough Search and Rescue cabin.

Barrel Caches

The piles of now mostly empty fuel drums that can still be found on the North Slope, and to a lesser extent on the Alaska Peninsula and the Seward Peninsula, are a legacy of past exploration and construction efforts in an era when logistical considerations and convenience trumped any concern for the environment. They nevertheless are an important part of the history of the state and are fascinating to visit. Most of the drums in the North Slope fuel caches were the old, heavy gauge, rolled crimp drums that were much more durable than standard drums. They were stamped "HUD" for "High Utility Drum" or "RIB" for "Reinforced Iron Barrel." They were designed for rough use, like rolling out of aircraft and throwing off sleds, and

Driftwood burning. After floods on the Utukok River damaged the airstrip in the early 1980s and bears destroyed the cook tent, the remains were cleaned up and burned in the mid-1980s.

even dropping into deep snow or lakes as a method of delivery. They were also widely sought after everywhere in Alaska for making wood stoves, and if all these thousands of empty drums had not been on the North Slope, they would have had some value.

There was an urgent need to find more domestic oil during World War II, and then to build the Cold War radar sites in the late 1950s. Most of the fuel caches on the North Slope were established to power the Cat trains that were used to explore for oil in Pet-4 between 1944 and 1953. Some very large drum caches, containing thousands of drums, were also established at DEW Line sites that were originally built 40-60 miles apart along the coast of northern Canada and Alaska and along the Alaska Peninsula and the Aleutian Islands. Because of improved radar technology, every other DEW Line station was abandoned within a few years after they were built and the buildings and drum piles were not removed from those abandoned sites until the 1990s.

Many of the drums in the fuel caches in northwestern Alaska were left full of fuel (mostly diesel), but over the years much of the fuel was used for stove oil by local people. During the late 1960s and early 1970s, wolf hunters (including then well known Bill Hutchinson of Bettles) were still using gasoline from those caches. Several of the caches in the remote southern and western portion of North Slope still contain fuel. I had the opportunity to investigate several of them during the late 1970s while working for ADF&G on the Western Arctic Caribou Herd and also during the early 2000s while flying photographers around the western North Slope.

My first experience with the large barrel caches was at Driftwood during the late 1970s and early 1980s. Although there were some old, empty drums from Pet-4 fuel caches left at Driftwood, the main cache of barrels was on the ridge about a mile or two southeast of the strip. Barrel caches were generally placed on ridgetops to avoid problems with spring floods and getting the barrels drifted in by blowing snow. In 1977, there were around 150 drums in the cache and at least 50 were still full. Most contained No. 1 diesel fuel but there were still several drums full of 100/130 aviation gasoline, and 115/145 octane aviation gasoline. There were also the remains of some boxed gasoline but the boxes were broken and the old square 5-gallon cans were empty and in poor shape.

Boxed gasoline was widely used in Alaska until the mid-1970s. It was produced by most major oil companies, including Texaco, Union Oil, and Chevron, and was the only approved container for carrying fuel inside an aircraft with passengers. Each box measured 15 ½ by 21 inches and was 15 inches tall. The bottom and sides of the box were made of ⁵⁄₁₆-inch pine and ends were made of ³⁄₄-inch pine. A box contained two square 5-gallon cans. The empty cans were very useful in the bush for roofing material and rodent proofing in cabins, funnels for refueling aircraft, and any application where sheet metal was needed. The boxes were widely used for furniture and shelving and have become a real collector's item. It was the end of an era when Chevron stopped producing boxed gas in the mid-1970s. Boxed gas was still available in Kotzebue from Arctic Lighterage until supplies ran out in 1979.

In 1979, after a USGS crew left the Rolligon at Driftwood, we were able to drive the Rolligon up to the barrel cache and pump diesel fuel from the full drums up into empty drums on the back of the Rolligon. This free source of old diesel fuel eliminated our need to bring in stove oil by plane or use our helicopter fuel for stove oil. However, we discovered the 25-year-old, syrupy-looking, amber colored diesel left sooty deposits in our oil stove and chimney. It burned much cleaner when we added some of the old gasoline to it. We also cut it with Jet-B, which contains two-thirds naphtha. A couple of times, when we were low on aircraft fuel, we actually used some of the old 100/130 avgas from the Pet-4 barrel cache. We didn't like to use it because of its age and because much of it had lost its color (it had turned clear). It also had 3-4 times as much lead as the 80/87 avgas we used in the Super Cubs and the Beaver and lead fouling of spark plugs was a problem when using any high-octane gas in low compression engines not designed for it.

Probably the most interesting drum cache I ever visited was near Omicron Hill, south of the Utukok River. I had been aware of the cache since the late 1970s but it wasn't until mid-June 2006 that I was able to explore it. I found a place to land on a ridge nearby and spent a couple of hours at the cache with a landscape photographer. There were about 125 empty drums and more than 50 drums full of diesel. Many of the empty drums had been chopped open with an axe and the contents removed by local residents as fuel for cabin stoves. At this particular cache there was also at least 50 boxes of DuPont Gelignite (similar to dynamite) explosive. The explosives

Inside Buck Maxon's Twin Beechcraft on a trip from Driftwood to Kotzebue in 1977. ADF&G was still using large quantities of boxed gasoline then. Boxed gasoline was very handy, especially because the empty boxes and cans continued to be useful for all kinds of purposes once the gasoline was used. The ultimate in recycling!

were used in seismic exploration to create underground shock waves to locate caverns that could contain oil or gas. The Gelignite had been packed in boxes that were 26 ½ inches long by 9 inches wide by about 18 inches high. Each box had contained two columns of six waxed tubes filled with Gelignite. The boxes were labeled "High Explosives, Dangerous, This Side Up" and the purchase order numbers stamped on the tops of the boxes were still legible where they had not been exposed to sunlight. The pile of boxes had originally been covered with canvas, but the wind and grizzly bears uncovered the pile. The bears had also broken open all the boxes and torn into the Gelignite canisters. Bears were still coming to the site and had very recently been rolling in the old broken canisters, the contents of which looked like dark brown sawdust. None of the canisters remained intact.

I was curious about whether the Gelignite still had any active ingredient left after the 50+ years it had been there, or whether the nitroglycerin had weathered away and become inert. I gathered up about a gallon of the brown sawdust material and made a pile of it. I then made an elongated pile of box wood next to the sawdust and started it on fire. I walked away about 50 yards and hid behind an empty drum while the little fire burned toward the old explosive. I wasn't too concerned about it exploding because even fresh Gelignite is stable, burns slowly when ignited, and can only be set off with a blasting cap. Much to my disappointment, the pile of old brown sawdust material just smoldered when the fire reached it. It didn't behave any differently than damp sawdust would have. There must have been some chemical residue that was attracting the bears, but whatever was left wasn't very flammable.

In the late 1970s, the Bureau of Land Management allocated money to document and clean up the old drum caches in Pet-4, but after the project was over and all of the money was spent, many of the drum caches remained, especially in the western and southern portion of the petroleum reserve. During the 1990s there was another large effort to clean up contaminated old DEW Line sites and it was much more successful. However, an abandoned ship in Demarcation Bay near the Canadian border that ran aground in a storm while delivering supplies for the DEW Line sites still remains. With the bureaucratic and cumbersome environmental and labor laws that affect everything on federal land in the arctic, cleaning up the remaining fuel caches will be very expensive.

A freighter abandoned after it ran aground in a storm in Demarcation Inlet during DEW Line construction in the 1950s.

Board from the top of a box of Gelignite. About 50 boxes of Gelignite and 150 drums of fuel had been cached at Omicron Hill near the Utukok River in the 1950s.

Western Alaska by Snowmachine

In the early 1990s, ADF&G Area Biologist Tim Osborne invited me to travel with him on his annual spring travels by snowmachine through his 75,000 square mile area in the upper Koyukuk drainage and Central Brooks Range. Tim was an adventurous traveler with a great deal of scientific curiosity. He also believed in traveling throughout his area and getting to know people personally along the way. The best way to do that was by snowmachine in winter because that was the way most local people traveled. There is always a lot to see and learn while traveling on the ground, so I was eager to accompany him, especially because we would also be going through winter ranges of the Western Arctic Caribou herd and I had an active research project going on the herd.

I flew to Galena in early March, and after a couple of days of preparation, we departed. Tim was driving a Polaris, liquid-cooled, wide track snowmachine and I was driving his older air-cooled Polaris 440 long track. On the first day, we passed through several thousand caribou on the 90-mile trail from Galena to Huslia, where we stayed with Tim's friends, Madeline and Cue Bifelt. The following day, we drove northwest to the Selawik Hot Springs on the divide between the Koyukuk and Selawik River drainages, another almost 100-mile day. At the Selawik Hot Spring, there was an "Eskimo cabin" and an "Indian cabin," built by people from both sides of the divide. Since we were coming from the Interior, we stayed in the "Indian cabin." The bathhouse at the spring was shared by everyone, but we were the only ones there at the time. After a long day of riding in cold, windy weather, it was great to soak in the hot spring. One unpleasant surprise, however, was that the threshold of the bathhouse door was aluminum and when you stepped on it, your wet foot instantly froze to the -20F metal!

On the third day, we woke up to low clouds and what looked like white-out conditions to the north toward the village of Shungnak. Tim wanted to stay at the Hot Springs one more day, but I convinced him that he knew the trail well and we would be in spruce trees most of the time, so off we went. We made it to Shungnak rather easily and since it was still early in the day, we refueled and headed towards Ambler, 28 miles further along the trail which parallels the Kobuk River but bypasses all the twists and turns of the river. Soon after leaving Shungnak, the weather deteriorated and we could only see a few hundred feet. We crossed a small lake and stopped for lunch in the shelter of some trees, hoping the visibility would improve.

After lunch, Tim started off first but he was driving into the wind and should have been driving with the wind. I caught up to him and convinced him to turn. After a bit, we realized we had certainly lost the Shungnak-Ambler trail and didn't know whether it was north of us or south of us, so we decided to turn onto the first creek that headed down towards the Kobuk River. We drove and drove and didn't come to the Kobuk River. We then checked the direction the small stream was flowing and found we were going up it rather than down it! By then we had almost 50 miles on our odometers, almost twice as many miles as it was from Shungnak to Ambler. At that point, we were clearly and hopelessly lost and decided to just camp for the night and try again in the morning. So, we turned around and started looking for a place to camp.

We soon came upon a nice-looking old mining cabin on a hill and I climbed up to take a look at it. Remarkably, it was completely filled with a giant old steam "donkey" engine ("donkeys" were big steam engines used by miners to power winches and belt-driven machinery and provide steam for thawing) with not even room to fit our two sleeping bags. We continued on a little further and found another smaller mining cabin filled with old empty drums and mining odds and ends. We threw enough of the drums out into the snow to make a couple of spaces for our sleeping bags and then brewed up a pot of nice, hot tea.

The next morning, we awoke to clear skies and very cold temperatures. By the time we got the snowmachines going, the still frigid air of the little hollow we were staying in was filled with engine smoke and smoke from our straining clutch drive belts. After a lot of pulling, revving and shaking, we finally got the machines moving and we were glad to be on the way again. We eagerly drove to the top of a nearby ridge to get our bearings but, much to our surprise, right below us was the village of Shungnak, a place we thought we had left far behind the previous day. We drove down into town to refuel again and ran into Billy Burnhardt, who I had met years previously on my first trip to Shungnak to count caribou. I told Billy about how we got turned around on the way to Ambler and he laughed and said, "Yeah, that can be a problem. The wind always changes directions about half way to Ambler."

We made the 28 miles to Ambler in a couple of hours and stayed with school teacher Nick Jans for about four days, giving talks in the school and preparing for the next leg of the journey. Tim entertained the school kids with a hunter education talk. One of his very effective props was an old .410 shotgun that had a nasty habit of firing if it was cocked and you set the stock down too hard on the floor. He first demonstrated that the gun was unloaded, and then when the kids weren't looking, he slipped an empty shell into it with a live primer. He normally then "accidentally" banged the "unloaded" gun stock

-first onto the floor and the primer would go off, scaring the kids and waking up those who were bored or not paying attention. Unfortunately, in the Ambler demonstration, the floor was carpeted and the gun wouldn't go off so Tim tried the teacher's desk instead. The desk wasn't strong enough and the butt of the shotgun broke right through it, so everyone in the classroom got a big surprise, including Tim. The teacher wasn't too happy about the destroyed desk but agreed that the presentation was very effective.

Our next leg of the journey was up and over the Redstone Pass into the Noatak River through the mountains to Anaktuvuk Pass. The first night, we bivouacked without a fire at the start of the Redstone Pass. Tim liked to travel light with easy to cook food. We largely lived on tea, Pilot Bread, salmon strips, moose jerky, and raw chocolate chip cookie dough (with a generous amount of whiskey added for antifreeze). The cookie dough also had twice the normal amount of butter for extra energy and it was rolled in waxed paper to help keep it from disintegrating with the constant jostling and bumping on the snowmachine sled. The only thing we really had to cook was the tea.

On the second night, Tim had planned to build an igloo in the Noatak Valley because it was going to be wide open and wind-blown. Neither of us had ever built an igloo before, but Tim had brought a copy of instructions with him, which he pulled out of his snowmachine suit. With Tim reading the directions and passing them on to me, I scurried around cutting snow blocks with my Shark-Tooth carpenter's saw. Once we had enough to start, we both set about building the spiraling circle of blocks about nine feet in diameter. Even though we were tired after a long day of traveling, building the igloo was great fun, especially when we put the final "key" block in place on top. By the time we finished, it was 10:00 pm with the light fading and the temperature dropping rapidly. Once inside, the igloo was beautiful and very bright with just the light of a single candle. I fired up the primus stove and we cooked up our long-anticipated cup of hot tea. Very quickly, the walls began to drip as the temperatures climbed above freezing inside. With the stove off, the walls stopped dripping and we had a restful night at what felt like just the right temperature. We had a thermometer with us and by morning it read -40F outside and +18F inside from just our body heat.

We hated to leave our beautiful igloo in the morning. We had grown quite attached to it. We later heard that people from both Anaktuvuk Pass and Ambler had found it and they thought it was very funny to see a central Canadian-style igloo in the Noatak Valley. No one in Alaska ever built snow-block igloos. It had taken us about three hours to build it and that seemed like a long time, but when I talked to a man from Aklavik in the western Northwest Territories a few years later, he told me that was actually not too bad. It usually took experienced people at least a couple of hours to build a good small igloo for overnight shelter.

The night after building the igloo, we stayed in an 8 x 10-foot wall tent in the Nigu River Valley. The tent belonged to Ben Hopson Jr. from Anaktuvuk Pass and he had invited Tim to use it. It was luxury! Caribou hides on the floor and a little sheet metal stove. Despite the -20F temperatures outside, we were basking in the warmth of the tent in our T-shirts, and drying things out as well. The igloo was nice, but it was hard to dry things out.

The following day, we arrived in Anaktuvuk Pass and Tim gave his hunter education talk without destroying any more desks. I also gave a talk about caribou and about the animals in the Brooks Range. One slide I showed was of an Alaska marmot (*Marmota Broweri*) and I used the Inupiat name "siksikpuk," literally meaning, big ground squirrel. I was surprised none of the kids knew about them or had even seen one because marmots live all around Anaktuvuk Pass in rocky areas. In the old days, they were an important fur animal for both local use and for trade. Times had changed!

The situation with caribou around Anaktuvuk Pass that winter was rather enlightening to me. Caribou were abundant and several thousand had arrived to winter right around the village in November. Despite heavy local hunting, the caribou stayed all winter. By the time we arrived there in March, everyone had all the caribou meat and hides they wanted and very little hunting was occurring. Once the village quieted down at night, the caribou grazed right up to within a few yards of people's houses. As the village woke up and vehicles and heavy machinery started driving around, dogs started barking, etc., the caribou slowly moved away about a half mile. The caribou were obviously very tolerant of the aircraft coming and going and all the other village activity, as long as they weren't being actively hunted.

The next day, we drove east through the Brooks Range to the North Fork of the Koyukuk and Tinyaguk Rivers, over to the Glacier River and then on to Wiseman, where we had dinner with Jack Reakoff and his family. Rather than staying in Wiseman, we continued on to Coldfoot, where, after a long exhausting day of getting stuck many times in deep snow, we rented a room at 1:00 am. Tim stayed up even later and made sure that the local Fish and Game contract vendor had all his questions answered. By the time Tim finally got to bed it was about 3:00 am and starting to get light again. Coldfoot is a 24-hour truck stop on the Dalton Highway and there is usually someone awake all night.

The following day, we drove to Bettles and I caught a plane to Fairbanks. Tim continued on for a couple more days to get back to Galena, completing a round trip of over 1,200 miles by snowmachine. It was a great trip and people really appreciated Tim's efforts at educating kids and providing support for the vendors. A little extra effort is really appreciated in the bush, especially when it comes from people usually viewed as bureaucrats.

Chapter 2

Weather

Weather is a pervasive force and constant concern in Alaska. When a friend at the University of Maine heard I was moving to Alaska in 1972, he said, "If you don't like weather, you won't like Alaska." He had lived in Fairbanks while going to school at the University, and he was right! Fortunately, I loved weather, all kinds of weather, or at least, I used to. Now I'm a bit more selective about the weather I like. Dealing with deep snow and operating machinery and aircraft below zero is not my idea of fun anymore. But the weather is one of the reasons I'll never permanently leave Alaska. I still love the change of seasons and the drama of the big Pacific storms.

One of the things to keep in mind with weather in Alaska is that weather records have only been kept for about 100 years, so that means new records are set almost every year. With Murphy's Law, it is very likely that the days you might pick for a hunting or fishing trip or a hike in the wilderness could include weather that will set new records. Many of the weather experiences I describe below occurred on days when records were set.

Weathered In!

I never consistently kept a journal, except for short periods of time on some projects. If I had, I'm sure a frequent entry would have been something like, "Weathered in again today…." During my first month in Alaska, I spent two weeks weathered in during snow and rainstorms in the Brooks Range in May and early June, usually a very nice time of year. It was a harbinger of things to come. During my first five years working for ADF&G on the Western Arctic Caribou

Herd in northwestern Alaska, I'm sure we collectively spent at least a couple of months at Bettles, Umiat, Driftwood, Kotzebue, and Kobuk waiting for weather to be good enough to fly. I first found it really fun telling jokes and stories, playing cards, reading, and checking on the airplanes. Once, in the village of Buckland, we arrived in March to radio-collar caribou, but spent ten straight days in a northwest windstorm and ground blizzard. The silver lining to that storm was that we got to know the local people pretty well and even played a challenge game with the high school basketball team.

During my first fall season with ADF&G, I was sent to the village of Kobuk with ADF&G Technician Ed Crain to try to count the caribou crossing the river near Ambler (see map on page 17). There was a major crisis with caribou in northwest Alaska because the Western Arctic Caribou Herd had crashed and the herd was a critical source of food for many people. As with many controversies and crises, there were major disagreements about whether there was a real problem and what or who was to blame. Being a new employee and still relatively new to Alaska, I really didn't have an opinion. I was just happy to have a job and I was very excited about being able to work on caribou in northwest Alaska.

Our assignment was to fly to Kobuk, rent a cabin, and count all the caribou crossing the Kobuk River. During the first day, by flying along the lines of migrating caribou, we were able to count about 29,000. Then the weather settled in, with a low ceiling, light snow, and rime icing; consequently, we had a couple of days off. On that trip, because of those two down days, I met three of the most interesting people I have ever met in Alaska. Guy Moyer was the first of those. He ran the store in Kobuk and owned the cabin we rented for $20 a day. The first evening in Kobuk, I went over to the store to pay Guy for the cabin. There were no phones in Kobuk then, but somehow Guy was expecting us. Guy had come into the country in the 1930s to mine for gold and trap. He was in his mid-70s when I met him and by then he had settled down to run the store in Kobuk. He also bought furs from the few people who were still trapping, and he sold hunting licenses for the state. I wish I had

ADF&G Wildlife Technician Ed Crain at Guy Moyer's rental cabin in Kobuk in 1977 where we spent many days waiting out bad weather. We counted about 29,000 caribou crossing the Kobuk River during the first week of October. At the time, there were approximately 75,000 in the Western Arctic Herd.

realized what a gold mine he was himself. I spent several evenings with him, sitting in his store until 10:00 pm, chatting about the old days and the changes he had seen. He seldom had a chance to talk to people other than the locals who had probably heard all of his old stories. So, he really enjoyed having a fresh audience. I will mention more about Guy in the chapter entitled "Trapping."

The second really interesting person I met while weathered in at Kobuk was Tony Bernhardt. His father was Albert Bernhardt, a German who had come to the arctic as a young man in the early 1900s. Albert had married an Eskimo girl and settled down to trap and run local enterprises in Teller on the Seward Peninsula. Tony was one of the youngest of 12 children and he settled down in Kobuk to run an Air Taxi and guiding service in the 1950s. He had a Helio Courier and a 125-horsepower Super Cub he put on floats in the summer. Tony had a diverse flying business. Besides providing transportation for local people, he also flew wildlife surveys for ADF&G, dropped off or guided hunters and fishermen, and hunted wolves in the winter time when there was no other flying to be done. Tony also served on the Board of Fish and Game in the 1960s and early 1970s.

Ed and I spent many evenings with Tony in his house overlooking the Kobuk River, listening to his stories and drinking tea. Tony became something of a local hero in the late 1960s and the 1970s when wolves were really abundant. During some years, he shot 50-100 wolves per year. There was a $50 bounty on wolves until 1968. Tony collected the bounty from the wolves he shot and turned the hides over to his wife to make parka ruffs to sell. Although there were no restrictions on shooting from the air until 1972, when the Federal Airborne Hunting Act passed, Tony generally did not shoot wolves from the air, preferring instead to land first and then shoot.

Tony told Ed and I that he had tried shooting from the air but he would get caught up in the chase and shoot the wolves in places where he couldn't land. He would then end up wasting a lot of daylight dragging dead wolves back to the plane. He said he found it was a lot more efficient to simply circle up high without disturbing the wolves and wait for them to get to a good landing area. He seldom took anybody with him because the plane performed better with just one person. Most of the time, the first hint the wolves had that someone was after them was the sound of the skis touching down on the snow behind them. Tony often got several wolves in a single landing, even with just his favorite .243 bolt action rifle.

Many people who were opposed to wolf control and wolf hunting were skeptical about whether it was possible to even "land-and-shoot." Even some ADF&G biologists believed that "land-and-shoot" was really "shoot-and-land" and thought people were using the term as a loophole to get around the Federal Airborne Hunting Act. I was also skeptical until I talked to Tony. Tony was a very honest, straight-forward person who had no intention of breaking the law. After I got my first Cub in 1979, based on what he told me, I also tried landing and shooting wolves. I found it to be quite easy and also quite safe. I did it successfully with my bolt action .30-06 but preferred my .223 Ruger Mini-14. Tony was absolutely right. Most of the time, the first thing the wolves heard was the sound of the plane's skis touching down in the snow behind them.

Tony landed his Cub on floats in some amazingly short places, including the little pothole lake in the middle of Shungnak. People loved it when they could take off on the river at Kobuk and be dropped right in downtown Shungnak to visit relatives after a ten-minute flight. In 1977, Tony had just recovered financially from a mishap with the Helio Courier. He was taking off on the river on skis and hit a stump with the right ski. The thing he disliked most about the design of the Helio was the big blind spot on the right side of the plane. After that wreck, I could see why. Other topics we discussed included the coming of snowmachines in the late 1960s. Tony thought they were a very useful tool that made life in the Bush a lot easier and they reduced the need for people to kill thousands of salmon and caribou for dog food, but he couldn't believe how the kids abused them, including his own son Billy. He said, "A machine like that would last me ten years, these kids will ruin one in two." Some things never change. Within a few years after I met him, Tony started spending winters in Hawaii and then retired to Anchorage. He had grown tired of fighting the extreme cold in winter.

The third person I met while weathered in at Kobuk was Joe Harvey. Joe was in his 60s when I met him in 1977 and was very much an Inupiaq subsistence hunter and trapper of the old tradition. He had a cabin in Kobuk but spent much of his time out on the land, running a trapline in winter up towards Selby Lake or fishing for sheefish and salmon in late summer and fall. A couple of years after I first met him, he invited me into his cabin one day in the spring. It was a simple log cabin, chinked with sphagnum moss, about 16 x 20 feet with a very small door and low roof. The only furnishings inside were caribou skins on the floor, gas boxes for shelves, a two-burner Coleman stove, a two-burner Coleman lantern, and one home-made wooden chair. In his shed outside the cabin were frozen sheefish, stacked like cordwood. In the snow outside his cabin there were also carcasses of wolves, wolverines, foxes, and marten, each with a little piece of dried fish in their mouths. I asked him about the fish, and he indicated it was food for their trip to the afterlife. Joe didn't speak much English in 1977, which was too bad because he was obviously a very capable and knowledgeable man and I would have loved to have him share some of his stories with me. Once he offered to sell me a stone seal oil lamp he said he found while clearing a trapline trail. All he wanted for it was $20, but I didn't even have $20 on me. The seal oil lamp had a chip out of it where he hit it with an axe. In those days, people dug artifacts out of historically used sites as a way to get a little extra money. That was all part of their "subsistence" way of life. The story about finding it while clearing trail might have been made up because some people were starting to be critical about digging and selling old artifacts.

I also remember being weathered in frequently at Bettles, either trying to get north or west to work with the caribou or trying to get back to Fairbanks. Bettles is a bit of a weather hole because it is surrounded by the Brooks Range to the north and an extensive range of wind-scoured hills to the southeast. During the late 1970s and 1980s being weathered in at Bettles in late winter was actually very enjoyable and I heard some of the most entertaining stories I have ever heard in my 49 years in Alaska. The period of aerial wolf hunting (that is, shooting from the air) was just over, but several enterprising pilots had figured out "landing-and-shooting" wolves and consequently there were usually several wolf hunters staying at the Bettles Lodge. It was a warm and friendly atmosphere with lots of stories, some no doubt exaggerated. Several of my favorites were about Bill Hutchinson, a former airport manager at Bettles and legendary aerial wolf hunter. Bill had been hunting wolves on the North Slope starting in the 1960s and occasionally flying support for the Cat trains of oil exploration crews. He had been using fuel from some of the old Pet-4 drum caches that were scattered around the western North Slope. He used a Citabria, instead of the more common Super Cub, and he was very good. He also mostly flew

Bettles, transportation hub of the central Brooks Range and base for wolf hunters during the 1960s, 1970s, and early 1980s.

alone and did the flying and the shooting by holding the stick between his knees while he shot. Unlike Tony Bernhardt, Bill Hutchinson preferred shooting from the air over landing and shooting.

When shooting from the air ended in 1972, Bill kept at it, with the full support of local people. He was charged once for illegally shooting from the air but acquitted by a jury in Fairbanks. It should have been an open and shut case, but at that time, there was not a jury in Alaska that would ever convict anyone for shooting wolves illegally. For several more years, Bill played a cat-and-mouse game with Fish and Wildlife Protection officers. Once, officers got an unusual tip from Bettles that Bill was sending a big shipment of gunny sacks full of illegally taken wolf hides to Fairbanks. Undeterred by the first unsuccessful trial, officers decided to try again. They needed some good evidence to charge Bill, like wolf hides full of buckshot holes, so they were waiting for the shipment when it arrived. When they opened the sacks, they were full of carpet remnants! It was an obvious prank, and almost everyone in Bettles was in on it. Bill died when he crashed his Citabria at the mouth of the Hunt Fork on the John River in 1975. I remember seeing the remains of the plane for many years when I passed through there while doing caribou work.

By the time I started working for ADF&G in 1977, Bill Hutchinson had been dead for about two years, but the stories about him just kept getting better. One evening in the Bettles Lodge, one of the locals who had known Hutchinson well, told a story about how Bill developed a very effective technique that involved roaring down on wolves from up high, unloading his shotgun at them and then pulling the plane up into a loop. Supposedly, while he was at the top of the loop, he would quickly reload and be ready to shoot when he leveled out again at the bottom. As you can imagine, there were a lot skeptics in the well-lubricated audience and a lot of good-natured guffawing, but the story teller swore it was true.

One of my most recent weathered in experiences was on the North Slope in 2016. We were doing surveys to document the distribution of wolverines all across the Slope and that year we based in Atqasuk to do the western third of it. We arrived there about the 10th of March with the temperature around -35F. We rented a house and stayed there 42 days to get in just 12 days of flying. There were frequent snowstorms and ground blizzards. Much of the time, we couldn't even see our airplanes that were parked less than a mile away. Fortunately, we had good Wi-Fi and there was an airport camera near the planes so when the visibility was bad, we could see the planes by accessing the camera site with our phones. We did get quite a bit of exercise shoveling snow, though. Like most government-built houses in rural Alaska villages, very little thought is ever given to designing them for local conditions. The entryway to the house in Atqasuk drifted in every time the wind blew and we had to dig it out almost every day. Fortunately, the outer door opened inward so at least we weren't trapped inside after every blow. Inward opening doors are generally not a good idea where there are bears around, especially polar bears, but drifting snow was much more of a concern at Atqasuk.

One of my favorite "weathered in" stories was about the ADF&G bear research crew at Driftwood in 1977. Biologists Harry Reynolds and Ron Ball, Ron's wife Maureen, and pilot Jim Rood had spent the entire summer at Driftwood, working on the bear project. It had been a very fun summer, but everyone was ready to leave and resume their lives. In late September, they wanted to locate all the radio-collared bears once more before heading back for the winter. It took ten days of waiting to get the one good day they needed to locate all of the bears. After finding all the bears, there was just enough daylight remaining to get to Kotzebue but the crew decided to spend one more night to avoid being in a big rush. The next morning, the weather was bad again and it remained bad for ten more days. By the time they left on about October 20th, they had spent 20 days cooped up together in the 12 x 16 wall tent, listening to the thundering of the army surplus oil stove, waiting for two good days of weather. Harry is a fun guy to be in camp with and really knows how to run a camp well, but you can only read the same books and hear the same stories so many times. It was particularly frustrating for Jim Rood because he could have been making money flying on other jobs. Everyone remembered that situation for years and went to extraordinary lengths to not get caught like that again.

Wind

Despite flying for many years in some of Alaska's windiest places during my career with ADF&G, including the North Slope and the Alaska Peninsula, I never had an aircraft damaged by wind, except at my home base. Wind is my least favorite of all of Mother Nature's elements so I have really enjoyed living in the Fairbanks bowl, which is usually a great refuge from the wind, except for spring dust devils and summer thunderstorms. I certainly had some unexpected and interesting experiences with wind though, and they are worth relating because I learned some valuable lessons with each one.

Alaska Peninsula

When a person first visits the Alaska Peninsula, it becomes obvious right away that wind is a force to be reckoned with. One immediately notices the small aircraft at King Salmon with vehicles parked in front of them to break the wind, cabins with ½-inch steel cables tying them down, pumice patches with no vegetation growing on them, lakes that have been elongated by the prevailing southeasterly storm winds, and below-ground revetments at the Cold Bay airport for parking large aircraft.

Once, in mid-June during the late 1990s, we experienced a storm with winds over 100 mph. We were doing a caribou calf mortality study on the Sandy River calving area of the Northern Alaska Peninsula caribou herd and living in a cabin belonging to Mel Gillis, a local guide. A commercial video outfit called Wild Things from Los Angeles was sharing the cabin with us. I reluctantly agreed to work with them, getting pictures of caribou and caribou calves, and hopefully of bears or wolves killing caribou calves. They had intentions of producing one of the first of the Alaska "reality" shows that were to become so popular. They agreed to share helicopter expenses and fuel. They also hired an Alaskan camp manager who was experienced at running camps under Alaska's often challenging conditions, so I hoped they would get the pictures they wanted without requiring too much baby-sitting. I'd had mixed experiences working with photographers and film crews. BBC, National Geographic, PBS, and Michio Hoshino were very good and fun to work with, and some other crews had been good too. However, a few were demanding, unprepared, and just too much trouble. The Wild Things photographers were actually fun to work with but Wild Things turned out to be a company out of Los Angeles that hired only freelance photographers and, in the end, the company refused to pay their share of the helicopter bill.

Around the first of June we rendezvoused in King Salmon and then headed down to the Sandy River, with a stop to refuel out of our drums at Port Heiden. When we arrived at Port Heiden, I noticed the town's large fuel storage tanks had just been painted bright white. It must have been quite a job to completely strip and paint the huge tanks. The runway had also been recently graded and it was nice and smooth, with a coarse sand and fine gravel surface. After fueling up, we flew about another hour down to Sandy River to get settled into the cabin and prepared for collaring caribou calves in the morning. I suggested to the Wild Things crew that they camp on a tundra flat, right in the middle of the biggest concentration of caribou cows so they would have the best chance of getting video from the ground.

The first days of the project went smoothly and we had about 20 newborn calves collared by the third day. I would take off in the state Bellanca Scout about 7:00 am to see if any of the calves died overnight. I would then radio back the location of any dead calves, and helicopter pilot Rick Swisher would bring Area Biologist Dick Sellers, or another member of the crew in the R-44 helicopter to see what killed the calves.

On the fourth day of the project, I climbed into the Scout at about 7:00 am, as usual, and headed out to find all the radio-collared calves. The sky to the southeast had an angry look to it, with a high

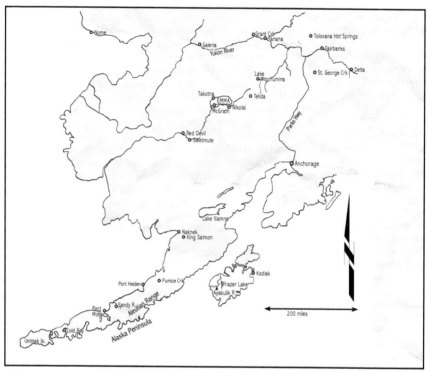

Alaska Peninsula and Southwest Alaska.

thin overcast and some lenticular (lens-shaped) clouds hanging just above the volcanic peaks of the Aleutian Range. What really caught my attention, though, was the occasional small swirls of volcanic ash coming down the sides of the mountains to the southeast. I kept an eye on the weather and located the first few calves, but the air was becoming turbulent and the distant rooster tails of dust were becoming larger and more frequent, so I gave up tracking the caribou and headed back to the Sandy River strip. It was only blowing about 15 mph when I landed but the wind was becoming unpredictable and gusty. I stopped the Scout next to some tall alders along the runway and ran to the cabin to warn the crew of the changing weather. I then got in with Rick and we flew over to the Wild Things camp to suggest they strike their tents and come back to the airstrip and cabin where they would find some shelter from the wind. They were reluctant to break camp because it had taken a whole day to get it set up and comfortable, but I assured them that if we were in for a regular Alaska Peninsula blow, they wouldn't want to be in the middle of that wide open tundra flat. They reluctantly started breaking camp and Rick said he'd be back in an hour to start flying them to the strip.

Back at the airstrip, I took a hand saw and cut a place in the tall alders where I could keep the Scout from blowing away. Three of us pushed the Scout back into the hole I cut and we tied it down securely to alder stumps. Rick started to move the Wild Things crew with the helicopter. The wind was about 15 and gusty and still not too bad at Sandy River, but the volcanic dust plumes coming down the sides of the volcanoes in the Aleutian Range were looking pretty serious. Rick finished hauling in the Wild Things crew and we all retired to the cabin for a late breakfast. I asked Rick if he wanted to move the helicopter behind the cabin but he said he thought it would be OK where it was.

While we were having breakfast the wind suddenly picked up and I went outside to move my sleeping tent to a more sheltered spot in the thick alders. I also asked Rick if he still thought the helicopter would be OK. He said, "Well, I'd like to move it behind the cabin, but it's too risky to start it with this wind; the main rotor might hit the tail boom." So, instead of moving it we decided to build a tripod out of alders to support the front rotor blade. We then secured the tripod with ropes tied to some pieces of angle iron we drove into the ground. At that point there wasn't much more we could do so we returned to the cabin to watch the blow develop.

By mid-afternoon I guessed it was blowing 30-40 mph at the strip, and the wind noise was considerable. The lenticular clouds over the Aleutian Range were huge and stretched as far north and south as we could see. By midnight, when it began to get dark, the wind around the cabin was really thundering and it was difficult to stand up outside. Our sleeping tents were all OK in the thick alders and both aircraft seemed to be doing fine. The Wild Things crew were very glad to be at the cabin with their tents in the alders, and not out on the open tundra. If they had stayed where they were, their tents would probably have been floating out in Bristol Bay somewhere. By late that first day, as the wind continued to increase, I was actually more worried about the cabin blowing away than anything else because it was relatively new, up on pilings, and not cabled to the ground like most cabins on the Alaska Peninsula.

The wind blew all the next day and we stayed in the cabin, playing cards, telling stories, and reading. It finally started to abate after the second day, and by the morning of the third day it was calm. After flying over the caribou calves and investigating two that died during the blow, we decided to go up to Port Heiden to refuel and haul more fuel back to Sandy River. I left Sandy River in the Scout with 15 empty gas cans and was the first one into Port Moller.

Instead of being the nice, smooth runway I remembered from the previous week, it was full of cobble-sized rocks and was anything but smooth. What had happened didn't dawn on me until I taxied past the big fuel storage tanks. They weren't bright white anymore. The sides facing the runway were bare metal and only the back sides were still white. Our fuel drums were the same way, bare metal on the windward side and blue on the lee side. The wind had blown so hard at Port Heiden that all the newly graded sand and gravel had blown off the runway and sandblasted everything down wind. Some of the windows in the terminal building were so chipped and scoured they were opaque, like frosted glass.

A couple of locals came by and I asked them about the wind. One guy said he had an anemometer on a little weather station at his house that registered 104 mph, before it blew away. I asked him what they were going to do about the sand blasted fuel tanks. He just laughed and shrugged and said, "Paint 'em again, I guess."

Wind shears (winds of different directions and velocities at different altitudes) are also a common phenomenon on the Alaska Peninsula, especially on the Pacific side of the Aleutian Range. They can be very dangerous for small aircraft. On the Alaska Peninsula, they are usually associated with mechanical turbulence (wind over rough terrain), mountain wave winds, or thunderstorms. Headlands that jut into the Pacific Ocean or valleys where strong winds are funneled are particularly bad. One can be flying along in calm air, come around a headland, and suddenly encounter moderate turbulence (turbulence that is occasionally strong enough for the aircraft to be out of control).

On one of my first trips to the Alaska Peninsula in late May 1995, I was radio-tracking caribou with Rick Swisher riding in the back of the state Scout as observer. While we were circling a radio-collared caribou I noticed the waves on one side of a small lake were going in the opposite direction to the waves on the other side. We both noticed that at the same time and I was extra cautious as I approached the caribou. We had to plan on an east wind, then a wind shear, and then a west wind. Fortunately, the maximum wind speed was only about 15 mph, but it was a real struggle to control the plane and still get a good look at the caribou.

Wind shears have caused many airplane wrecks on the Peninsula. Wind shear was a likely cause of the only serious accident involving an aircraft owned by ADF&G. (Not counting one fatal accident in the mid-1960s that involved Fish and Wildlife Protection Officer LeRoy Bahuslov, when the enforcement division was still a part of ADF&G). In the ADF&G wreck on the Alaska Peninsula, two fisheries biologists were flying at low level near Port Heiden in a Super Cub. Both biologists sustained serious head injuries when their plane crashed because of severe turbulence and wind shear. ADF&G has an outstanding safety record with its aircraft since statehood. Of all government agencies, state and federal, ADF&G also has had the least bureaucratic training and safety program. It's pretty good evidence the increasingly formalized, bureaucratic, and unbelievably expensive federal government aircraft safety programs aren't the answer to aircraft safety. ADF&G always had a policy of not hiring pilots but rather expected its employees to learn to fly on their own and get their first 200 hours at their own expense. They were then worked into the flying program under the tutelage of more experienced pilots.

Weather

The Alaska Peninsula has several wind-related geological formations that clearly show even a casual observer that wind is a major force there. These include "pumice patches", elongated lakes, and drifts of volcanic ash. The pumice patches are areas of barren gravel with no vegetation that occur from Lake Iliamna southwest to the end of the Peninsula. They make great landing areas for aircraft with large tires, but the light volcanic gravel can be hard on propellers. When the wind blows hard, one can see the gravel in a pumice patch moving and understand why many areas are bare of vegetation. The Alaska Department of Public Safety owns a cabin at Pumice Creek and there are several other privately-owned cabins on the large pumice patch there. Not surprisingly, Pumice Creek is a notoriously windy place, and all the cabins there are cabled to the ground with ½-inch steel cables. I experienced several big blows while doing caribou work there during the 1990s and early 2000s.

On May 25th, 1998, we flew in to occupy the cabin at Pumice Creek and set up our sleeping tents for a project to determine why the Northern Peninsula Caribou Herd was declining. It was the last day of the brown bear season and several groups of hunters were coming in from outlying cabins to Pumice Creek to be flown back to King Salmon. Several complained about the atrocious weather that occurred during the last ten days of the bear season. They experienced intense snow squalls, strong winds, and below freezing temperatures. We arrived on the first nice day. However, the next day, the wind picked up and though we had our tents set up in the lee of the cabin, within two days, several of the tents had blown down. The tents were Barney's Bomb Shelters and designed for rugged conditions, but they were no match for the winds of the Peninsula. Three days after our arrival, the wind stopped, the sun came out, and the temperature climbed steadily. We then had five days with high temperatures in the mid-80s and the black flies came out in force. Both the wind and the black flies were bad enough to keep us in the cabin when not flying, but at least we could still work when we just had the black flies to deal with.

The extensive "pumice patches" on the Alaska Peninsula are formed by wind and are great places to land, but the light gravel can cause extensive damage to propellers.

State cabin and field camp at Pumice Creek on the Alaska Peninsula. Wind and bears were our two biggest concerns.

North Slope

From May 1977 to September 1982, ADF&G ran a field station in the western Brooks Range at the old Driftwood airstrip. Strong winds usually came from the south with approaching warm fronts, or from the northeast because of frequent arctic high-pressure systems over the Beaufort Sea to the north. The airstrip was aligned with and somewhat sheltered from the strong south winds, but during strong northeast winds we were grounded from flying because of the crosswind and because of frequent ground blizzards in winter. These ground blizzards were often quite localized.

In April 1980 I had been waiting in Fairbanks for weather to improve before making a trip in a Cessna 185 to Driftwood. The crew at the camp had been reporting blizzard conditions for several days. Other reports indicated the weather on the North Slope was generally good so I departed anyway. When I flew over the camp, I could see straight down and there was just a narrow band of ground blizzard just around the wall tent frame. I landed into the wind and out of the blizzard about a half mile south of the camp and then taxied the half mile through the blizzard. The crew were quite surprised that I had arrived. They saw me fly over and assumed I had seen how bad it was and continued on to Kotzebue. I had a hard time convincing them the weather was actually good everywhere except at the tent camp. From their perspective it had been horrible for days.

In early March 1980, we were working out of Driftwood on wolverine and caribou projects and had a 12 x 16-foot wall tent set up over a sturdy frame for cooking, and three 8 x 10-foot wall tents on frames for sleeping. One day in the early afternoon, the wind started to pick up from the northeast and we soon realized we were in for a pretty good blow. I tied down the ADF&G Scout (N88417) with two 55-gallon drums of fuel under each wing and one under the tail. We also checked the security of the tents and parked our two Skidoo Elan snowmachines so they wouldn't get drifted in or packed full of blowing snow. By early evening it was blowing so hard I could hardly stand up outside when I went to check on the Scout. She was lifting off the ground and straining on the ½-inch nylon ropes during the strongest gusts and moving the drums backward a little at a time. It was impossible to dig into the frozen ground to bury a deadman, so I just rolled three more fuel drums over and tied two of them between the landing gear and another one on the tail. By moving backward, the tail of the plane had started to climb the dirt berm along the runway and the angle of attack of the wings was reduced, so the plane had less tendency to want to fly, which was a good thing. With the additional drums tied to it, and the tail half-way up the berm, she looked pretty secure.

As I lurched and stumbled my way back to the cook tent to get out of the wind, I noticed one sleeping tent next to the cook tent had torn and was starting to blow off its frame. Before I got to it, I saw a sleeping bag billow up into the air and fly away through the naked part of the tent frame. The sleeping bag was quickly followed by a sleeping pad and some other miscellaneous pieces of clothing and personal gear. With help from others in the cook tent I secured most of what was left in the sleeping tent and left the ripped wall tent canvas in a pile on the lee side of the tent. I hoped the wind wouldn't pick up any more, because we were about at the limit of what we could take. Losing the cook tent and frame would have resulted in a survival situation with the whole crew crammed into the remaining two sleeping tents. The temperature was around 10F, so it wasn't particularly cold, but the wind chill was extreme. Fortunately, the remaining two sleeping tents were across the runway in the lee of some willows, so I was pretty confident they would survive. We went to bed about 10:00 pm, as darkness descended with the wind still screaming, roaring, and thundering.

Everyone slept in the next morning, partly because we couldn't really work in the blasting wind and partly because it was pretty tough to crawl out of our nice, warm bags with no heat in the sleeping tents. About noon, the wind gusts started to lessen and after a good meal in the cook tent we were ready to inspect the camp for wind damage and see what we might have lost besides the sleeping bag and pad. The one sleeping tent needed some pretty extensive repairs but I had extra canvas and a Speedy Stitcher awl. Fortunately, the plane was fine, so I took off and went looking for the sleeping bag. I found it fetched up in some low willows about a mile downwind from camp. Nearby, I also noticed a fuel drum that must have blown out of our empty drum pile. I landed and loaded the drum and the sleeping bag into the plane and flew back to camp. It actually turned out we had lost three empty fuel drums, one of which I found and later recovered with a snowmachine from two miles downwind.

Another wind experience I had on the North Slope was during the 1979 Porcupine caribou census. We were staying in the old abandoned DEW Line buildings at Beaufort Lagoon, about 40 miles southeast of Barter Island. The caribou aggregation was spectacular that year with essentially the entire herd of 105,000 caribou in two groups spread between the Kongakut River and the Jago River on the 4th of July. Research Coordinator John Coady had just finished the aerial photography of the aggregations with the ADF&G Beaver, and the next step was to conduct composition counts (counts to determine the age and sex composition of the herd) of the caribou from the ground with spotting scopes. The caribou were moving rapidly east and we wanted to catch them before they got too far into the Yukon. Although we had permission, and often landed in the Canadian Yukon Territory without clearing customs each time in those years, the caribou could easily move 50 miles in a day and the logistics would get increasingly complicated the longer we waited.

I began shuttling three crews of two biologists each (including me) with the ADF&G Scout. I made five quick trips to get the six of us out to three different gravel bars along the Clarence River ahead of the rapidly moving aggregations. The weather was spectacular, not a cloud in the sky, and temperatures of about 80F at 1,000 feet and 70F at ground level. There was no wind and the mosquitoes were terrible. After a couple hours watching tens of thousands of caribou go by, and classifying and photographing several thousand, Jim Davis and I thought we must have seen the whole herd. It certainly was a spectacular movement of caribou. We were getting ready to pack up and head back to the plane when I noticed the horizon fill up with more caribou. We sat back down, got out the spotting scope again, and got ready to classify some more. For the next couple hours, tens of thousands more caribou went by and then it finally looked like the spectacle was over.

It was a good feeling to have a major caribou census and all the composition counts done, and it had been a very long day. Jim and I headed back to the plane, strolling nonchalantly along the edge of a small lake, chatting about the caribou spectacle we had just observed. Suddenly, we began hearing a rushing sound behind us. We both turned around and saw a line of whitecaps moving down the lake toward us from the northwest. For a brief moment we stood there in disbelief before I yelled, "The plane!" and took off running towards the Scout that was parked on a gravel bar a couple hundred yards away. It wasn't tied down and that sudden wind was threatening to blow it into the nearby Clarence River. Although the wind beat me to the plane, it was only blowing about 20 mph when I got there, jumped in and started it up. Jim got in, I gave it the gas, and we were airborne in less than 100 feet.

We flew back to Beaufort Lagoon against the wind with a ground speed of about 50 mph. I hovered in to the strip, let Jim out and took off straight ahead with essentially no ground roll. The trip back to the Clarence was pretty quick, with a ground speed of about 150 mph. Fortunately, at ground level it was only blowing about 35 and it was relatively smooth, so I was able to hover down and land, stopping in about 30 feet; I just held the brakes with the engine at high idle while the passenger climbed in. On the second to last load, Ken Whitten was my passenger. As he got out of the plane at Beaufort Lagoon his blue foam sleeping pad slipped out of his hand and blew off down the runway. He sprinted after it but it was hopeless. The pad was going about twice as fast as he was. He found his pad three years later during the 1982 Porcupine caribou census. It was washed up on the beach about two miles to the east.

By the time everyone was back at Beaufort Lagoon, the temperature dropped from 70F to 35F. The abrupt change in weather was the result of a rapidly moving arctic cold front coming in from the northwest and the drop in temperature was partly a function of the wind coming straight off the pack ice. In those years there was always ice at Beaufort Lagoon in early July. There is seldom ice there now.

Kodiak

There are lots of stories about bad winds on Kodiak Island. I experienced two bad blows there, both on deer hunting trips. While neither was life threatening, they nevertheless were exciting and uncomfortable.

In early October 1985, two friends (Ed Crain and Mark McNay) and I decided to try to hunt the south end of Kodiak Island to get some big buck deer. Sitka black-tailed deer (14 of them) had been introduced to Kodiak after being captured near Sitka in 1924. Two subsequent transplants of two deer from Prince of Whales Island in 1930 and nine deer from near Kake in 1934 completed the effort. The deer were placed on the north end of the island and had been slowly expanding their range towards the south end of the island. They did not reach the south end of Kodiak until the 1960s. Because they were occupying new, relatively ungrazed range, the deer on south Kodiak had a reputation for big antlers. We asked our air taxi pilot to take us to an area that had not had much deer hunting. He chose the lower Ayakulik River, which was popular for salmon fishing but hadn't received attention from deer hunters.

We were pretty excited to be in an unhunted spot in deer nirvana in relatively nice weather. The first order of business was setting up our six-man dome tent. Unfortunately, all the flat places were either completely exposed to the prevailing southwest wind and/or right next to major bear trails. The spot we finally chose was both completely exposed to the wind and about 15 feet from a well-used bear trail with fish remains scattered around—not exactly an ideal situation for bear safety or weather considerations. Coho salmon were still running in the river and bears were actively feeding on them. Fortunately, the bears were hunted there and had a healthy respect for people. We really wanted to be camping in the thick alders, sheltered from the wind and away from the bears but all those areas had giant tussocks. It would have taken at least an hour or more to chop out the tussocks and cut enough grass to make a good flat place in the alders. We were anxious to get out hunting while it was not raining, so we opted to take a chance on the wind not blowing too hard in the week we planned to be there.

For the first five days and nights, our choice of a camp site was fine. Winds were light and I never saw a single bear. That changed on the sixth night. We began hearing the wind pick up around 10:00 pm. At first, the tent fly was just flapping, then it was really flapping. Finally, we could hear the really bad gusts coming before they hit, and when they hit, the tent collapsed down on top of us. After the first few williwaw gusts slackened, the tent sprang back up, but after the next few gusts we began to hear tearing sounds and then I started feeling the broken end of a tent pole hitting me on the head. I felt around in the dark for the broken tent pole end and held onto it to prevent it from tearing up my sleeping bag and the remains of the tent. Mark and Ed did the same, and for the rest of the night we all just lay in our sleeping bags, wide-awake, hanging onto the broken ends of the tent poles. With the tent now completely flat, the wind gusts couldn't really grab hold of it and there wasn't much danger of it blowing away into the river with us in it. Another good thing is that there wasn't much rain with the wind so we were staying relatively dry.

After what seemed like a very long time, it began to get light. As soon as we could see, we crawled out of the wet, collapsed pile of nylon that used to be the tent. As it became light enough to see the sky, we could see dark clouds coming in from the southwest and it looked like a serious rain was in store. We immediately began chopping out the tussocks and cutting the tall Kodiak grass with our hunting knives so we could make a sheltered flat place in the alders for our backup two-man tent. An hour or so later we had the tent up and our sleeping bags in it. Then, with all three of us crammed into the 2-man tent we spent the next couple of hours catching up on some welcome sleep. If we had just spent an extra hour or two on the first day preparing a better tent site, we could have avoided the miserable night spent clutching the broken tent poles and the two last nights crammed into the little two-man tent. Lesson learned!

My other Kodiak wind experience occurred during another deer hunt to Frazer Lake in October 2003. Four of us, including Fish and Game biologist Tom Paragi, helicopter pilot Toy Cambier, and my son Toby rented the U.S. Fish and Wildlife Service cabin at the north end of the lake. The first morning of the hunt, we climbed aboard our two inflatable boats—my Grabner two-man kayak and a rented inflatable canoe. It was a beautiful calm morning, so we paddled about one-third of the way down the lake and climbed up high to look for deer. (We figured we better try up high because the previous party at the cabin had hunted for a week and not seen a single deer, or so they had written in the cabin log.) By the end of the day, Toby and I had two deer, including a very nice buck, and headed back down to the boats. Tom and Troy were already there, looking out at the lake surface that had blown up into serious looking whitecaps. We debated about what to do, but decided we had to try it because we weren't equipped to spend the night. We loaded two deer into the inflatable canoe and Toby and I took the two halves of the big buck in our kayak. We headed along the shore just far enough out to get a good paddle full of water. Although the waves were a good two feet high and about all our kayak could safely handle, it wasn't too dangerous because we were right next to shore. The inflatable canoe was more sea-worthy than the smaller kayak, even with two deer in it, but it caught the wind more and it took more effort to drive it forward. We made it about a half mile before the waves kicked up even more and we were paddling into a wind of about 25 mph. When we rounded a small point with over a mile left to go it was clear that forward progress was no longer possible, so we pulled the boats out.

It was rapidly getting dark, so we decided to turn the boats over and sleep under them and wait for the wind to go down. If we'd had warmer clothes or a couple of sleeping bags the plan would have worked, but about 1:00 am we were so cold that we were having to get up and do jumping jacks to warm up. At about 2:00 I heard Troy say, "Hell with this, I'm walking to the cabin." Toby agreed, saying, "Yeah, I'm going with you." Well, that settled it, Tom and I were not going to stay behind, shivering all night, alone with the bears. We all got up, pulled the boats into the thickest bushes and headed along a bear trail, single file, groping along with our headlights on. The guy with the best headlight and rifle at the ready took the lead and the other three followed, carefully stepping in the footprints of the person ahead.

It only took us about an hour before we could see the cabin; we were much warmer than when we started walking, but there was one final obstacle. The cabin was on the other side of a chest-deep, ice cold, stream. We all took our clothes off in the cold, howling wind and made the crossing. Emerging on the other side, we ran naked for the cabin. We had left the heat on in the cabin and a stew on the oil heater on low, so we immediately had warmth and a ready-cooked, warm meal waiting. After a couple of beers and hot bowl of stew, we hit the sack and slept in until 10:00 am. By then the wind had died and it was a simple matter of hiking back for 45 minutes to the boats and the deer.

For the last 150 yards we gave Toby the .375 H&H magnum and let him lead the way. We figured he was the most expendable—the rest of us had families and/or jobs. Fortunately, no bears were waiting for us and we loaded the boats and had a leisurely paddle back to the cabin on the now calm lake. Usually, it is not possible to leave a deer overnight on Kodiak. Nine times out of ten, bears will find it and there will be nothing left, or worse, a bear on the carcass lying in wait for the returning hunter. Although we had been unlucky with the wind the day before, we were lucky with the bears overnight.

Ropes and Tiedowns for Airplanes

The subject of ropes and tie-downs frequently comes up with pilots in Alaska's windy places. The best way to secure an airplane is to tie it down behind some sort of windbreak, but that's not always possible. The next best thing is to use spoilers on the top of the wings to cause turbulence over the wing and thus reduce the lift that the wing produces. Before spoiler wing covers were commercially available, I made my own spoilers out of Dacron fabric tubes and filled the tubes with moss or gravel.

You not only need to prevent a secured aircraft from trying to fly during a windstorm, you also have to prevent it from being blown away sideways and backwards, so some kind of tiedown is always needed once the wind is above about 20 mph. I have used all kinds of methods of anchoring a plane, but mostly now use a combination of Duckbill anchors and spoiler wing covers. In winter, it is often not possible to drive Duckbill anchors into the ground. Once, at the village of Atqasuk, we went to the dump and got four pallets, covered them with snow, and then poured water over the pile. The snow-filled pallets froze solidly to the ground and our planes survived 40-50 mph wind gusts several times during the 42 days we stayed there in March and early April. Ice screws or a hole in the ice with a deadman frozen in also work well on lakes. Another method that works in summer is to carry a small sturdy shovel and dig a hole to bury a feed sack filled with rocks.

A method I have sometimes used to secure aircraft on village runway aprons is to bring along a short piece of quarter-inch cable with an

Preparing the 90-horsepower Piper Cub for wind after landing in the White Mountains to go sheep hunting. We hiked down to tree-line to get spruce trees to use for "spoilers" on the wings.

"eye" on one end, a stop pounded onto the other end, and a cable clamp. Many of Alaska's village runways are gravel and were often constructed with cable tiedowns buried in the gravel pad of the parking aprons. The problem is that during the first winter after construction, the grader or loader that is used to clear the snow also breaks off the cable eyes of the original tiedowns. When I find those old, broken cable ends, I simply clamp my portable cable eye to the old cable.

Rope size is a frequent subject of discussion among pilots too. Half-inch nylon rope works fine most of the time but I know of a case where a windstorm in the western Alaska Range broke the half-inch tie-down ropes of a Super Cub and it was a total loss. That pilot now uses five-eighths-inch nylon ropes. The only serious wind damage I had on one of my airplanes happened at my home base at Chena Marina in relatively wind-free Fairbanks. The damage was caused by a dust devil that flipped the plane over because the

Damage to my Super Cub caused by a dust-devil at Chena Marina in late April 2007. After flying for many years in some of Alaska's windiest places, the only wind damage one of my planes ever sustained was in relatively wind-free Fairbanks because the tail was not tied down.

tail was not tied down. The wings were solidly tied with half-inch nylon rope, and both wing ropes held without breaking. Although the ropes held, both steel tiedown ring loops on the Cub broke and so did one of the metal channel pieces holding the main strut to the wing. The plane was a total wreck, with all four lift struts buckled and three out of four wing spars bent, all because I had not tied the tail down.

Flying Backwards

People talk about Super Cubs coming from the factory with a built-in headwind. It sure feels like it on long flights, especially when there is a real headwind anyway. In good weather, it is possible to try out different altitudes to find the most favorable winds, especially now with GPS. By watching the groundspeed readout on the GPS and comparing it with the airspeed indicator, a pilot can instantly tell how much headwind or tailwind exists at a given altitude. It was much more difficult to read the wind in flight before Loran and GPS came along.

In bad weather, a pilot often has no choice but to forge ahead into strong headwinds and turbulence. Once, on a Civil Air Patrol search near the village of Tanana in March 1975, I was riding in the back of a Super Cub in fairly windy conditions. Dan Holleman, a research scientist at the University of Alaska and flight instructor, was flying. We were searching for two missing marten trappers who were reported overdue by family members. We had come from Fairbanks in record time with a very strong tailwind. After several hours of searching, we found two people on snowshoes walking along the old Tanana-Allakaket trail about 15 miles northwest of Tanana. We made several low passes and they just waved that everything was OK each time, so we continued on our way and began heading back towards Fairbanks in the afternoon. We climbed to about 2,500 feet to avoid low level turbulence but noticed almost right away that our ground speed was very low. In fact, when I marked a big rock formation below us and looked at it in relation to the window frame of the aircraft, it was clear at that altitude and heading we were actually going backwards! I yelled up to Dan, "Hey Dan, I think we are going backwards!" (We didn't use intercoms during the 1970s.) I saw him looking at the ground, after about half a minute he yelled back, "Yeah, I think we are too!" By climbing higher, we just ended up going backwards faster, so Dan made a gradual turn to the south and we picked up forward speed, but we were going about 60 degrees to the right of our course to Fairbanks. We were just in a bad area, where the northeast wind funnels down the Yukon near the mouth of the Tanana River. By flying about 20 miles south we were able to get out of the strongest head wind, but we still had to stop in Manley Hot Springs to refuel. In those days, Cy Hetherington and his wife Daisy ran the store and an aircraft repair station and they also sold 80/87 and 100/130 avgas.

The area around the mouth of the Tanana River is a notorious area for bad winds and the river itself has been affected by wind over the eons of its existence. Wind has blown the river sideways in the area of Squaw Crossing, resulting in multiple, frequently-changing shallow channels and Aeolian (wind-generated) sand dunes in the woods south of the river.

Fortunately, we didn't have to fly in that bad northeast wind around the village of Tanana the next day because the search was called off. The two men we found turned out to be the missing trappers and they walked into Tanana the evening before. They said they crashed the plane in a snowstorm, but were uninjured and just decided to walk out to Tanana. There were rumors the plane was never found, which sounded a little fishy, and we wondered if it wasn't some sort of insurance scam. I never did learn the real story.

The only other time I came close to flying backwards was while trying to fly south from Healy through Windy Pass in 2000 to bring supplies to my wife, who was raising two baby wolverines in the Alaska Range east of Cantwell. I tried to go direct from Fairbanks up the Wood River but it was too turbulent, so I tried Windy Pass. The Windy Pass route wasn't as turbulent, but by the time I got close to Healy, my ground speed on the GPS was about 30 mph. That particular Super Cub cruised at 85 mph, so the headwind was about 55 mph. Since it wasn't too bumpy, I decided to continue, and near the highway bridge south of Healy my ground speed had fallen to 18 mph, making the headwind there about 67 mph! Once through that narrow section, my speed gradually increased and in Windy Pass proper my ground speed was about 45 mph. I turned east along the south side of the Alaska Range and there was just a gentle wind out of the south at about 15 mph. It was a long, nerve-wracking flight, but at least the trip back only took a few minutes because my groundspeed was 120-140 mph.

Tailwinds

Strong tailwinds can be just as memorable as strong headwinds, but they are a lot more fun. In 1980, I was preparing to radio-track caribou for the Western Arctic Herd census that was likely to occur around the 4th of July. I was in Fairbanks and planned to fly in an ADF&G Cessna 185 to Cape Lisburne, track half of the radio-collared caribou, and meet Jim Davis at the Driftwood field camp about 60 miles southeast of Point Lay. I talked to Jim on the side band radio in the ADF&G office and headed for the 185 that was parked at Phillips Field. He said he was leaving Driftwood to go and track the other half of the caribou near Point Lay. I took off in the 185 and climbed to 8,500 feet on a heading for Cape Lisburne. When I went by Indian Mountain, I calculated my ground speed (using elapsed time and measured distance on the map) and found that I was doing about 175 mph. The normal cruise speed of the 185 at that altitude was about 145 mph indicated airspeed. I climbed to 12,500 feet, waited about 15 minutes, and then calculated I was going just over 200 mph ground speed. I flew from Fairbanks to Cape Lisburne, tracked my half of the caribou, and landed at the Driftwood field camp before Jim got back from tracking his half of the caribou. I got a pretty good laugh at the look on his face when he landed and I told him I had already finished my half of the tracking and been back at camp for 30 minutes when he arrived.

The most remarkable sustained tailwind I ever had while flying a Super Cub was on a trip I made from Ketchikan, Alaska to Walla Walla, Washington. In early October 2012, I was planning to ferry my Super Cub down from Petersburg, Alaska to Enterprise, Oregon, with an overnight in Prince George, B. C. The problem was that Petersburg was fogging in at about 5:00 am every morning, and the fog wasn't lifting until about 3:00 pm. So, on the 6th of October I flew to Ketchikan, where there was no fog, and launched for Prince George on the morning of the 7th. After filing a flight plan and completing all the absurdly bureaucratic electronic manifests required by U.S. Customs and the relatively simple phone calls required by Canadian Customs, I took off and climbed to 7,500 feet to clear the Coast Range and get above a fog layer. After leveling off at 7,500 feet, I noticed I was doing about 120 mph ground speed. Pretty nice, a 35-mph tailwind! Then I starting thinking. With that kind of tailwind, I might be able to make Oroville, Washington and avoid having to clear customs. So, I turned the plane toward Oroville and climbed to 11,500 feet, the highest legal VFR altitude for an easterly heading without having to use oxygen. After leveling out, my ground speed was 125 mph. At that relatively high altitude I would also save fuel.

The weather was clear as far as I could see and when I got cell phone reception over interior B. C., I checked the weather in Oroville and Pasco. It was clear there too. After flying for about three hours, I was certain I could make Oroville without refueling so I watched my cell phone and the next time I had a signal I cancelled my Canadian Customs request and I also called customs in Oroville and told them I would not need their services either. About two hours out of Oroville, I plugged Walla Walla into the GPS and turned toward it. I could easily make Walla Walla too, so I continued on. When I crossed the Washington border, I called my friend Ed Crain and asked him to meet me at Martin Field airport near his house in Walla Walla. When I landed at Martin Field, I did some quick calculations while waiting for Ed. I had flown 866 straight line miles from Ketchikan to Walla Walla in 8.2 hours for an average ground speed of just over 105 mph. Because of the various zigs and zags along the way, my ground speed was actually a little higher than that. I used only 57.4 gallons of fuel (or exactly 7.0 gallons per hour) and the plane carried 66 gallons, so I could have made Enterprise, Oregon (or even Boise, Idaho). It was a spectacular weather system, probably the kind that black brant (geese) wait for when they fly non-stop from Cold Bay, Alaska to northern California.

Floods

Most major floods in Interior Alaska occur in the early spring because of ice jams, like the ice jam floods on the Yukon that devastated Eagle in 2010 and Galena in 2013. August floods, caused by days of heavy rain are also quite common and can be just as devastating, like the famous Fairbanks flood of 1967 and Allakaket/Alatna flood of 1994. On a much smaller scale, there are unpredictable break-up, ice jam, or rain-caused floods that are just a fact of life for hunters, fishermen, and outdoorsmen in Alaska's back country. Most of them are never even reported because of Alaska's vast expanses of wild country. I never had a serious situation involving flooding in my first 40 years of flying around Alaska, working for ADF&G or on my own hunting and fishing trips. That all changed on the 21st of June, 2013 on the Utukok River, when I was caught in a sudden and unexpected flash flood in the western Brooks Range. It was one of the most dangerous and frightening experiences I've ever had in Alaska and it's one I'll never forget.

My wife Audrey and I were helping German photographer Uwe Anders and his wife Christina with a documentary about the national parks of the United States. Uwe was trying to get movie footage of caribou swimming rivers with their young calves in June. It is not possible to get pictures like that in Alaska's national parks, so we were on state land along the Utukok River in northwest Alaska. We were using my Super Club to land on gravel bars ahead of groups of caribou that were just about to cross the river. We had arrived on the 14th in clear weather, and it remained cloudless until the 20th. Uwe had lots of good footage of caribou swimming the river, with all the drama that goes along with those crossings, i.e. cows picking a bad place to cross and their calves ending up stranded under a cut bank, calves losing their mother in the crossing and then recrossing the river to the side they started from, etc. Some of it was pretty heartbreaking and we couldn't resist helping a couple of calves up a cutbank rather than watch them die.

Uwe finished filming on the 20th and we arranged for a charter with Golden Eagle Outfitters in Kotzebue to pick up Christina and Uwe, while Audrey and I planned to fly back to Fairbanks in the Cub. The charter was for the 22nd so we were planning to take the day off on the 21st and relax around camp. It was just before the mosquitoes became intolerable and after almost all of the caribou crossed the river on their way to the Lisburne Hills to the southwest.

On the evening of the 20th, we saw the first major cloud build-ups of the summer, and there was some lightning towards the Brooks Range and light rain at our camp. We went to bed about 11:00 pm with the sun still shining from under the cloud layer in the northwest. When I first checked the river in the morning at around 7:00 am, it had come up about two vertical feet but was still about 75 yards from our tent and the parked airplane, with at least another 15 vertical feet to go before it threatened our camp site and landing spot.

During the day, the river started to fall again and I never gave it another thought because the clear weather returned overnight and there was not a cloud in the sky until about 3:00 pm that day. By 8:00 pm, however, there were major build-ups in the Brooks Range and lightning began to flash. The lightning put on quite a show; the clouds turned blue/black in the southeast, and we lay in our tent watching and photographing. It started raining at our camp about 10:00 pm but the rain was never heavy and it slacked off after about an hour. At 11:00 pm, I checked the river level one last time and noticed it had risen about a foot. Although the clouds and lightning were more extensive and dramatic than during the previous evening, it looked and sounded like the thunderstorms were over and we went to bed shortly after midnight. I heard the rain and some wind pick up again about 1:00 am, but assumed it was just a local squall and didn't bother looking outside.

At about 2:00 am, I heard Uwe's bear alarm fog horn blaring. I assumed there was a bear in camp and grabbed my 12-gauge shotgun from beside my sleeping bag. I unzipped the tent fly and looked toward Uwe's tent about 50 feet away and slightly below ours. I was stunned by what I saw. The river, now a raging brown torrent, was lapping at the edge of our tent and flooding Uwe's. The water had risen nearly 20 vertical feet in a couple of hours. We were now on an island with raging brown water all around. The only remaining dry ground was a willow patch near the airplane and about 400 feet of the highest part of the gravel bar where the plane was parked. I yelled at Uwe and Christina to get all of the valuable camera equipment and for Christina to get to the airplane. I anticipated having to take three loads in the Cub to a nearby ridge as fast as possible. We threw as much as we could in the back of the plane and Christina climbed in. I started the plane, and with minimal warm-up, took off and headed for a level spot on a ridge I had noticed a few days before. The flight was only about five minutes. Fortunately, it is light all night in June in northern Alaska and I could see the ridge was indeed a suitable landing spot as I came in to land. We threw everything out of the plane and I took off straight ahead and roared back to the gravel bar at full throttle. When I got there, the part of the gravel bar I departed from was under water but I saw Audrey standing in low willows motioning me to land there instead. I made one quick circle to look at the spot and then landed. I stopped as short as I could and then back taxied to my landing point. As soon as I opened the door, Audrey ran up to the plane and dove into the baggage compartment with our tent and a couple of sleeping pads. She already knew that only one more trip was possible. I yelled for Uwe to come to the plane and get in. He ran up to the plane and asked, "Is this safe?" I replied, "No, it's not safe, but it's your only chance. Get in!"

He got in and I fired up the plane and roared off through the thinnest part of the willows. There was a gusty crosswind from the north, so as soon as the plane was flying, I made a right turn into the wind to gain as much airspeed as possible. I only used about 400 feet to get off even though the plane was full of fuel with two passengers in back. Once we were in the air, the emergency was over and we could relax.

The river was a sight to behold. Carbon Creek, usually a placid tundra stream with very little flow, was about 200 yards wide and roaring straight down its valley cutting across all the normal twists and turns. Where it joined the Utukok, it was blasting across the Utukok River onto the tundra on the other side. Five miles upriver, Disappointment Creek, which is much larger, was doing the same thing. The sheer volume of water coming down Disappointment Creek was astounding. It must have rained many inches in the northern foothills of Brooks Range, and with the ground still frozen a few inches under the surface, there was no place for the water to sink in. I had been working, off and on, in that part of Alaska since 1976 and I'd never seen evidence of flooding like that. I'm sure it was something like a 100-year flood but it never even made the news.

The three of us made an uneventful landing on the ridge and Christina was surprised and relieved to see us all get out of the plane. Over many years of flying small aircraft in Alaska, I have developed the habit of always looking for places to land—just in case. I noticed this ridge several days earlier and the thought had crossed my mind that it might make a good emergency landing spot if the gravel bars along the river had bad winds or high water. That instinct saved Audrey and Uwe. When I flew over and checked our gravel bar on the Utukok the next day, the willows were all flooded and there was no dry ground anywhere. I finally landed there two days later to see if some of our abandoned gear could be salvaged. The gear was gone and the drift-line was about two feet up in the willows on the highest part of the gravel bar.

I cancelled the Cessna 206 charter with Golden Eagle Outfitters in Kotzebue and told Jared Cummings about the flood. He was surprised because he said the weather had been fine in Kotzebue. I then ferried everyone to the Copter Peak strip and had the 206 fly Uwe and Christina from there. While we were camped at Copter Peak waiting for the 206 to arrive, Uwe asked me why I hadn't thought the river would flood. In hindsight, it was a rather embarrassing question for which there really wasn't a good answer. After the black clouds and lightning show in the Brooks Range, I should have stayed up for several more hours and watched the river. One thing's for sure, I'll never take thunderstorms for granted again.

Another more recent flood I experienced was in 2020 while deer hunting in Southeast Alaska. This time, the flooding was forecast. We planned to travel by boat to hunt out of a Forest Service cabin for the last couple of days of October and first few days of November. As my son Toby and I were listening to the marine forecast on the evening of the 30th, I was beginning to think we might want to change the plan. They were calling for as much as eight inches of rain over the weekend and winds gusting to 40 mph. I suggested cancelling the boat trip and hunting out of our house in Petersburg instead. Toby gave me a disdainful look and said emphatically, "We are sticking with the original plan!" I guess that's the difference between being old with lots of unplanned adventures to think back on and being young and looking forward to new adventures.

Fortunately, the forecast for the Friday we planned to depart was for light winds in the morning and no rain until later in the day. We had a nice boat ride in and got to the cabin with no trouble at about 2:00 pm. We then went hunting and Toby shot a nice buck. Just as we got back to the cabin at dark on Friday evening, it started to rain. It was rainy and windy all night, but nothing out of the ordinary. I didn't sleep well because I was worried about the boat anchored in front of the cabin. I didn't know the anchorage very well and thought the anchor might drag causing the boat to end up banging on the rocks on shore.

In the morning, it was raining hard and starting to blow harder, so we ran the boat across the bay to the lee shore about a half mile from the cabin. We pumped water out of the boat but I didn't keep track of how much rainwater accumulated over night. The anchorage there was much better because I could tie the boat solidly to a big spruce tree and then anchor the stern out to keep the boat away from shore. However, that evening it started to really pour with rain and the wind picked up to about 30-35 mph. I wasn't worried about the wind anymore, but still didn't get any sleep worrying about the incredible volume of rain that was coming down and how much rain it would take to sink the boat. On Sunday, about noon, Toby went over to pump out the boat and measured how much water had accumulated in it. He pumped out 180 gallons of rainwater. When I calculated how much open area there was in the back of the boat, it would have had to rain about eight inches over that Saturday night to get 180 gallons of water in the boat.

We went hunting in the pouring down rain on Sunday morning.

Every deer trail was a stream, every little stream was a river, and the muskegs were ponds and slop. It was impossible to walk quietly in heavy rain gear, making squishing and sucking noises with every step. We returned to the cabin for lunch and I contemplated not going hunting in the afternoon because of the buckets of rain coming down. However, I didn't feel like staying at the cabin either, so I reluctantly went out to a spot about a mile from the cabin and sat down. As I sat down on a squishy tussock, it was hard to even think seriously about calling or hunting deer. The drumming of the rain on the hood of my rain jacket drowned out every other sound. I was just getting out my deer call, when I caught a movement ahead. There stood a big buck, broadside to me at 20 feet. I raised my rifle and even though my scope was set on one-power, all I could see was hair. I just pointed the rifle in the general direction of the buck's chest and fired. The buck ran off at high speed and left no blood trail because the rain was washing away the blood as soon as it fell. After searching for 15 minutes, I finally found the deer, piled up under a small spruce tree. It appeared to have died while running at full speed. It was the second biggest Sitka black-tail I ever shot.

When we checked the weather records at Petersburg upon our return from the trip, about 8 inches of rain had fallen in all three days of the storm. It was record rainfall, but it was also clear that much of the water in the boat must have come from rain falling on the roof of the boat and then working its way into the back of the boat. A month later, there was another record-setting storm. During those two rainstorms, several new landslides occurred, and in the December storm, a house in Haines was carried out into Lynn Canal with two people inside it. The one good thing about the trip was I learned that no matter how much it rains overnight, it can't rain enough to sink a boat. But, a tarp for the back of the boat and an automatic bilge pump will be along on my next boat trip!

The Perfect Storm

One of the best things about living in Alaska is the extreme changes in weather from season to season and from year to year. Animals are generally well-adapted to these weather changes and weather extremes, but even for these highly adapted animals, there are weather events that are so far out of the normal range of extremes that animal movements and populations can be greatly affected. When I first arrived in Alaska in May 1972, wildlife populations had just been devastated by two extremely severe winters with alternating heavy snowfalls and periods of extreme cold. The winters of 1970-71 and 1971-72 caused statewide declines in moose, caribou, goats, deer, and also sheep in some areas. In Southeast Alaska, deer numbers were reduced to such low levels that some hunting seasons were closed for 16 years in the Petersburg area and biologists even tried bringing deer from Admiralty Island to get the deer population going again. Biologists had an idea that these two winters were exceptional at the time, but the long-lasting effects were not fully appreciated for years to come.

In 1992, another record-setting weather event occurred in Interior Alaska. This time, it was not only a severe winter, but a record-setting early snowstorm preceded by, and followed by, a series of severe winters. Like the severe winters of the early 1970s, the effects of these weather events were long-lasting, especially for caribou, and particularly for caribou in the Delta Herd in the central Alaska Range. The September storm is widely remembered by those of us who were around Fairbanks in the early 1990s and also by the hundreds of hunters that were stranded in remote hunting camps for as much as two weeks before they were rescued. The storm was also the subject of several scientific papers, including a very good one by USGS biologist Layne Adams and his colleagues.

Prior to the storm, a series of winters with deeper than normal snow had begun in 1989 and caribou mortality in the central Alaska Range had increased as a result. Then, on 15 June 1991, Mount Pinatubo erupted in the Philipines, causing global cooling. In 1992, green-up in Fairbanks did not occur until 25 May, about two weeks later

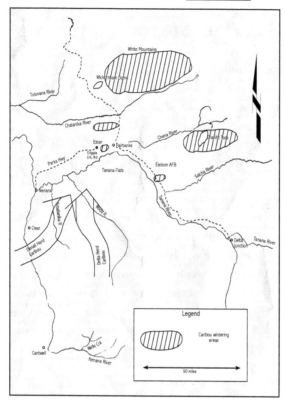

Movements and wintering areas of caribou from the Delta and Denali caribou herds during the "Perfect Storm" in September 1992 and the winter of 1992-1993.

than normal. The summer of 1992 then seemed fairly normal, but mean daily temperatures were about five degrees cooler than the long-term average.

I picked up some friends who were moose hunting on the Tanana Flats on September 9th, and it had been a beautiful, warm fall day, with the fall colors just starting to peak. The wind changed to the northwest that night however, and the temperature began to fall. By late on the 10th, the temperature was below freezing in Fairbanks and from then until the end of the month, the mean daily temperatures continued to fall from about ten degrees below normal to more than twenty degrees below normal. A strong storm from the northwest moved in along a warm front that was pumping moisture in from the Bering Sea. The result was an unprecedented snowstorm that began on the night of September 11th and continued for 11 days. The first three days of the storm were the worst, with about 40 inches of heavy, wet snowfall at the Denali National Park weather station.

During the first day of the storm, the snow did not stick much in Fairbanks and we thought it would melt. But, by the third day of the storm, it was clear that winter had arrived early and there was about 24 inches of snow on the ground in the hills around town. The mostly green leaves had frozen onto the trees and the heavy wet snow accumulating on them was causing the limbs of birch, poplar, and aspen trees to break off. Birch trees were particularly badly affected and whole stands of birch were bent over. Many of these trees remained bent over for years. Power was out throughout Fairbanks, and people were driving around with chain saws in their trucks to help clear trees and limbs from roads. Several snow-covered birch tree limbs were hanging over my power supply line. Under the circumstances, the only solution I could think of was to shoot the limbs down with my 12-gauge shotgun and .30-06 rifle. I used up most of the old ammo I had accumulated over the years, but I saved my power service line.

I had been planning to fly out to the Alaska Range to go moose hunting with two friends to get meat for the winter, but we soon gave up on the idea and decided instead to go hunting by boat on the lower Teklanika River southwest of Nenana. While we were out there hunting there was more than two feet of wet snow on the ground. We got one yearling bull but decided to end the hunt early and go back to Fairbanks to deal with the downed trees, the deep wet snow that was still accumulating, and the power outages.

The snowstorm finally abated on September 22nd and I flew out to find the radio-collared Delta Caribou Herd south of Fairbanks. I usually didn't fly my radio-collared caribou in September, mostly because people were hunting in the Alaska Range then and I didn't want to disturb hunters by flying around the caribou. However, I knew caribou movements could be affected by sudden snowstorms so I was beginning to wonder how this freak storm might be affecting their movements. I found almost all of the radio-collared caribou, and most of them were in the Totatlanika drainage in the Alaska Range. Three days later, on September 25th, I received a call from Layne Adams, a biologist working with caribou in Denali Park. He had been out doing composition counts and found a large number of Denali caribou on the northeast corner of their winter range southwest of Clear Air Force Station. The caribou were streaming north and east and it sure looked like a very abnormal movement was in progress. I flew again on the 28th of September and was quite surprised to hear most of the radio-collars within just a few minutes after I took off from Chena Marina. The caribou were on the Tanana Flats further north than I had ever seen them. About half of them were piled up along the south bank of the Tanana River between the mouth of the Wood River and Fairbanks and the rest were scattered across the flats as far south and west as Clear. It turned out the Delta caribou moved north and west from the Totatlanika and mixed with the Denali caribou that were moving north and east. So, the two herds were now all mixed together—something I had never seen before (in the fourteen years I had been studying them).

The Tanana River was pretty high and full of pan ice. I guessed it would be a significant barrier to the caribou and they probably would be reluctant to cross. I flew again on the 29th, still expecting to find the caribou along the south bank of the Tanana, but almost immediately, I heard some of the radio-collared caribou north of the river. I tracked in on the signals and the first radio-collared caribou I found was in a group of about 200 filing through a subdivision along Cripple Creek Road heading towards Ester. Over the next few days several thousand caribou crossed the Tanana River. Some headed northeast as far as Granite Tors and others went north to Wickersham Dome and the White Mountains. Other groups settled down to winter in the Fairbanks area.

Several hundred must have crossed the Tanana just east of Fairbanks and some of those were having trouble crossing the Eielson Air Force Base boundary fence. Several groups were standing forlornly along the Richardson Highway wondering what to do next. As soon as I noticed this, I called the base and explained the problem. I must have talked to the right person because the next day several panels of the security fence had been removed and the caribou were on their way. Many moved on through the base and continued north, but about 300 decided that Eielson was a fine place to winter and settled down in a good lichen patch right off the east end of the runway. I visited them several times and collected fecal samples to see what they were eating. With the jets thundering overhead, it was very loud in there and I had to wear hearing protection. The caribou didn't seem to mind at all. Unfortunately for them, a lynx discovered them and over the next four months it killed several, including one of my radio-collared males that was about eight months old. I never had one of my caribou killed by a lynx before but I read that it was common for lynx to kill caribou calves and yearlings in Newfoundland. The caribou remained on the base all winter and finally headed back to the Alaska Range in early April. After the caribou left Eielson, the removed sections of the security fence were replaced.

Another group of about a hundred caribou decided to winter in the valley on the north side of Chena Ridge about a half mile east of the Gold Dredge. This group of caribou remained there from about mid-October to early April. Most people had no idea there was a group of caribou wintering there. At the time, it was an isolated spot with no roads or houses but the area was no more than a mile long by half a mile wide. Like the ones that wintered at Eielson, they stayed until early April and then headed south, back across the Tanana River and across the flats to the Alaska Range.

The freak September storm resulted in the deaths of many caribou, some from unexpected causes. I found one radio-collared caribou killed by coyotes in the Standard Creek area of Goldstream Valley. When I went in to investigate the death, I found the radio-collar had accumulated a soccer ball-sized lump of ice and snow that weighed about ten pounds. The coyotes apparently realized there was something wrong with the caribou and attacked it. The caribou put up quite a fight because there was a trampled area of bloody snow about 100 yards long leading down to the carcass. I had never seen an ice ball like that on any other radio-collars on caribou.

In early October, I was in the ADF&G office on College Road when ADF&G Technician Bob Hunter told me he just had a call from a woman who lived on Murphy Dome Road. She said there was a caribou caught in her volleyball net. I grabbed an old, used radio-collar and Bob and I headed right out there. As we pulled into the driveway of the house, we saw the caribou immediately. It was a cow and she had tangled her antlers in the net while trying to walk under it. We had no trouble wrestling her down and putting a radio-collar on her. I had no way of knowing if she was from the Denali Herd or the Delta Herd, but after spending the winter in the White Mountains around the Big Bend in Beaver Creek, she migrated back to calving area of the Delta Herd in Wells Creek. She calved there for at least the next four years.

The return migration of the Delta and Denali caribou that wintered north of the Tanana River was not nearly as noticeable as the fall migration across the Tanana. The spring migration occurred over the months of March and April and most caribou bypassed Fairbanks. There were some exceptions though. During the last week of March or the first week of April, a group of about 200 caribou emerged from the woods behind Beaver Sports and came out on College Road. A state trooper soon arrived on the scene and escorted the caribou along College Road to University Avenue, where they turned left and continued south on University Avenue to the Chena River. The group then found their way down onto the frozen Chena River and continued down the river to its mouth and then crossed the Tanana River.

In mid-April I also got a phone call from Department of Transportation staff about a caribou up against the highway fence near the junction of Lathrop Street and the Johansen Expressway. I went to look at it and decided to just leave it alone and hope it would wander away that night. It was a yearling male and looked pretty depressed and confused, but I hoped it would relax at night when the traffic died down and figure a way out. It was still there the next day, however, so I immobilized it and took it in the back of a state pickup to the south end of Cowles Street where I released it onto the ice-covered Tanana River.

All of the radio-collared caribou from the Delta and Denali herds that survived the winter eventually made it back to their respective normal ranges in the Alaska Range. A few were pretty confused by the ordeal though, including one Denali caribou that lived with the Delta Herd for most of a year before returning home.

During the early 1990s, there were few fences and other barriers to caribou movement and the thousands of caribou that left the Alaska Range in late September and early October were able to make it through the Fairbanks metropolitan area and then return in the spring. The only fence that caused a major problem was the Eielson Air Force Base security fence. With increased fencing along highways and greatly expanded subdivisions all around Fairbanks today, caribou would likely have much more trouble. These kinds of movements occur very rarely though. I asked several old timers who were in Fairbanks as far back as the 1930s if they remembered anything like that movement. Bill Waugaman, a former big game guide, told me that he saw something similar in the early 1940s. He was the only one I talked to who remembered a movement like that.

As I continued to study the Delta Caribou through the 1990s and early 2000s, it became clear the series of bad winters that began in 1989, and the "perfect storm" years of 1992-93, had major long-lasting effects on the caribou herd. During this period, all of the older radio-collared caribou (those over ten years old) died, caribou calves were smaller, and three-year old females did not produce as many calves. The size of the Delta Herd had been much too high in 1989 (over 10,000 caribou) and that also contributed to the long-term effects of the bad years. Caribou in the Denali Herd, which had not been nearly as high, recovered much more quickly when the bad winters were over.

Chapter 3

Wolverines

F ew people know wolverines well, but those who do have found them to be one of the most fascinating of all northern carnivores. In North America, they received little attention from wildlife biologists until Maurice Hornocker began studying them in northern Idaho during the early 1970s. It was a time when they were at an all-time population low in the Lower 48 states. Audrey, conducted the first detailed life history study of wolverines in Alaska from 1978 to 1983, when she worked on her Ph.D. project based from the ADF&G field camp at Driftwood airstrip on the north side of the western Brooks Range, one of the most remote areas of the United States. She had determined such basic things as how large their home ranges are, when they have their kits, where they den, what their major foods are on the North Slope, and how far they are likely to disperse as they reach adulthood. Since those early studies in Alaska, there have been major studies in most of the wolverine's circumpolar range, including studies in British Columbia, Alberta, the Northwest Territories of Canada, Sweden, Norway, the northern Cascades of Washington state, Montana, and Idaho.

In Alaska, I participated in four wolverine studies over the last 49 years, including 1) Audrey's Ph.D. project—the Driftwood study, 2) the first study of wolverines in the coastal rainforest of Southeast Alaska during 2005-2010, 3) a large wolverine survey headed by ADF&G biologist Craig Gardner in Interior Alaska during 2006, and 4) a large survey of the distribution of wolverines across the entire North Slope during 2013-2018 sponsored by The Wildlife Conservation Society. During 2004 and 2005, I also flew our Super Cub to Red Lake, Ontario to work on extensive wolverine surveys in Ontario, Labrador, and Manitoba also sponsored by the Wildlife Conservation Society. It was all fascinating and exciting work and even more enjoyable in some ways because I didn't have the responsibility for much of the planning and writing. That largely fell to others, especially Audrey. All of those projects were very well-documented in technical reports and published scientific papers but there were many enjoyable stories that have never been published. In the sections below, I relate some of those stories more or less chronologically, project by project, with a mix of the fun and the science.

The Driftwood Study, 1978-1983

Audrey based her Ph.D. project out of the ADF&G field camp I helped to build in 1977 at the old Driftwood airstrip. I related the history of this airstrip in the chapter on North Slope Adventures. Basically, we had a 12 x 16-foot wall tent on a frame for the cook tent and three 8 x 10-foot wall tents on frames for sleeping tents. Other studies were based there too, including full-time on grizzly bears and wolves, and part-time on caribou and moose. Much of the money for the studies was appropriated by Congress for studies by the Bureau of Land Management (BLM) after Pet-4 (Naval Petroleum Reserve No. 4) was renamed NPR-A (National Petroleum Reserve Alaska) in 1976. BLM contracted much of the work to ADF&G and USGS. (See map on page 17).

That part of northwestern Alaska has a long history of human use. For at least a couple of thousand years, there were various small groups of people numbering up to several hundred or perhaps more using the area seasonally, especially the upper Utukok River, Howard Pass, and the upper Killik River. In historic times, the decline of the Western Arctic Caribou Herd in the 1880s resulted in the inland portions of the North Slope being abandoned by people. By the early 1900s, almost all the people north of the Brooks Range lived along the coast where they were greatly affected by imported diseases and a great deal of historical knowledge was lost. The gradual recovery of the caribou herd and the desire to get away from disease problems along the coast led some of the remaining Nunamiut to move inland around 1930. After 1950, the inland people that were scattered around the central Brooks Range and central North Slope settled permanently in Anaktuvuk Pass. Simon Paneak, an elder and

ADF&G field camp at Driftwood in winter. Audrey did the first study of wolverines in Alaska using radio telemetry.

co-founder of the village of Anaktuvuk Pass, had learned to speak English at an early age and worked with several anthropologists, archaeologists, ethnographers, and biologists, including Robert Rausch, Nick Gubser, Laurence Irving, and Helge Ingstad. Thanks largely to his cooperative relationship with these scientists, much of the historical information on human use of the central North Slope has been preserved. There is much less information for the western North Slope, but it appears the area was never reoccupied by people after the exodus to the coast in the 1880s. The next period of human activity on the western North Slope was between 1944 and the early 1960s, when geologists with the U.S. Navy and the U.S.G.S. explored the area for oil. From the late 1960s until 1977, when we set up the field camp at Driftwood, there was almost no recent use of the area by people, except by occasional wolf hunters. Most of the signs of human presence, besides the occupied villages and DEW Line sites along the coast, consisted of old drum caches, abandoned equipment, and abandoned buildings at old DEW Line sites and at Umiat, and old airstrips that were being slowly washed away or being reclaimed by the tundra.

As snowmachines became more reliable during the early 1980s, people again started traveling long distances inland from the coastal villages of Wainwright and Barrow. Over the five-year period we operated the field camp at Driftwood, we were essentially the only people using the area, except for occasional use by geologists. It was uncommon to see any aircraft not associated with our projects, and we only saw evidence of one group of people traveling in the area in winter. As a result, the area felt very remote and wild and we had to be completely self-sufficient.

Audrey had a series of wall tents and two Ski-Doo Elan snowmachines for her winter work to the south of the camp in the northern foothills of the Brooks Range. When I was not actively working on the caribou project, I stayed at Driftwood, maintaining the camp and helping with the wolverine project. Because of the weather, including fog and low clouds in summer and wind and extreme cold in winter, and the remoteness of the location, logistics were about 80% of the work in all the projects. Driftwood was a four to six-hour flight from Fairbanks and a two-hour flight from Kotzebue. The only weather reporting points that were helpful in planning flights were in Bettles and Umiat, hundreds of miles away. The only heat sources we had at the field camp were an oil stove in the cook tent, a propane stove in one of the sleeping tents, and gasoline catalytic heaters for preheating the aircraft. For lighting, we had Coleman white gas lanterns. The only communications were with the single-sideband HF radio in the cook tent powered by a truck battery. At that time, all of ADF&G regional offices had base station HF radios and the field camps had battery operated portable HF radios. Portable generators were generally not available and seldom used, although we did have a very small one at Driftwood for charging batteries. Reception of the HF radios was variable and depended on atmospheric conditions and interfering radiation from sunspots and other unknown phenomena. Sometimes we could talk to the Fairbanks office just fine and other times not at all. ADF&G only used three frequencies so it was possible to listen to a lot of the department radio traffic, especially in summer when all the fish weirs, hatcheries, and canneries were operating. Sometimes, if it was important enough, we asked people at other locations to relay messages to Fairbanks for us.

We operated the Driftwood field camp from early February until late November. Opening up the camp in February was always a chore. We would arrive late in the day after a long flight from Fairbanks or Kotzebue. When we arrived to set it up, the runway was generally drifted in and not suitable for large aircraft, the tents had to be dug out of snowdrifts where they had been packed into snap-lid drums the previous November, the oil stove had to be unwrapped and set up, etc. Very often, we had to accomplish all those chores with the temperature well below zero and the wind blowing. It was always a big relief to get the cook tent set up and the oil stove going so we could finally have a warm drink, some food to eat, and feel some warmth after a very long cold day. Generally, after a couple of days of hard work, with the tents set up and the snowmachines running, the outhouse dug out, water melted, and snowdrifts on the runway dug away by hand, the camp was really quite comfortable even in the coldest temperatures. Operating comfortable camps on the North Slope is a lot of work and is a specialized skill that takes a while to learn. Learning to maintain camp equipment, radios, small engines, aircraft, and other equipment is critical to making arctic projects a success and it requires knowledge of electronics, carpentry, small engine repair, operating all sorts of tools, and a general knowledge of physics and engineering. None of those skills are learned in courses taught to wildlife students. Collecting the biological information that is the actual goal of the work ends up being a small part of the total project. Fortunately, by the time fellow technician Ron Ball and I were asked to set up the Driftwood field camp for ADF&G, I had been in Alaska for five years, hunting, trapping, camping, flying, and operating snowmachines in the cold of Interior Alaska. I also built a cabin in Canada with my parents while I was in high school and the cabin in which we lived in Fairbanks. I also had built a wall tent camp for trapping at Minto, so I knew the basics of frame construction and winter operations that depended on small engines and aircraft.

During the first three years of the wolverine project, the main focus was on trapping wolverines in live-traps and putting radio-collars on them. We checked the traps from the ground every day with the Elan snowmachines. We did catch some of the wolverines by darting them from a helicopter whenever the helicopter was available and was not being used by other projects. Darting wolverines from a helicopter had never been attempted before. They are a small target, but it turned out to be possible, although I do remember someone setting the new record for the number of misses in a row.

The more we learned about wolverines, the more they fascinated us. They are amazing diggers, especially in snow. All the dens we found were in tunnels in the snow, some as much as 90 feet long. We dug out several of their dens after the females had moved their kits to other sites when the snow started melting. I got a lot of exercise shoveling snow. We once tried to catch a wolverine by digging it out of the snow and in the process, we learned just how good they are at digging. We had been following a set of very fresh tracks with the Super Cub when we came upon the animal. Almost as soon as it saw us, it decided to dig into the snow instead of running. When we saw it starting to dig, we decided to try to catch it and radio-collar it. I quickly landed, grabbed a scoop shovel I had tied on the wing strut, and started digging. I dug as fast as I could for a while and then stopped to listen. I could hear the scratch, scratch, scratch of the frantically digging wolverine in the snow below me so I kept digging. After I had gone about six feet down into the snow drift I finally gave up. I was exhausted, dripping with sweat, and certainly no match for that master digger.

Another time, we were flying along, following a fresh set of tracks and came upon the wolverine with its back end sticking out of a hole in the snow. It wasn't moving and appeared dead, so we landed right next to it. The wind was blowing about 15 mph and the snow was blowing a bit. Audrey got out of the plane, walked up to the apparently dead wolverine and reached down to touch it. At that point, it burst out of the hole with a loud huff and ran away. Audrey looked into the hole and found the remains of a ground squirrel

Audrey with a six-week old wolverine kit dug from a den near Driftwood in March 1979. Audrey found that wolverine kits are born surprisingly early and usually in snow dens, from late January through late March.

frozen into the tundra. The wolverine was so intent on digging out and eating the frozen ground squirrel and we landed so quietly in the wind and soft snow the wolverine didn't even notice. That was one of the first hints about how important ground squirrels are to wolverines on the North Slope.

We found that wolverines spent a lot of their time hunting ground squirrels, especially in mid-to-late summer when there are lots of young squirrels around. On several occasions, we flew circles for hours around radio-collared wolverines, watching them hunt. They very quickly learned the airplane was not a threat as long as we stayed a few hundred feet in the air, and after just a few hours of circling they completely ignored the slowly circling Cub. Their usual method of hunting ground squirrels was to rush a ground squirrel mound and try to surprise the squirrels and either catch one right away or get them trapped in shallow holes and then dig them out.

ADF&G grizzly bear research biologist Harry Reynolds tries to photograph a wolverine hiding in a meltwater tunnel near Driftwood in 1979.

Some of the shallow holes had two entrances with just a shallow tunnel in between. The wolverine would dig into one tunnel and then quickly run over and dig into the other one. The squirrel would eventually panic and run for it. Sometimes the wolverine got it but other times the squirrels would get away.

We also watched a wolverine try to catch a young caribou calf. Driftwood is on the southern edge of the main calving area of the Western Arctic Herd and there were often small groups of caribou passing through in late May and early June. The wolverine we were circling spotted one such small group and gave chase. Wolverines are not particularly fast runners, nothing like wolves, so it could just barely keep up with the caribou that were slowed down by their young calves. The wolverine gained on one of the calves but when it got to within about 30 feet of the calf, the mother caribou darted around and started chasing the wolverine, kicking at it. At first, the

Unloading wolverine live-traps from the ADF&G Beaver at Driftwood in 1980. I learned to fly it in 1980. The Beaver is still (2021) an important part of the ADF&G small airplane fleet, especially for caribou censuses.

wolverine tried to ignore the mother and focus on catching the calf but it finally had to defend itself. Once the wolverine turned on the mother caribou, she lost her nerve and ran away from the wolverine. Caribou are about the least aggressive member of the deer family but they will defend their calves from small predators like foxes and eagles. Wolverines are just large enough and dangerous enough that female caribou would apparently rather run than fight. Although we didn't realize it at the time, wolverines are actually pretty good at catching adult caribou in late winter.

Raising Wolverine Kits

In 2000, Audrey got to do something she had always wanted to do with wolverines. She obtained two young wolverines, a female and a male, and she raised them for several months. She also got a permit from ADF&G to raise them in the mountains of the Alaska Range and observe the development of their behavior. Audrey named them Deborah and Denali, after two of the highest peaks in the Alaska Range. She bottle-fed them in Fairbanks for a few weeks, and then we took them to Wells Creek on the south side of the Alaska Range near Cantwell. It was a late break-up, so we had to go in by helicopter around the third week of May. We set up a base camp with a wall tent and kept the wolverine kits in a portable steel cage at night to protect them from wolves, bears, and other wolverines. Audrey stayed with the kits full-time but I had my job to attend to and mostly visited the camp on weekends.

As they grew older, we led them around on walks during the day to investigate their surroundings. At first, they were most interested in wrestling with each other, so it seemed like they were either eating, sleeping, or wrestling. Towards the end of June, they began to get more interested in their environment and liked to chew on, and play with, shed antlers and other objects they found. They also started to take a real interest in lingering snow beds, which are a very important part of the lives of adult wolverines in the wild. Adult females often den in snow beds and all adults cache their food in rock piles and snow beds. They loved the snow when we were out walking and they would rush to a snow bed and wrestle, play, and slide like bears.

As the kits grew older, I was glad I parked the Super Cub a half mile from the camp, because the wolverine kits loved the plane. Whenever they saw it, they'd run over and try to climb all over it. I was worried about their sharp little claws and teeth scratching the paint and poking holes in the fabric. One day in late July, when they were getting quite grown up, we were on a walk and I made the mistake of getting a little too close to the Super Cub. They both saw the airplane at the same time and dashed for it. They started climbing all over it and after a minute or two I had them both by the scruff of the neck, one in each hand, and started running away from the plane. I managed to get them about two hundred yards away from the plane and dropped them on the ground. I tried to get their attention with a shed caribou antler to get their mischievous little minds off the plane. It worked for a couple of minutes and then I saw

Denali glance over towards the plane and immediately start running towards it as fast as he could go. He beat me back to the plane and Deborah was right behind me. I had to peel them both off the plane once more and make another run with the squirming, growling kits. That time, I carried them off behind a little hill so they couldn't see the plane. That worked, and they eventually forgot about it and started wrestling with each other instead.

Their physical abilities developed quickly from all the play fighting and by mid-July they were very athletic. Denali was the more outgoing of the two and especially liked to play a game with me where I would walk bent over next to a big boulder and he would leap from the boulder onto my back. I tried walking further and further from the boulder and he learned to leap further and further. He could easily leap 10 or 15 feet to land on my back. It gave me a good appreciation of how wolverines could leap up onto the backs of caribou or moose to attack them.

In early August, the kits began getting independent quickly and they were sometimes reluctant to come back from under snowdrifts or rocks, and we realized within a couple of weeks we wouldn't have any control of them at all. According to the permit, Audrey was not supposed to release them in the wild, so she ended the project about the 5th of August. Audrey wrote an unpublished report about the project and a TV special was filmed for Canadian public television. The wolverine kits were returned to their owner in western Washington and Audrey visited them every couple of years. They clearly remembered her all their remaining lives. Denali died of a tumor when he was ten, but Deborah lived to be sixteen, when she died of old age.

The young wolverines Audrey raised could be a real handful. We were often glad when we put them back in their pen at night so we could get some rest.

Wolverine Surveys in Canada

After the summer of helping to raise the wolverine kits at Wells Creek in the Alaska Range, the next major wolverine project was a survey of wolverines in Ontario, Labrador, and southeastern Manitoba. In 2004, fellow Fairbanks pilot Marty Webb and I flew our Super Cubs to Red Lake, Ontario to continue a wolverine research project started by Audrey and Justina Ray of The Wildlife Conservation Society (WCS) in northern Ontario in 2003.

We left Fairbanks in early February at the start of a pretty severe cold spell. Fairbanks wasn't too bad, but Whitehorse was about -25F when we landed. When we went to take off in the morning it was -40F and as we were about to depart, the rush hour traffic caused ice fog to form. The visibility went below a mile (the minimum allowed for flights under Visual Flight Rules) and we were delayed for a couple of hours waiting for it to improve. Fortunately, the flight from Whitehorse to the next stop, Dawson Creek, was only a little over five hours, so the delay was not a major problem and it was a little warmer in the air than it was on the ground. When we flew over Watson Lake, we could barely see the town, it was buried in ice fog and it looked damn cold. Dawson Creek was about -30F when we landed, and the next two stops, Fort McMurray and The Pas, were about the same. When we arrived at Red Lake after five days of flying, it was a balmy +10F and the sun was strong. We were both feeling relieved to be out of the extreme cold and in the relatively mild southern latitudes, so we got a pretty good laugh out of one of the comments made to us by a local in the hotel bar. He heard we were Americans and had just arrived in Red Lake. He was quite concerned and said, "You boys better be careful, you're in the North now!" We just thanked him for his concern and mentioned that we'd just come down from Alaska and flown for five days in temperatures below -30F. He said something like, "Oh, OK then, I guess you know what real cold is like."

Marty and I both had a lot of experience snow-tracking animals from the air in Alaska and he had come down to Ontario the year before

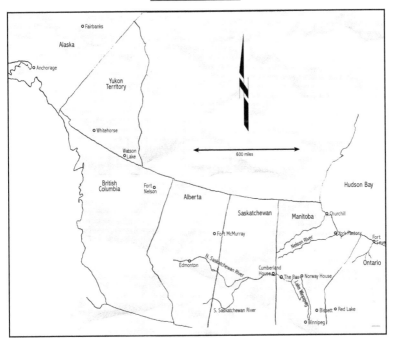

Northern Canada and the route we took to get from Alaska to Red Lake, Ontario and back in 2004 and 2005.

and had some local experience as well. Ontario was all new to me, but we had flown low enough on the way down to see animal tracks and I was getting used to the differences in track patterns of animals in the Canadian boreal forest compared with those in Alaska. By the time we were done with the two years of the tracking project, I noticed some really interesting differences in the appearance of tracks in the boreal forests of Manitoba and Ontario compared with Alaska. Wolverine tracks looked the same, but the tracks of wolves, caribou, and moose were noticeably different. Wolves and moose are smaller in the southern boreal forest compared with their counterparts in Alaska, but caribou are larger. It is sometimes possible to confuse caribou and wolf tracks in Alaska, but we never had that trouble in Ontario. There were also deer tracks that could sometimes be confused with wolf tracks in Ontario. Fishers were also present in the southern portions of Ontario and I was initially concerned about telling their tracks apart from wolverine tracks. It turned out not to be a problem. Fishers have much smaller feet and

127

Wolverines have distinctive tracks that can be easily recognized from the ground or from the air. Photo by Roblyn Brown.

sink deeper into the snow than wolverines and their track pattern is also quite different. They also commonly climb trees, so if there is any doubt, you can always track one to where it has climbed up or jumped up into or down out of a tree.

After working with wolverines and getting to know them pretty well in Alaska, it was enlightening to study them in a completely different environment. One of the first things I noticed was that wolverines in Ontario pay much more attention to beaver lodges than they do in Alaska. Beaver meat is a high-energy "sweet" meat and therefore highly desired by carnivores. All the carnivores in Alaska pay some attention to beaver lodges, but most of the wolverine tracks I followed in Interior Alaska just passed by lodges. In contrast, it seemed like wolverines would always go out of their way to check beaver lodges in Ontario and we found a couple of lodges where wolverines bored a hole into the south side and dragged beaver out and killed them on the ice. It was rather dramatic to see the big blood smears in the snow in front of the beaver lodges with wolverine tracks all around. One of the local Cree names for wolverines translates into "beaver-eater." An explanation may be that the sun is much stronger in Ontario and the south sides of the beaver lodges must be thawed a lot of the time. In Alaska, the mud incorporated into beaver lodges is solidly frozen all winter and probably more difficult for wolverines to break through until spring, when the south sides of the lodges begin to thaw. With warmer winters in Alaska as a result of climate warming and an increasing and spreading beaver population, beaver may become a more important winter food for wolverines in the future.

Besides the historical trapping records collected by the Ontario Ministry of Natural Resources and its predecessors, there had really been no effort to collect information on wolverines in Ontario before WCS began their wolverine work in the early 2000s. Many people today think of wolverines as a mountain or arctic animal, but historically they ranged completely across the boreal forest on the Canadian Shield in eastern and northern Manitoba, practically all of Ontario and Quebec, and all of Labrador. By the late 1920s, wolverines were gone from all of Labrador and Quebec, and they were restricted to the northwestern portion of Ontario. Caribou had declined to a very low level in Quebec and Labrador, and because the northern parts of those provinces are so biologically poor, wolverines had very little to eat and were probably quite vulnerable to trapping. By the time the Wildlife Conservation Society started their studies on wolverines in Ontario, it was pretty clear wolverines were expanding their range again, reinvading areas where they had been absent for decades.

During the extensive wolverine surveys we did in Ontario, we stayed in several First Nations villages and regional centers as well, including Attawapiskat, Webequie, Pickle Lake, Kapuskasing, Sioux Lookout, and Moosonee. We had the opportunity to talk to many First Nations elders and to Bush pilots, and their stories were all enlightening and entertaining. One universal theme in all the stories was how much the north had changed, with the most rapid change occurring in the 1970s. Until then, the economy of First Nations villages had largely been based on trapping and commercial fishing in the winter, and sport and commercial fishing in the summer. Most of the access to the villages had been by float planes in summer and ski planes in winter, with some use of winter sled roads in northern Saskatchewan, Manitoba, and northwestern Ontario. By 1980, that had all changed and the economy was entirely based on government welfare and providing local services. A formerly externally-focused, resource-based economy transformed into a largely inwardly focused village-based economy. In 2004, it was pretty clear that although the whole of northern Ontario was divided into hundreds of registered traplines belonging mostly to First Nations people, almost none of them were being actively trapped. That went a long way to explain why wolverines were again expanding their range. Because they rely heavily on scavenging, wolverines are easily caught in any baited sets and in traps set for wolves.

In 2004, when we were doing the wolverine surveys, the price of marten was averaging around $75 a pelt and marten were abundant in most areas of Ontario where we flew. In fact, there were often marten tracks right up to within a few hundred yards of the houses in the village, but almost no one was trapping. I asked several people why that was and the universal answer was, "Trapping is hard work and a difficult life, and people don't need to do that anymore." It still didn't explain why no one was trapping the local marten where they could have been home every night.

We met one very enterprising man in Attawapiskat. Marius Kataquapit was running the local hotel, along with several other businesses in town. He agreed to spend an evening with Marty and I discussing the old trapping lifestyle, how it used to work, and why it would never work again. Marius was born in 1938 and in his late teens started to run a trapline. He trapped off and on for many years. His main trapping area had been around Akimiski Island in James Bay. He often got a later start than other trappers because he had to wait for the water in James Bay to freeze between the village and the island. He had some hair-raising stories about thin ice and also one about catching a polar bear cub and being chased by its mother until he was forced to stop his snowmachine, unload the cub, and speed away. He said he had pretty much stopped trapping in the early 1980s and now ran the hotel in town, working seven days a week. Although he really missed trapping and it had been an important part of his life, it was indeed a tough life if you worked at it full time. Most trappers flew, boated, or canoed out to their traplines just before freeze-up in October, trapped with dog teams, snowmachines (after the late 1960s), or on foot until Christmas, and then flew back in to town for a few weeks around the holidays. Wives and grandparents raised the children and ran the household when their trapper husbands or sons were away. Then, when trappers returned at Christmas, wives were expected to help flesh and stretch the pelts the trapper brought in. After the holidays, the trappers returned to their 'lines until spring. There was lots of work for commercial airplanes on skis and floats in those days. Older men who lived the trapping lifestyle remembered it fondly and certainly missed many aspects of it. Marius believed that making a living by trapping was just not possible anymore.

During the 1970s, the Canadian government embarked on a massive program to build large gravel airstrips in the villages and provide services, including improved schools, community centers, television, public housing, and other amenities. That was the end of the trapping and subsistence lifestyle. Almost no one was willing to live the lonely life of a trapper and the wives would no longer tolerate their husbands being away most of the time in winter. A very few people would continue to do some village-based trapping, but most registered First Nations traplines would never be used again. There have been some government and industry-funded programs to restart trapping, but as soon as subsidies end, so does the trapping effort. The chronically low fur prices of the recent past will ensure what little trapping is done will primarily be a hobby or recreational pursuit. Another problem now is that the First Nations villages have grown substantially since the 1970s and even if fur prices rebounded, the fur resource would be too small to support the much greater number of people that now reside in the villages.

Everyone we talked to had heard of wolverines and talked about them with concern bordering on fear, and/or with respect. In western and northwestern Ontario, people accepted them as part of the local fauna, but to most people in central and eastern Ontario, they were mostly a mystical creature of the distant past. We often asked the question about wolverines in different ways. One evening, we asked if anyone in the village of Webequie sold moccasins. Three old women got the word and came by our house in the evening with some beautiful crafts to sell. Webequie is geographically in northeastern Ontario, and Marty had seen wolverine tracks on the outskirts of town when he arrived. I first asked the three women, "Are there wolverines around Webequie?" The answer from all three was a firm "NO." I then asked, "Were wolverines around in your father's or grandfather's time?" The answers again were firmly, "NO." One of the women could see where the questions were going and said, "We don't have wolverines around here, but we don't like them!" Her comment strongly implied they certainly did not want them back. We then got down to the business of buying some moccasins and local crafts made with fur. Some items were beautifully made and trimmed with beaver or rabbit fur. We asked if the fur was obtained locally and they said no, it was mail ordered from Goldberg's in Seattle. It was pretty clear that although trapping was a thing of the past, the older women still enjoyed their handicrafts. As we were leaving Webequie the next day, both Marty and I saw wolverine tracks within a few miles of town. In the years since those surveys, wolverines have expanded even more and I'm sure, by now, everyone knows that wolverines are back, whether the people actually wanted them back or not.

I had not appreciated how wild the province of Ontario was until we flew over most of it in 2004 and 2005. Away from the villages and the southern road system, we rarely saw any sign of people. In Alaska it is common to see or hear aircraft when one is on the ground almost anywhere in the state. From the air it is also not uncommon to see snowmachine tracks. In contrast, there are very few private airplanes in Ontario and people don't seem to travel across country with snowmachines. One reason is that the bedrock granite of the extensive Canadian Shield has been cut through into steep canyons that create barriers to ground travel. It is also much less productive country than most of Alaska or the adjacent Canadian prairie provinces, so there is much less reason for people to be there, except for fishing in the summer.

In much of northern Ontario there is very little for carnivores to eat. A few moose and scattered small groups of woodland caribou are about all there is for large game. As a result, there are also few wolves, except further south where logged areas and hardwood forests begin, and where deer and moose are both present and more abundant. The beginning of the hardwood forests south of Red Lake was also the end of the wolverine range. One surprising thing we did find was there are huge numbers of sharp-tailed grouse throughout the Hudson Bay Lowlands. There are fair numbers of sharp-tailed grouse in Alaska, but they are uncommon in the western U.S. and sought after as a game bird. I didn't realize the stronghold of the species was the boreal forests of Canada where we saw them in large numbers over huge areas.

We had lots of opportunity to visit with people around Red Lake, often when the weather was bad or the tracking conditions weren't good enough to fly surveys. There were some notable differences and similarities in the way of life and the way people expressed themselves in Ontario compared with Alaska. Although Red Lake and Fairbanks had a similar feel because both are essentially at the end of the road system, I didn't get the same feeling of independence and freedom I get in Alaska. One day, I was slowly driving a borrowed snowmachine to make a nice, packed runway on the lake when a local friend walked out on the ice and said, "You better not let the police catch you doing that." I looked at him and then I looked back at the area I had just packed and said, "Well, I must be doing something wrong, but I have no idea what it is." He pointed to his head and said, "Helmet!" Apparently, it was illegal to drive a snowmachine without a helmet. We saw lots of kids driving snowmachines recklessly at high speed around the lake and heard a story about one of them running over and killing a cross country skier, but apparently, driving recklessly was OK, as long as you wore a helmet.

Another difference in Canada is that people couldn't just get in their airplane and go flying like they can in the U.S. Even though it was a relatively remote area, there were mandatory radio frequencies monitored remotely from Winnipeg and some kind of flight plan is always required in Canada. Controllers were always asking, "What are your intentions?" whenever they heard you on the radio. At first, I found it a bit annoying and felt like saying, "None of your business!" But I soon got accustomed to it and realized it was just a different way of doings things in a different country. In Canada, a "Company Flight Note," meant just telling your wife or any other responsible adult where you are going and when you will be back, and it fulfills the flight plan requirement. But you have to let the authorities know you have one. Canadians don't have a right to free use of their airspace like people in the United States do. There are also landing fees at most airports east of the Yukon and BC. It is no wonder general aviation has never caught on in Canada the way it has in the U.S. It has been strangled by user fees and overregulation.

Despite the tighter controls over flying and requirement to wear a helmet while driving a snowmachine, the long arm of bureaucracy was present at Red Lake in other ways too. I became friends with a local Conservation Officer who was very interested in the wolverine project and in snow-tracking animals. He also really liked airplanes and I could tell he was dying for a ride in our Super Cub. I offered to take him up one day but he said, "You know, I'd really love to go, but because of Ministry policy, I'm not allowed to." So, I said, "Well, let's go on your day off then," to which he said, "I'm not supposed to do that either. The ministry has a policy that provincial employees are not allowed to fly in aircraft smaller than a Turbo Beaver, even during their days off." I told him I'd never tell anyone if he did fly with me. He was sorely tempted, but politely declined the offer. Another even more bizarre thing he told me was that another recent ministry policy was that if he was driving a snowmachine on the ice, he was required to stop every 200 feet and drill a hole to test the ice thickness. He said if he strictly obeyed that, it would be pretty hard to do his job and he would be the laughing stock of everyone else out on the ice, so he just didn't go out on the ice anymore. Apparently, the new policy was implemented because a provincial employee grooming snowmachine trails had fallen through with his snowmachine and drowned. Bureaucrats love to protect themselves from liability by coming up with silly policies that make no sense at the field level.

One of the other local issues was the ice roads that are built in mid-winter. These ice roads had their advantages and disadvantages. It made life easier around Red Lake when the local ice road on the lake was built because people could avoid having to drive way around to settlements and summer houses on the other side of the lake. On the other hand, the ice roads that reached First Nations villages to the north were something of a mixed blessing. People from the villages could easily drive into town and hang around the bars and cause trouble. There was a bar in the basement of our hotel, the Red Lake Inn. When I came out of the hotel one Saturday morning after the ice roads were completed, I saw a blood trail coming up the basement steps from the bar and going to the sidewalk. At the sidewalk junction, the blood trail went both directions. After following it a couple of hundred yards one way, I saw an older Native man sitting forlornly in the sun on a bench with a big, blood-soaked bandage on his head. I didn't follow the blood trail the other way but suspected I'd find something similar. Apparently, there had been a wild, drunken brawl in the bar the night before and there had been several casualties.

One other bone of contention with the ice roads was that First Nations people competed with non-native locals while ice fishing on Red Lake. Unlike Alaska, where everyone living in an area must generally obey the same hunting and fishing regulations, First Nations people in Canada are not bound to follow any regulations, except for endangered species. The bag limit for non-native walleye fishermen at Red Lake was two per day but First Nations people were allowed to catch all they could and then sell them. The same applied to moose. There was a tightly controlled fall hunting season and bag limit of one bull moose, and people enjoyed seeing moose unmolested during the rest of the year. After the ice roads went in, the local roadside moose that people enjoyed seeing ended up as gut piles on the side of the road. Inevitably, the racially-based rules caused some grumbling and an underlying current of racism and resentment.

We also ran into differences in terminology. Bush pilots and trappers in Alaska are always concerned about "overflow" when flying on skis in winter. To people in Ontario, it is "slush", the word "overflow" being unknown. "Slush" was a major problem and persisted for weeks at a time, making it sometimes difficult for us to find places to land and take a break. When we asked about what it would take to make the "slush" go away, the local pilots said it would take wind or rain. Either or both would destroy the insulating quality of the snow and allow the water that was on top of the ice, but under the snow, to freeze.

Marty and I also had a few humorous exchanges with government officials in Ontario. The first one was in the village of Attawapiskat on the west shore of James Bay. There is no all-season road but the area was beginning to get some attention because of the recent discovery of diamonds about 50 miles to the west. While we were there, the Lieutenant Governor of Ontario arrived and was listening to the concerns of local people about the proposed mining development on Crown lands. When I saw the new guest in the hotel, I didn't know who he was or what was going on, but he came over to talk to me one evening and said, "Hello, what are you doing in Attawapiskat?" So, I told him about the wolverine surveys. He gave me a rather puzzled and questioning look but didn't ask any more questions, so I said, "And what are you doing here?" He said, "I'm the Lieutenant (pronounced, "lef-tenant") Governor of Ontario", and then he quickly added, "And being an American, you probably don't even know what that is." I certainly wouldn't have had a clue, except I had just read something about the visit and asked a local what the "Lieutenant Governor" was. So, the Lieutenant Governor was pleasantly surprised when I immediately replied, "Of course I know, you are the Queen's representative in the province of Ontario, and I'm very pleased to meet you, sir."

Another funny exchange we had was in the town of Moosonee at the south end of James Bay. We had just arrived late in the day and fueled up to depart for Labrador City in the morning. An Ontario Provincial Police (OPP) officer was in the airport terminal and he came walking over and glanced out the window at our two Super Cubs sitting on the ramp. He asked, "So you're Americans, eh? What are you doing in Moosonee?" I told him we were flying wolverine surveys by tracking them from the air. No one we had talked to in Canada had ever thought of doing that or even realized it was possible, so it wasn't surprising the OPP officer was skeptical. Being a good, nosey cop, he wanted more information, so he asked, "So how do you do that, exactly? You must have to fly pretty low, eh?" I replied, "You don't have to fly too low. In fact, it actually works better if you stay around 400 or 500 feet, or higher, so you can see a bigger area." Instead of helping, that explanation got him even more confused and I could tell he was beginning to think our surveys must be some sort of a scam being foisted on unsuspecting Canadians by a couple of American shysters. At that point, I started to get a little concerned, especially because Marty had not been able to get his required work permit when he came through Customs and Immigration in Whitehorse. The Immigration office was only open from 10:00 am until 2:00 pm Monday through Thursday, making it virtually impossible for someone flying from Fairbanks to get a work permit without spending at least one extra day in Whitehorse. Not having much patience for silly bureaucratic rules, Marty had just blown it off and come anyway. It also finally dawned on me that the OPP officer was thinking we must be trying to identify individual paw prints from the air, so I said, "We aren't actually trying to see the paw prints, we identify the animals by their track patterns in the snow." At that point, Marty jumped in and talked about needing good sunlight, how the patterns of tracks are quite easy to identify, and that we do this all the time in Alaska. We could tell the guy was still a bit skeptical, but it was such an unlikely story that he probably thought we couldn't possibly have made it up, so he just told us to be careful and went on his way.

In 2005, we were contracted by the Labrador government to fly wolverine surveys in that province too. The government was thinking about reintroducing wolverines there but they wanted to be sure they were really gone. The last wolverines were trapped in Labrador during the 1920s and there had been no confirmed reports of them since then. The "Traditional Ecological Knowledge" obtained from First Nations elders was contradictory. There continued to be stories and unverified reports, but to most biologists, it was clear that wolverines had been gone from Labrador for about 80 years. There may have occasionally been a few long-distance dispersals from western Ontario or wolverines escaped from captivity in Quebec, but there certainly was no breeding population left in Quebec or Labrador.

We got to Labrador by first flying to Moosonee at the south end of James Bay. We ended up waiting a couple of days there for suitable weather and had a good look around. Moosonee is an historic place, especially the old Hudson's Bay Company (HBC) post of Moose Factory that sits on an island in the Moose River. The post was the second HBC post in Canada and dates back to 1673. It operated almost continuously as mainly a fur trading post until around 1960, when the store was modernized.

From Moosonee, we flew across James Bay and landed at the village of Waskaganish, formerly called Fort Rupert. Fort Rupert was the first HBC post in Canada and was established in 1670. I had read several books about the history of the HBC, so it was exciting to see where it all started. The HBC essentially owned about one-third of Canada for 175 years before it relinquished its royal charter to all the lands drained by waters flowing into Hudson's Bay in 1847.

A direct flight from Moosonee to Labrador City was just a bit too far for our Super Cubs so we carried an extra five gallons of fuel

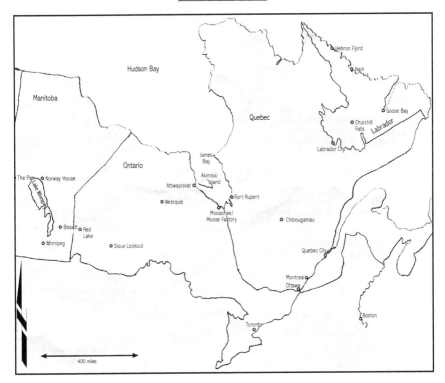

Eastern Canada and the places we visited during wolverine surveys in Labrador, Ontario, and Manitoba during 2005.

and added it at Waskaganish. The rest of the flight was nonstop and it was one of the most desolate pieces of country I have ever flown across. For the first three hours we did see quite a few wintering caribou and we crossed the giant power lines coming from the James Bay Hydro Project, but then we flew for hours in sunny weather without seeing any signs of people or tracks of animals larger than red squirrels, except for a very occasional marten track.

We spent several days in Labrador City, waiting for sunlight and good tracking conditions. Labrador City and neighboring Wabush were company towns until the 1980s and are centered around the huge iron mines there. One of the largest buildings (in area covered) I have ever seen was in Labrador City. We could see the building from 40 miles away and Marty and I discussed on the radio what it could possibly be. It turned out to be essentially a small city enclosed in a single building that looked to be a about a mile long. Once we realized how consistently bad the weather is in Labrador, the building made sense.

Labrador is an amazingly desolate place. The underlying bedrock is all granite, there is very little soil, and the province sits at the end of the two major storm tracks in North America. Storms that form at the base of the Rocky Mountains (called "Alberta Clippers"), track east across Canada to Labrador, and the storms from the south ("Nor-Easters") track north up the eastern seaboard to Labrador. Finding stretches of good weather in Labrador required a good deal of patience.

From Labrador City, we worked our way northeast for seven hours to the village of Nain, searching for wolverine tracks but recording the tracks of other animals as well. We saw very few tracks at all, particularly of animals larger than marten. Nain is the northernmost village on the Labrador coast and we also waited there for many days in bad weather. I have spent a good deal of time in northern villages in Alaska and the Yukon, but they were nothing like Nain. The kids in town were largely out of control. They had vandalized the new school, were constantly trying to break into the hotel to steal things, and RCMP officers had to enlist people at the airport to watch our Super Cubs to keep them from also being vandalized by village kids. A pack of unruly kids hung around in front of the entrance to the bar, which was also the entrance to the hotel, yelling four-letter words at people going in and out. As we went in, Marty mumbled something about wanting to put some of those kids over his knee. They clearly had encountered no meaningful discipline in a long time. A bouncer was on duty full time to keep the kids out of the hotel and the bar, and all the windows were barred to keep the kids out of the hotel rooms. The more time we spent in Nain, the more it seemed like a village version of "Lord of the Flies."

On our first trip from the airport to the hotel, Marty and I passed a small building with all the windows and doors barred but the front door standing wide open. I asked one of our accompanying six-year olds, "Is that the jail?" He replied, "No, that's the beer store." So,

I asked, "Why is it all barred up, but the door is open?" He said, "They used to lock the door, but then people were just taking chain saws and cutting holes through the walls to steal the beer. So now they just sell all the beer in one day and leave the door open so people can see there is no more beer." It seemed like some of the adults were in need of supervision too!

Besides the unruly kids, Nain was a challenging place from which to operate airplanes. The runway was situated at the end of a sloping ridge that came down from a higher mountain to the northwest. With the prevailing west winds coming down off the high interior plateau, severe downdrafts and wind shears occurred right at the end of the runway. There was a wind sock at each end of the runway and they often indicated opposite wind directions. One day we watched a turbine single engine Otter on wheel skis as it came in to land on the lagoon. When it was about 100 feet in the air, a sudden wind shear caused it to bank 90 degrees to the left and plummet toward the ice on the lagoon. The pilot applied full power and just barely saved it from crashing. I talked to him a little later and he remarked, "I really hate coming into this place, even in good weather. The lagoon is better than the runway, but not by much."

I did talk to an older man who said he once owned a Piper PA-12 which he kept in a sheltered spot on the shore near his house. He said it was great to use for flying around fishing in summer and going out to get supplies, but he was always worried about the weather. About the third year he had the plane, it was destroyed in a windstorm. He asked me if I thought our Super Cubs were going to survive Labrador. I told him that between the kids in Nain and the wind in the rest of the province, I was a little worried about that too.

One thing that happened in Nain was that I met the CEO of The Northwest Company. The company was formed out of remaining parts of the Hudson's Bay Company and had consolidated all of the Northern Stores in Canada and all of the Alaska Commercial Company stores in Alaska. I asked him about Sailor Boy "Pilot Bread." A big smile came across his face and he said, "Oh, you'd know about that, eh? You're from Alaska." I told him I knew all about Pilot Bread and the inventor of the ovens that were used to produce it. It was really popular in Alaska. I asked if they sold it all over northern Canada too. He told me it was just in demand in Alaska, the Yukon, and western NWT and it was unknown in the rest of northern Canada.

From Nain, we flew about seven more hours of surveys and spent two nights at a cabin at Hebron Fjord. We refueled there from drums that had been barged up from Nain the previous August. From Hebron Fjord we covered the northern tip of Labrador and a small part of adjacent Quebec, then it was back to Nain and then on to Goose Bay where we spent several more days waiting for weather and flying surveys to the southeast. Goose Bay is a large military and civilian airport. Since World War II it has also served as a departure and arrival point for small aircraft flying across the Atlantic to Europe. There were both Canadian and American aircraft mechanics there who mostly issued overweight approvals for aircraft heading across the Atlantic. I asked one of the mechanics if he had ever seen someone fly a Super Cub across the Atlantic and he said no. He had seen just about every other kind of aircraft do it, but no Cubs.

In 1980, the base at Goose Bay was expanded to be a major NATO training center for low-level flying. The flying activities soon became controversial because Native people complained the jets disturbed caribou. Years of controversy ensued and most of the training had just been shut down when we arrived there in March 2005. There were vast rows of hangars and housing facilities that were sitting unused.

I also remember a conversation with a Conservation Officer (CO) at Goose Bay. He was white but he was married to a Labrador Inuit woman. He said that although he was in charge of enforcing hunting regulations, it really wasn't much use because most people in Labrador are now exempt from all hunting regulations because they are either covered by First Nations treaties or are Metis (mixed blood), who have now also been exempted from hunting and fishing regulations. He said that people usually hunt in groups and someone in the group will invariably be exempt. If a CO tries to enforce anything, the exempt member of the group will claim any game taken. He said his exempt son even did that. There seemed to be so little game in Labrador besides the large number of marine mammals, especially polar bears, that I wasn't sure enforcement would really make much difference anyway.

By the time we left Goose Bay and started heading back to the southwest toward Quebec, we had not seen any wolverine tracks. We had seen a few wolf tracks and some marten tracks, especially in the range of hills south and east of Goose Bay. Beaver appeared to be relatively rare too. The only animals that appeared to be really abundant in Labrador were polar bears and seals. Marty and I didn't fly over the ice much, but we found polar bear tracks on shore in several places. Audrey and I even found one place where a polar bear sow with cubs appeared to have been hunting caribou. We followed those tracks for a few miles and finally found the bear out on the near-shore sea ice surrounded by a huge blood smear that covered about an acre. She had just killed a ringed seal and the two little cubs were all covered with blood and having a grand time. Judging from the abundance of polar bear sign, Marty and I figured we could have counted quite a few polar bears in a few hours if we had really been trying. The harvest limits for polar bears in Labrador had been set at four bears per year. Based on the sign we saw along the vast stretches of uninhabited coast, those harvest limits seemed absurdly low and certainly not biologically based.

After spending about two weeks in Labrador to do six days of flying, we left and headed southwest, surveying toward the Labrador boundary and then on to our next planned overnight stop at Chibougamau in west central Quebec. However, just as we were nearing Churchill Falls, we started running into heavy snow. With the visibility down to around a mile or less, we headed directly toward the Churchill Falls airport and decided to spend the night there. We taxied onto the ramp of the airport next to a gigantic hangar and were discussing what to do next, when a little man-door in the hangar opened and a man walked up to us and said, "If you're spending the night, would you like to put your planes in the hangar?" Next thing we knew, the giant hangar door opened. We rolled the two little Cubs into the hangar, next to two Twin Otters, a giant helicopter, and several other airplanes. Then the same man said, "We can arrange rooms for you at no cost and if you'd like, and we can also arrange a guided tour of the Churchill Falls Hydroelectric Plant." Justina (Marty's observer and biologist with the Wildlife Conservation Society), Audrey, Marty, and I just looked at each other with big grins and said almost simultaneously, "Well, sure!" Then the man said, "You can get some food in the cafeteria but I'm afraid you'll have to pay for that yourselves." No problem there!

Churchill Falls is one of the few remaining true "company" towns in the world. Nalcor Energy owns everything, including the airport, hangars, housing, gymnasium, curling club, school, grocery store, restaurant, hotel, and library. Despite being a Sunday night, our personal guide arrived at our hotel room at 8:00 pm and gave us a tour of the power plant. When the construction project was completed in the late 1960s, Churchill Falls was the largest hydroelectric station in the world. Five parallel 12-foot diameter penstocks had been drilled 1,000 feet down through solid granite to a power house at the bottom. The power house was completely subterranean and also carved out of the granite rock with five 200-ton generators inside. The giant control room is 900 feet underground and accessible only from the top with elevators. The scale of the project and the precision with which it was built are truly astounding, especially considering it was all done before computers, with 1960s technology.

We left Churchill Falls the next morning, much refreshed after our warm welcome there. Just after we crossed the border into Quebec, Audrey and I saw our first fisher track. I had just remarked that there didn't seem to be any fishers in Labrador. From the border onward we started seeing more and more sign of furbearers and moose and it was nice to see the country becoming more productive again. At Chibougamau, we were told by the manager of the fuel company that he had not sold any 100LL avgas in over a year. There are so few small aircraft in Canada and almost all the larger planes have turbine engines and use jet fuel.

Our next, and final, tracking job in Canada in 2005 was to go over to Bissett in eastern Manitoba and try to see if wolverines were also present and expanding their range south towards Winnipeg. Audrey and I did that job alone, with just one Super Cub. (Marty had left to gone back to Alaska.) Bissett had been a gold mining town that had largely closed down when the biggest mine ceased operating in the early 1980s. We parked the Cub on frozen Rice Lake and tied it to the float dock. We were able to buy avgas from the company which ran floatplanes there in the summer. The first day we were there, I told Audrey I would work on the plane for a bit and then walk the three miles back to the Forestry bunkhouse where we were staying.

On the way to the bunkhouse, I passed by the liquor store and decided to stop in to see what was on offer, and to buy a six-pack of beer. The proprietor turned out to be quite a character. He asked me what I was doing in town and I told him. I could see his mind working and then he said, "You know where the real money is in flying, don't you?" I said I didn't. He turned and pointed to the wall of hard liquor bottles behind him and said, "It's right there." He then pointed to a big bottle of Canadian Club whiskey and said, "You see that toddy right there? Here, that's a $25 toddy. Up in Norway House that's an $100 toddy." I told him that was undoubtedly true but there might be people who would object to me running liquor up to Norway House (which is a First Nations community on the northeast corner of Lake Winnipeg). He didn't say anything and then changed the subject to caribou, and said, "Have you ever noticed how caribou only come in groups of two, six, nine, and twelve?" He seemed quite serious, so I wasn't sure what to say. I mumbled something about never noticing that with caribou, but I was starting to feel like I should hurry up and buy my six-pack of Molson and head for the door. Before I managed to get away, he did tell me he had actually been an officer with the Royal Canadian Mounted Police (RCMP) in Norway House for several years. I walked down the road shaking my head, thinking that here was a retired RCMP officer trying to get me to run liquor to the Indians, or that the guy was completely crazy and making it all up. I talked to a couple of

Manitoba biologists later and they just laughed. They said that yeah, the guy was indeed totally crazy, but pretty harmless so far. They had never heard that he was retired RCMP.

We did end up finding two or three sets of wolverine tracks in the area between Bissett and Lake Winnipeg so it did appear that wolverines were probably expanding their range in southern Manitoba as well. From Bissett south there was logging and regrowth of hardwoods so consequently there were quite a few more moose than in most of northern Ontario. There were also quite a few more wolves too. We weren't sure how much farther south wolverines were likely to go in eastern Manitoba. In Ontario, once we got into extensive logged areas with deer, more moose, and more wolves, wolverines were noticeably absent.

One thing we discovered in Manitoba was that coyotes occur around old burns where jack pine regeneration is occurring. We had been seeing fox-like tracks and they were driving us crazy because they just didn't look right. We finally found a pair of coyotes lying on a knob surrounded by small jack pines in an area with lots of snowshoe hare tracks. It turned out the coyotes on the fringe between the prairies and the boreal forest have figured out how to make a living on snowshoe hares and are completely dependent on them, like lynx are.

At the end of the 2005 surveys, we headed home to Alaska in early April. With the longer daylight, it was an easy four-day trip and we flew a slightly different route. I always wanted to see Cumberland House on the Saskatchewan River because of its historic significance as the first major inland post of the Hudson's Bay Company. The HBC remained on the coasts of James Bay and Hudson Bay for the first hundred years of its existence but then expanded inland to compete with the rival Northwest Company and freelance American trappers. Cumberland House was established in 1774 and served as a major center for the fur trade and for the pemmican trade that fueled the fur brigades. It was a strategic location because, within a few days paddling and portaging, travelers could either be headed west toward the Rocky Mountains, northwest to the Athabasca country and the McKenzie River, northeast to the Churchill River and Hudson Bay, or east and south to the Great Lakes and Montreal. We saw a couple of old abandoned HBC style buildings with trees growing up all around them along the Saskatchewan River and I would have loved to get on the ground, but there were no safe places to land. We flew back toward Alaska on the divide between the boreal forest and the prairies. To the left there was agriculture and road systems and to the right there was granite, lakes and rivers, pine and spruce forest, and wild country.

During the first couple of years of the wolverine survey and other snow-tracking projects in Ontario, Manitoba, and Labrador, there was essentially no paperwork involved, other than the documents needed to fly commercially in Alaska. We flew under the North American Free Trade Agreement with active support from an upper-level supervisor with Transport Canada. Starting in 2005, things became more and more bureaucratic. Work permits were required, lists of all modifications that had been done to the aircraft were required, an expensive permit from Transport Canada was required, agreements with a maintenance base were required, etc., etc. The last time we attempted to fly down and do wolf surveys in Manitoba in 2016, the paperwork took over three months to complete and most of it was redundant and meaningless. The relentless march of bureaucracy!

Wolverines in the Rain

In 2006, Audrey was invited by ADF&G Area Biologist Rich Lowell to start a wolverine study on the Alaska mainland across from Petersburg. I agreed to help as a full-time volunteer. Wolverines are commonly found along the entirety of coastal mainland Alaska and British Columbia, but like mountain goats, wolverines were not able to colonize most of the islands of the Alexander Archipelago after the last ice age. Even Revillagigedo Island, which is separated from the mainland by only about a mile of water, was not colonized by wolverines or mountain goats. Despite their relative abundance on the mainland and the long history of trapping them, there had never been a study of wolverines in the rainforests of Southeast Alaska or British Columbia.

Wolverines

The study was suggested and encouraged by Dave Benitz, an enterprising and concerned local trapper who had some doubts about whether he was sustainably trapping wolverines on his trapline at Thomas Bay and LeConte Bay. He agreed to stop trapping wolverines for five years while Audrey completed the study. He also freely shared his local knowledge and worked hard as a volunteer to make the project a success. He was really interested in knowing how many wolverines were in the area, what their home range sizes were, and how productive they were—all the things biologists need to know to manage a population of furbearers and make sure they are not being over-trapped. Many local residents in Petersburg make a living from commercial fishing, guided hunting, and other resource-based, outdoor activities. To some people, trapping is also an important winter activity that keeps people active during the long winter and also provides a secondary source of income. Good trappers are highly respected in the small communities of Southeast Alaska for their knowledge and boating skills, and the fact that they help control wolf numbers, especially during and after bad winters when wolf predation on deer can be severe.

In the fall of 2005, taking advantage of some very high tides to use the ADF&G landing craft, Audrey and I took eight prefabricated timber live-traps to sites around Thomas Bay. Over a couple of months, we moved into the ADF&G cabin at Thomas Bay, erected the live-traps, and set up camera traps to determine how many wolverines were using the area. We also chartered a local helicopter in Petersburg to set up camera traps from Le Conte Bay to Port Houghton. Pilot Wally O'Brocta and one of his sons took an active interest in the project. It was great to have all that cooperation from local people and their cooperation contributed to the success of the project and also made it much more enjoyable.

We moved over to Thomas Bay full time in November 2006 and within a month we had all the live-traps and camera stations operating. We soon had a routine established. We'd get up early, have a quick breakfast, and then go by boat to check the live-traps. The traps were made of six-inch square Sitka spruce timbers with a top door (roof) that dropped down when an animal pulled on the

Trapper and hunting guide Dave Benitz with Audrey at Thomas Bay near Petersburg in Southeast Alaska. Dave was instrumental in getting the first study of wolverines started in Southeast Alaska.

baited trigger inside. We didn't catch anything, except a couple of marten, for about a week. Then we caught two wolverines in one day. Much to our disappointment, however, they both escaped by chewing holes overnight in the walls of the traps. We got a very good deal on the timbers, partly because some of them were not entirely sound and had some punky spots. For their size, wolverines are very strong and also have strong jaws, but we were unpleasantly surprised they ate through the six-inch timbers overnight. After that discovery, we lined all of the traps with two-inch hemlock boards. We probably should have built the traps out of hemlock to begin with. Hemlock is denser and has tough, stringy fibers compared with spruce.

Within a few months, we made a couple of other improvements, including trap monitors that activated and broadcast a line-of-sight

VHF radio signal when the door of the trap closed. After I attached the receiving antenna to a 30-foot pole, we could hear the signals from all of the live-traps, except one, from our base cabin at the south end of the bay. The one trap we couldn't hear was left unset. The other improvement was to get a better boat. We had been using a 16-foot Lund skiff. Because we had to be prepared to go out every day regardless of the wind and weather, the Lund just wasn't safe enough. A couple of hair-raising trips across the bay in two-foot waves with freezing spray was enough. Our good friend Doug Larsen was the ADF&G Regional Supervisor in Juneau, and he arranged the use of a 20-foot aluminum Workskiff with a hard windshield and canvas top. After I spent a couple of days fixing the boat by installing floor boards, resealing the water tight compartments, and installing a marine radio and my aircraft GPS, it was the perfect boat for the job.

Just by sheer luck, we happened to do the wolverine study right when a cyclic series of severe winters occurred. A weather cycle, called the "North Pacific Oscillation" (NPO), sets up a pattern of heavy precipitation accompanied by colder than normal temperatures roughly every 20 years. In the years when the NPO results in heavy winter snow, it can be devastating for wildlife, especially for deer and mountain goats. In the Petersburg area, the most memorable of those events were the winters of 1970-71 and 1971-72, but most of the winters between 1968 and 1974 were also worse than normal. Deer became functionally extinct over large areas of the mainland and islands around Petersburg. In some areas, the hunting season on deer was closed for 16 years. The winters we chose to do the wolverine study at Thomas Bay, 2006-10 were all mostly severe, particularly 2006-07, when snowfall set new records. Roofs collapsed, boats were sunk in the harbor at Petersburg, and there were major avalanches on the mainland. During the months of February and March, I shoveled the dock and the boat at Thomas Bay almost every day. If I hadn't shoveled the boat, I'm sure it would have sunk after several days of snow accumulation during major storms.

We certainly had some adventures with the boat and I learned a lot about boating in winter in Southeast Alaska. I'm sure many of our adventures would be considered pretty routine by the intrepid local

Our base cabin at Thomas Bay. Former ADF&G Area Biologist Ed Crain discusses the wolverine study with Audrey.

trappers who go out in small boats every week all winter, year in and year out, but they were pretty exciting for us. I'll just relate a few of the more memorable ones.

As part of our evening routine, we listened to the marine weather forecast and then tuned in to listen to all the trap monitors around 10:00 pm. Listening to the weather forecast was usually entertaining, especially the long-range forecast, which was often pure fiction. On the other hand, we listened to the trap monitors in the evening with a mixture of hope and anxiety. We always hoped to catch a wolverine, but heaved a sigh of relief when none of the monitors were broadcasting. The thought of having to run the boat all the way to the end of the bay in the dark and the cold in bad weather wasn't very pleasant, especially when we were already tired from a long day. After losing the two wolverines at the beginning of the project, however, we didn't want to take the chance of leaving a wolverine in one of the traps overnight.

Trapper Dave Benitz prepares dinner, while I skin a beaver for wolverine bait and Area Biologist Rich Lowell observes.

One evening, the monitor on a trap at the far end of the bay was beeping. It was snowing lightly and pitch dark outside but not especially windy. We put on all our winter clothes, gathered up all the gear we needed to process a wolverine, and headed for the boat by the light of our headlights. I had established several safe GPS tracks around Thomas Bay just in case we needed to go boating in the dark, so as soon as we left the dock, I steered along one of the tracks that would take us to the trap at the far end of the bay. In the daylight, we could have gone on step at about 25 mph, but in the pitch dark without being able to see the water ahead of the boat, there was too much chance of hitting a log or a chunk of ice, so we went at a more prudent speed of about 6 or 7 mph. It took an hour to get across the bay while navigating solely by reference to the GPS. When we were within about 50 feet of shore, I could use our strong flashlight to pick up the shoreline and any rocks showing above the surface. We anchored the boat and then I got my inflatable kayak

The dock at Thomas Bay in early March 2007. Winters during the period of the wolverine study were unusually severe.

down and gave Audrey and the gear a ride to shore. I then went back to the boat to make certain it was secure and in deep water before going to help deal with the trapped animal, whatever it might be. As I was paddling back to shore, I started hearing some choice four-letter words coming out of the dark from the direction of the trap. That was a very bad sign because Audrey almost never uses that kind of language. When I got up to the trap, there was actually good news and bad news. We had caught a wolverine, but Audrey had forgotten the receiver and it was critical for making sure the radio-collar was working before releasing the wolverine. We had to come up with Plan B. We finally decided on drugging the wolverine, putting it on the boat, and taking it to another bay, where we had a portable trap made out of a piece of plastic culvert pipe. We would then put the drugged wolverine in the culvert trap, take it to the cabin overnight, and then take it back to where we had captured it in the morning.

Wolverines

The wolverine was a particularly feisty female and it took us a while to jab her with drugs. We finally got her down, out of the trap, and sleeping peacefully in the bottom of the boat. Then it was another hour of boating in the dark with reference to the GPS. I had a GPS location for the portable trap and a GPS track that got us most of the way there. The beach at that particular bay was a smooth cobble beach, but it was obstructed by a field of submerged boulders. I had to be able to nose the boat in to shore because the portable trap was heavy and had sharp pieces of metal on it so I didn't want to put it into the inflatable kayak. As I was very slowly motoring in with the big engine tilted up, shining a light out ahead, looking for boulders, I started hearing a scuffling sound inside the boat. It was the wolverine rapidly coming awake! Audrey started yelling, "Get some drug, get some drug!" I put the boat in neutral, put down the big light, and with my headlight, fumbled for a syringe and the bottle of Ketamine we had ready. It seemed like forever, but it probably only took about 30 seconds to get the syringe loaded and the wolverine jabbed. Meanwhile, Audrey was holding the snarling, squirming female by the scruff of the neck. After the female was injected with the Ketamine, Audrey dropped her and she squirmed around in the bottom of the boat for a few minutes before she quieted down again.

I turned my attention back to the boat and the rocks. We were drifting about 50 feet from shore, so I looked all around for rocks with my big light and then gave us a little burst of thrust to get to shore, dodging a couple of big, mostly submerged boulders on the way in. While Audrey held the boat, I went for the trap, got it loaded in the boat, and pushed off. At least on that sloping cobble beach there was little chance of getting hung up, even with the outgoing tide. As soon as possible, I got the boat turned around. I'm always leery of backing up in shallow water. If you do hit a rock going backwards, you are leading with the propeller and likely to do more serious damage than if you hit a rock going forwards. After another half hour of GPS boating, we arrived at the dock and got the wolverine collared and back into the trap. By the time we got to bed it was about 2:30 am. Audrey named all the wolverines we photographed and collared. This one was "Mariner" because of her long boat ride.

Over several winters of boating around Thomas Bay and going into shore frequently to work on wolverine traps, collar wolverines, and run the string of camera stations, I only managed to get the anchor line stuck once and hit a rock with the propeller once. Sometimes it was better to anchor off shore and go in with the kayak, but if there was an incoming tide, it was often more convenient to just pull the boat in to shore and put the anchor on shore. Shallow bays were the most challenging. The difference between high and low tides in much of Southeast Alaska can be around 25 feet. With the higher tides, at mid-tide the water is rising or dropping about an inch per minute, so it is very easy to get a heavy boat stranded on the dropping tide.

Once, in a particularly shallow bay, we parked the boat at low tide, stretched a long length of anchor line out to shore and then went to work on one of the traps. I went back to check on the boat about every 20 minutes to pull in slack line as the tide came in. After about my third check, with the tide still coming in rapidly, I pulled on the anchor rope but it was stuck. The water was getting deeper fast and at that point we only had a couple of options. We could either wait about six hours or so for the tide to cycle and go back down and then go out and free the anchor line, or I could swim out to the boat and try to drive around whatever the line was stuck on and pull it loose. Waiting six hours in the 35F weather wasn't a very attractive thought, and there was always the possibility if we waited for the outgoing tide, the boat would get hung up on a rock. Then we'd have to wait another eight hours or more to free it. I decided swimming was the best option.

I had on low rubber boots, a float vest, and heavy winter coat. I took off the heavy winter coat and waded out towards the boat. I was about waist deep with 50 feet to go when I started swimming. Adrenalin does amazing things and after what seemed like just a few strokes I was at the boat. The high gunwales were no obstacle at all. Before I knew it, I vaulted over the side and was standing, dripping wet on the deck. I started the motor and used the power of the boat to pull the anchor line in several different directions before it finally popped loose. Although I was completely soaked and had no heat in the boat, I never really got cold over the next hour it took us to get back to the cabin. I probably could have gone another hour before getting seriously cold, but I was glad to put on dry clothes and get a hot drink once we got back home. Later, at low tide, when we looked at the spot where the anchor line hung up, there was an old beach log, so that was probably the cause of the fouling.

A rapidly dropping tide is always concerning when going in to shore, especially in shallow bays. Although it is no problem letting aluminum-hulled boats go dry, lots of things can go wrong. The most concerning is getting a boat hung up on a boulder that could actually tip the boat so far sideways it will flood with water before righting and floating on the incoming tide. Fortunately, over the five years of the wolverine project we never had that happen. We did get the boat hung up twice, and had to wait about six hours to get going again, but that was a relatively minor problem. It was just cold and boring, waiting in the dark for the tide to come in. Boating back to the dock in the dark following a GPS track was always a bit exciting, but I got quite used to it and found it easier to operate a boat by reference to the instruments in the dark than to operate an airplane by reference to the instruments in bad weather. With a boat you only have two dimensions to worry about instead of three, and unlike an airplane, you can always stop the boat if you need to.

By the end of the project, we identified at least 33 different wolverines that lived in the area from Le Conte Bay to Port Houghton. We identified them both from their unique color patterns of fur on their chest and from DNA collected at the camera sites. We also found the locations of two dens that were both up fairly high in elevation and we photographed several different lactating females, one which brought her kits to a camera station. One resident male traveled all the way from the north side of Thomas Bay to Cape Fanshaw, a distance of 35 miles. I tracked the six collared wolverines frequently in winter but seldom saw them because they were mostly in thick timber. They did spend quite a bit of time around avalanche chutes and we suspected they were looking for goats that had died in avalanches.

One of the methods we use for identifying individual wolverines from pictures is now widely used in other wolverine studies as well. It involves attaching a short horizontal pole to a tree with bait suspended over the end of it on a cable. The wolverines climb up the tree, go out the pole, and then stand up to reach the bait. When they stand up, they expose the underside of their neck, chest, and belly and trigger a trail camera, which takes photographs. The pattern of yellow/orange-colored spots on the underside of their necks and chests is unique for each wolverine. With a good picture, we could also determine the sex of the animal and whether a female was nursing kits.

We also learned something about how deer escape from wolverines and probably from wolves too. Once, when I tracked a radio-collared wolverine to the shore of a bay, I noticed a dark object creating a small wake about a hundred yards from shore. It turned out to be a swimming deer the wolverine chased out into the water. I watched the deer as it swam in a wide arc back to shore. Even if there are no islands to swim to, by swimming out far enough to be out of sight and then curving back to shore the deer has at least a chance of leaving its pursuer behind. Judging by their distribution in Southeast Alaska, deer are probably better swimmers than wolves or wolverines.

In 2009 I was offered the position of Deputy Commissioner with the Department of Fish and Game in Juneau. It was a difficult decision to give up the exciting field work on the wolverine project and spend interminable hours in meetings trying to solve largely intractable problems. The job also involved dealing with difficult people and difficult political considerations. I finally agreed to accept the job and resolved to do the best I could while continuing to work on the wolverine project on weekends. I moved one of our Super Cubs to Juneau and then either flew down to Petersburg on Friday afternoons and came back on Sunday evening, or I took the ferry down and back if the weather was bad. In those days, the ferry was convenient because I could board in Petersburg, sleep on the ferry overnight, and then arrive in Juneau around 7:00 am in time to go straight to the office. Audrey continued to work, mostly alone, on the wolverine project.

The hard winters that occurred during the wolverine project probably provided more than normal food for wolverines, particularly because of the avalanches and deep snow that likely killed many goats. The deer suffered heavy losses too and many starved on the beach fringe. Goat surveys did not show much decline in goat numbers but deer were devastated, especially around Petersburg. During the spring of 2007, we counted about 150 live deer along the beach from the cabin to Wood Point, a distance of about 8 miles. They were a miserable looking bunch, and if there had been even a single pack of wolves around, most of the deer would likely have been killed in a few weeks. The fact that a trapper caught most of the local wolves right before the bad winters started probably saved enough deer that they recovered well after the bad winters were over.

The wolverine project at Thomas Bay ended in 2011, but Audrey continued to keep track of individual wolverines for several more years when their hides were brought in by trappers for sealing. Several published papers resulted from the study, and a PBS special called, "Chasing the Phantom" included a segment on it.

We were sorry to see the project at Thomas Bay end. It was a good life, away from civilization, with lots of daily exercise. Besides the long days and hard work of building and modifying the wolverine traps and checking the traps and cameras, there were some fun routines as well, like checking our shrimp and crab pots, and watching wildlife while trolling for king salmon. I tried shrimping all around the bay but never found a great location. We were mostly after spot prawns that live on underwater cliffs or areas with boulders and rocks. We were always able to catch a few, including some really big ones. The biggest I measured was 10¼ inches from the rostrum to the end of its tail. That record held for many years among shrimp enthusiasts in Petersburg until someone finally got one south of Petersburg that was 10½.

Based on recommendations from a friend who used to live in Petersburg, I tried hard to catch winter king salmon in Thomas Bay. Winter kings are revered as the best tasting of all salmon. Thomas Bay

A wolverine "run pole" designed to make wolverines stand up so their chest patterns and underbelly can be photographed. Thomas Bay 2006.

was rumored to be a great spot for winter kings and we occasionally saw people trolling there. I fished by trolling with an open 16-foot Lund that was loaned to us by a friend in Petersburg. I knew that fishing would be slow and I'd have to be persistent. After the first 20 hours of trolling without a bite, I resolved to continue until I caught something. Audrey quickly stopped going along and I didn't blame her. I was out there hour after hour in freezing temperatures, whenever there was daylight and free time, dressed in all the clothing I could get on under my rain gear, often with rain and snow coming down. Finally, after 80 hours of trolling, I thought I had one strike, but if it had been a fish, it got off. I'd get back to the cabin, barely able to move I was so cold. I continued until I eventually had 120 hours of trolling without a fish to show for it, and then I finally gave up.

North Slope Surveys

Deer are good swimmers and use their swimming ability to escape from wolverines and wolves in Southeast Alaska. If there are no islands to swim to, deer will swim in a wide arc back to the shore.

In 2014, The Wildlife Conservation Society wanted to expand wildlife research in coastal Alaska and the neighboring Russian Far East as part of their Arctic Beringia Program. One of the species they were interested in was wolverines and they contracted with us to survey the distribution of wolverines across the North Slope from the Canadian border to Point Lay. I had flown extensively on the North Slope doing caribou work and working on wolverines and moose surveys during the late 1970s and early 1980s and then again on more caribou work in the early 1990s. Flying on the North Slope can be stressful and challenging because of white-outs, fog, wind, short daylight, and extremely low temperatures. Another challenge is there are only two good places to base an airplane there for winter flying, Umiat and Galbraith. At least the new wolverine surveys were to be conducted in late March and the month of April when daylight is not a problem. The main challenge was that we needed good conditions for seeing wolverine tracks in the snow, which means at least some soft surface snow and bright enough light to see shadows.

Over the next few years, we based from Barrow (now Utqiagvik),

Atqasuk, Umiat, Kavik, and Galbraith. We used two Super Cubs for efficiency and safety. The second Cub was flown by Mark Keech with his wife, Tina as observer. Tina and Mark were both experienced at working in remote areas of Alaska. Having two husband/wife teams worked out really well and made it much easier to endure days and days of down time, waiting for weather.

In 2017, we based in Atqasuk for 42 days and managed to get in 12 days of tracking flights. Atqasuk is just far enough inland that it can be just out of the worst of the coastal weather, but it is just far enough north to be on the coastal plain where there are no willows that can provide a valuable visual reference when flying in white-out conditions. One day, we took off in bright sunshine and headed south into the foothills of the Brooks Range, where we spent seven hours documenting tracks of wolverines, wolves, caribou, muskox, and other species. On the return flight to Atqasuk, we started running into whiter and whiter conditions until we could no longer see tracks. It then became a question of getting safely back to Atqasuk with the small amount of remaining fuel we had left. White-outs are an ever-present problem on the North Slope in winter and they can be completely disorienting, even when the visibility is relatively good. Even with a thin overcast, the general gray/white features of the terrain blend together so that no horizon is visible. There are few dark objects on the North Slope, unless there are caribou or willows around. For VFR (visual) flying, seeing the horizon is very important and is often taken for granted south of the Brooks Range. Mark and I both had good GPS units, modern digital gyros and artificial horizons, and instrument ratings, so we were able to make it back into Atqasuk safely. One of the instruments we had was the Dynon D-2 that has an eight-hour internal battery that can also run off aircraft power. It provides an artificial horizon, turn and bank indicator, ground speed, altitude, digital compass and other information. On the North Slope, where there are no obstacles or towers to worry about, it is possible to fly safely, using a moving map GPS and an instrument like the Dynon for backup in case you run into whiteout conditions. When I first saw the Dynon D-2 at the Oshkosh Airshow in 2016, the Dynon rep told me that a man had walked into his booth the day before and bought five of them. When he had asked why the guy wanted five, the answer had been, "Me and my four friends all fly Airbuses and the instruments sometimes all go blank. We need the portable Dynons for backup". It was either a great sales pitch, or a reason to think twice about flying in an Airbus.

We honed our snow-tracking skills working on the North Slope. When the conditions are marginal because of either less than perfect lighting or very little fresh snow, it takes total concentration to avoid missing animal tracks. We found that we were able to distinguish the tracks of all the larger mammals like moose, caribou, muskoxen, wolves, and wolverines. With practice and concentration, it was even possible to distinguish between the tracks of arctic foxes and red foxes. Arctic foxes have slightly smaller feet than red foxes and a more erratic way of traveling. Arctic foxes live primarily within about 30 miles of the coast, probably because they are adapted to harder, more windblown snow, but red foxes are everywhere. We saw wolverines or their tracks over most areas of the North Slope, but tracks were uncommon within about 50 miles of Utqiagvik. There is renewed interest in hunting wolverines and the newer four-stroke snowmachines are so efficient that traveling all over the North Slope is now feasible. From the mid-1970s through the mid-1980s it was rare to see snowmachine tracks anywhere on the North Slope further than 30 miles from villages. From 2014 to 2018, we commonly saw snowmachine tracks wherever we flew on the North Slope.

During many years of surveying and tracking caribou, moose, and wolves and generally flying around the North Slope, we collected quite a few observations of wolverines and how they hunt and scavenge. In the early 1980s, I had seen two places on separate occasions southwest of the Prudhoe Bay oilfield where a wolverine chased one or more caribou in circles and eventually killed one. I assumed those were unusual cases where a wolverine discovered a caribou that was debilitated in some way.

Also, in the early 1980s, I was flying down the Anaktuvuk River with fellow caribou biologist Ken Whitten, when we noticed a concentration of wolverine tracks in the snow. We circled around to investigate and found an odd-looking brown lump in a stand of cottonwood trees. It

Operating in extreme cold and wind in the coastal areas of Alaska and northern Canada in winter can be very challenging.

looked like a moose carcass but it appeared to be partly suspended in a tree. We landed to investigate and found it was a young bull moose that had been rubbing his antlers on the trees and got them caught between two cottonwoods that were growing up in a "V" on the edge of a cutbank (see photo on next page). The moose apparently panicked and jumped off the cutbank and hung himself by his antlers. His rear end was about a foot off the ground and wolverines had hollowed him out from the bung hole up. The moose hung himself in the fall and by the time we found him in April, he still looked like a moose but most of the internal meat was gone, the wolverines having worked inside to hollow him out all winter. I continued to assume the two cases of predation on caribou and this one case of scavenging on

Poorly designed government houses in northern and western Alaska allow snow to drift in front of doors and entryways, resulting in endless snow shoveling every time the wind blows.

an accidentally killed bull moose were just aberrations, and not real indications of how wolverines make a living on the North Slope.

Then, in the early 2000s, we followed up on a report from fellow pilot Marty Webb of a single wolverine killing an adult bull moose in early April on the North Slope. We had flown to the site and looked at the tracks, examined the carcass, and camped next to it for over a week. There was no doubt about it, a wolverine definitely killed a 2-year-old bull moose by repeatedly jumping on its back and chewing on the top of its neck. It doesn't sound like an effective way to kill a big animal like that, but apparently it was enough to wear the moose down. At that time of year, moose probably don't have much energy reserve. During the week we camped next to the carcass, at least two wolverines came by to feed on it and we got several good photographs.

During the wolverine study started in 2014, we began seeing more and more cases of wolverines actually hunting caribou and a pattern emerged. First, Mark and Tina found two places where a single wolverine had run after caribou and killed them after chases of five to ten miles, longer chases than I had seen with wolves. The next year, Audrey and I found where a wolverine surprised a small group of caribou while they were resting on the edge of a large lake. The wolverine chased the group of caribou around most of the perimeter of the lake, across the end of it, and up a hill next to the frozen lake. Just before summiting the hill, the wolverine caught a yearling in a strenuous uphill chase. We found the wolverine just starting to feed on the kill. We landed and photographed the tracks from the ground. The power, speed, and persistence of the wolverine over the five-mile chase were impressive, especially the final uphill chase. Imagine running for five miles and then sprinting uphill for two hundred yards and still having the energy to kill a caribou with just your teeth! Unbelievable!

We thought we had seen it all as far as the incredible endurance and persistence of wolverines, but in 2018 we found an even more amazing chase scene. Audrey and I were flying north from Galbraith towards the coast just east of the Prudhoe Bay oilfield when we cut the tracks of what I thought were two caribou. We weren't at the start of our tracking transect so I wasn't fully focused on identifying the tracks. Audrey suggested going back. I resisted going back but then turned around and agreed to take another look. I quickly changed my mind on the second look and thought it was actually the tracks of a single wolf chasing a caribou. After about a mile, we decided the tracks were likely those of a wolverine chasing a caribou. The wolverine was going at a full gallop, which was why the tracks looked like running wolf tracks. After four more miles with some remaining doubt about whether the pursuer was a wolf or a wolverine, we came upon the wolverine on the caribou, which it had just killed. We left the wolverine alone and backtracked the chase some more.

After backtracking it for five miles beyond the spot where we first found it, we decided we were using up too much fuel and gave up. But, since the wolverine and the dead caribou were not too far out of the way to the start of our transect, we decided to take one more look. When we got back to it, the wolverine had finished cutting the head off the caribou. I was impressed! We hadn't been gone much more than 10 minutes. With a good, sharp hunting knife, it takes me about 5 minutes to remove the head from a caribou carcass when I'm butchering it. Just imagine, running for over five miles, then sprinting for five more miles to finally overtake a caribou, and then killing it and cutting off the head. The ultimate Ironman contest! We thought that was the end of an impressive story, but it wasn't.

After we started our tracking transect (a prescribed flight line), I called Mark on the radio and told him about the wolverine chase and the dead caribou. I also told him we had to break off the backtracking because it was taking us too far out of the way, but the place we left it was close to where his last transect would end. After we both got done and landed at Kavik to spend the night, Mark told us the rest of the story. He and Tina picked up the tracks of the wolverine and the caribou at the GPS location we provided. They backtracked the chase for 27 more miles! The wolverine found the caribou on the north side of the Sadlerochit Mountains in the Arctic National Wildlife Refuge. It chased the caribou west across the Canning River, running along either right on the caribou's tracks or up to a quarter mile to the side. The chase had definitely been continuous without any breaks or resting. In some places the tracks were indistinct in windblown snow but there was little doubt the wolverine and the caribou had run continuously for 36½ miles, almost to the Prudhoe Bay oilfield. We wrote an article about all the long chases we found, and it was published in the Canadian Field Naturalist. It had become clear that, despite their relatively small size (maximum of about 45 pounds for males), wolverines actively hunt and kill caribou.

Stormy

In 2010, Audrey and I began thinking about finding a place where

Carcass of a moose that hung itself between two cottonwoods on the Anaktuvuk River. The moose looked whole but was completely hollowed out by wolverines. Photo by Ken Whitten.

we could spend a few months outside of Alaska during mid-winter to get a break from the cold, dark winters in Fairbanks. We had a few criteria that had to be met. For both of us, the place needed to be rural, accessible from a small airport, and affordable. For me, the place had to be close to good bird hunting, particularly good chukar hunting, and without too much snow to shovel. For Audrey, it had to be near good wolverine country.

We had traveled through Northeast Oregon in the mid-1980s and liked the area. Audrey liked the look of the Wallowa Mountains and thought they looked like wolverine habitat and they were not too far from known wolverine ranges in Idaho. We bought an old derelict house in the town of Flora in 2008 and fixed it up. It served as our base of operations in Oregon. After spending a couple of months making the house livable, we decided to put out trail cameras in the Wallowa Mountains to see if there were any wolverines. Like many

Landing on the North Slope to investigate a caribou killed by a wolverine. We found that wolverines are willing to chase caribou for up to 40 miles before killing them.

other places, there were rumors of wolverines, but the local county biologist with the Oregon Department of Fish and Wildlife (ODFW) Vic Coggins didn't put much credence in the rumors, although he couldn't say for sure they weren't there. I was also skeptical and agreed with Vic. You'd think if there really were wolverines in those mountains, there would have been some concrete evidence. A picture, a dead body, pictures of tracks in the snow, someone catching one in a bobcat trap, etc.

We put out about 15 cameras all around the Wallowa Mountains starting in October 2010. Despite his skepticism, Vic was all in and provided snowmachines, freezer space, a permit to pick up road kills, etc. I liked Vic as soon as I met him. He was a non-bureaucratic, practical-minded, dedicated conservationist and a very good naturalist. Unlike many long-time agency biologists, Vic still maintained his enthusiasm for wildlife, conservation, and new ideas.

Wolverines

Tracks showing how a wolverine killed a caribou by overtaking it in an uphill chase after a five-mile run.

Audrey and I hiked, snowshoed, and snowmachined many miles that winter setting out and servicing cameras. We started checking them in March and by the middle of April, we had obtained lots of pictures of other carnivores in the Wallowa Mountains but none of wolverines. It was starting to look like Vic and I were right. I took a break to go turkey hunting with our friend Rich Lowell, who had worked with us on the wolverine project at Petersburg. We came back to Flora one day and I proudly bragged to Audrey, "I got a turkey!" Audrey bragged right back, "Well, I got a wolverine!" I certainly lost that bragging contest. We looked at the pictures and they were great. There was no doubt about it, Audrey found the first wolverine in Oregon in 17 years. The previous official record was from the 1980s, when a trapper who had worked for ODFW caught and released a wolverine from a bobcat trap in the Steens Mountains. Because the new wolverine had been discovered during a snow storm and he was dark colored, Audrey named him "Stormy". Some people don't like naming wild animals, but it's

Dead yearling caribou killed after the five-mile chase.

hard not to come up with some sort of meaningful name when there are just a few animals you are working with.

By early summer, we had pictures of three different wolverines in the Wallowa Mountains, two of which were males for sure. Over the next several years, only one of them continued to be photographed. It was an exciting find and not without some local controversy. We heard one rumor that we had actually brought wolverines down from Alaska. It was just too much of a coincidence that two Alaskan biologists had, "all of a sudden", discovered wolverines in the Wallowa Mountains. There was another rumor that the whole story about wolverines in the Wallowa Mountains was made up by environmental groups to stop trapping or logging, potentially another spotted owl situation.

Most people were pretty excited though. This mostly mythical animal had returned.

During the second winter, Stormy created a bit of excitement. A bobcat trapper called Vic to report he inadvertently caught a wolverine in one of his bobcat sets. He had heard about the recent pictures of wolverines in the Wallowa Mountains and wanted to do the right thing and set the wolverine free, but he was a little concerned about the danger of doing it himself. After all, wolverines were supposed to be a particularly "ferocious" animal. Vic had wolf duty and couldn't get away so he asked if we would go and release the wolverine. Audrey and I stopped by the office and picked through a random assortment of drugs and syringes and chose some Ketamine and then went to rendezvous with the trapper. We drove with him to the set, and sure enough, there was one frightened and angry Stormy with the toes of his right front foot caught in the little bobcat trap. I fashioned a "jab stick" out of a willow that I whittled down to fit into the plunger of the syringe and gave Stormy some drugs. Once he was asleep, we weighed and examined him. His toes seemed alright, but it was cold and they could have been frozen, but otherwise he was in good condition and judging by his very good-looking teeth, he was probably just three years old. After a close-up look at the peacefully-sleeping Stormy, the trapper, Audrey, and I had a good laugh about just how "ferocious" he was. We suggested not telling the story about him being trapped, but it was just too good of a story to keep quiet about and it spread rapidly from the Lostine Tavern. After all, how often does a person get to catch a "ferocious" wolverine, let it go, and live to tell about it!

Stormy has now been photographed in the Wallowa Mountains for over ten years. He is apparently a bachelor and no other wolverines besides him have been photographed since the first year of the camera study. After he was trapped, he did lose two toes, so his tracks can also be easily identified. Other solitary bachelor male wolverines have also been located in the western states since 2005, including one in the California Sierras and one in Rocky Mountain National Park in Colorado. The one from Colorado dispersed north after several years in Rocky Mountain National Park and was eventually shot by a rancher in North Dakota. A real traveler.

As I write this story in 2021, Stormy is becoming an old wolverine but he consistently shows up on the camera stations that are now being run mostly by volunteers Scott Shively and Kayla Dreher, and ODFW biologist Brian Ratliff.

Bobcat on a wolverine "run pole" in the Wallowa Mountains in eastern Oregon. We obtained lots pictures of other carnivores in the Wallowa Mountains during the wolverine camera study there.

"Stormy" in 2011. He was the first wolverine documented in Oregon in 17 years.

Chapter 4

Bears

B ears are amazing creatures. Over millions of years, they have figured out how to survive on almost every imaginable food and have also evolved to avoid dealing with seasonal food shortage by crawling into holes and starving. It is astounding to me that bears can be as abundant in Alaska as they are, and abundant they surely are. They are present throughout the state and after the last ice age were able to swim out and recolonize all of the islands in Alaska, except the Aleutians west of Unimak Island. In many ways, bears are the most important land animals in Alaska, and anyone who works in wildlife management or conservation, or participates in outdoor activities, has to deal with them, one way or another.

There are three species of bears in Alaska: polar bears, brown/ grizzly bears, and black bears. I have had very little experience with polar bears, so in this chapter I'm talking mostly about brown/ grizzly bears and black bears. Most people who know Alaskan bears draw a distinction between brown bears, which are thought of as coastal bears, and grizzly bears, which occupy Interior areas away from the coast. Ecologically, the main difference between them is that "brown" bears have access to fish runs and grow larger in size as a result. The difference between brown bears and grizzly bears gets a bit confusing, because some Interior grizzlies also have access to salmon runs and can grow almost as large as coastal bears. In this chapter, I largely use the terms interchangeably unless I'm trying to make a particular point about coastal versus Interior bears. The Boone and Crocket Club has wrestled with how to classify brown bears and grizzly bears for the purpose of comparing trophy size. The current dividing line between "brown" and "grizzly" is the crest of the Alaska Range until you get to

Bears

Houston Pass in the western Alaska Range where it becomes the 62-degree line of latitude. It is an imperfect division but probably the best that can be done.

Like the size differences among brown and grizzly bears, there are also major differences among black bears across the state, largely for the same reasons. Coastal black bears that have access to fish runs also grow much larger than Interior black bears. Some of these coastal black bears weigh over 500 pounds, considerably larger than any Interior black bears and most Interior grizzlies. There are color differences too. In the eastern Interior of Alaska, around 20 percent of all black bears are actually brown (cinnamon) and the proportion of cinnamon bears declines as you go west. Out of about 125 black bears that were captured around McGrath in 2003 and 2004, only two were cinnamon bears. Glacier bears, also called blue bears, are another color phase of the black bear, although they are much less common than cinnamon bears. They occur only along the northern panhandle of Alaska up to about Cape Yakataga. Like color phases in wolves, there is some evidence that bears can change color over time, adding even more confusion to the picture.

Despite several decades of intensive study, biologists still largely don't know what causes bear numbers in Alaska to increase or decrease. For the most part, black bear populations seem to remain fairly stable in most areas of the state, but the difficulty and expense involved in counting bears, or even in determining their relative abundance, has created doubt about whether or how much their populations change. During my 49 years in Alaska, I have not personally seen that numbers of black bears have changed in Interior Alaska, but recently, biologists working around Galena and in the Kobuk Valley have discovered an unexpected crash and partial recovery in local black bear numbers, so there is still a lot to learn. Black bears occur essentially everywhere in the Interior. Cabins, gas jugs, snowmachines and ATVs, and anything else left out in the country will eventually be found by black bears and likely destroyed unless precautions are taken.

In contrast to black bears, for which there is scant evidence of major changes in population size and distribution, it is quite obvious to me

175

that grizzly bears are now much more abundant and more widespread in Interior Alaska than they were in the 1970s and 1980s. I came to that conclusion, based not only on my personal observations but also on conversations with Native people and experienced hunters, and with other biologists throughout the Interior. The occurrence of a grizzly at the dump in Fort Yukon used to be a noteworthy event, and I never saw grizzly tracks on the river bars along the Yukon River in the 1970s and 1980s. Now there are grizzly tracks, including tracks of sows with cubs, on practically every gravel bar one flies over in summer. Similarly, people hunting moose along the Koyukuk River from Huslia down to its mouth at Koyukuk Village used to be able to hang a moose on meat poles along the river for days at a time without worry. Grizzlies have now made that very risky and they are common along the river where formerly they were rare. Some people I talked with believe the increase in grizzlies has resulted in a decline in black bears.

A few biologists who used to work on bears in Alaska have expressed opinions and fears that there is too much hunting of Interior grizzly bears and coastal brown bears and that bear numbers will eventually decline like they did in the Lower 48 states in the late 1800s. So far, all of the information collected by ADF&G indicates just the opposite. There are no grizzly or brown bear populations that have been reduced by hunting, even when the goal was to deliberately reduce bear numbers with hunting and trapping to improve moose calf survival. Like wolves, bears have proven to be extremely resilient to harvest and can tolerate harvest rates that are much higher than the maximum long-term harvest rates possible for moose, caribou, and other ungulates. Several grizzly bear populations in Alaska have been shown to tolerate harvest rates around 15 percent per year without declining. One of the reasons is probably that male bears kill lots of bear cubs and many of the bears that are taken by hunters are those males that do the killing. Several studies have shown there is higher cub survival in bear populations that are heavily hunted. So, unlike animals such as moose and caribou, bear populations are somewhat self-regulated by intraspecies (bear on bear) predation. When there are lots of bears and lots of males, few cubs survive.

Conversely, when bear populations are low, or when hunters kill large males, many cubs survive.

Female bears (sows) with cubs are very concerned about protecting their cubs from large male bears (boars). The presence of large boars also keeps sows with young cubs away from salmon streams and other important feeding areas. Audrey and I saw one interesting example of this in the Brooks Range in 1972. We were watching a sow grizzly and her yearling cub feeding on the carcass of a caribou. After a couple of hours, the sow noticed a boar approaching. She immediately started running away and tried to get her cub to follow. The cub was distracted with a piece of caribou hide and wasn't following fast enough. To solve that problem, the sow ran back and picked up the hide and took it with her. Then she ran up the hill towards our camp at full speed, trying to get away from the male. I grabbed our .30-06 rifle and stood in plain sight to let the sow know she was running towards us. She took one look at me and another look at the boar and veered just enough out of the way to miss our camp. She was obviously much more concerned about the boar killing her cub than she was about me or our camp. That area was so remote at the time that I doubt she had even seen a human before. She certainly knew how dangerous that boar was though.

During hundreds of hours of flying bear surveys in Alaska, I have always been impressed at what female bears will do to protect their cubs from males. It is not uncommon to see sows and newborn cubs in the highest peaks of Alaska's mountain ranges, surrounded by nothing but rocks and snow, far from any food. Many of these places are accessible only to mountain climbers with ropes and technical climbing gear. (Bears have natural "crampons" on all four feet so these areas are much safer for them than for humans.) Male bears sometimes hunt these areas looking for cubs to kill and females to breed.

Because bears are so abundant and widespread in Alaska, anyone working outdoors, hunting, fishing, hiking, or camping needs to be concerned about bears, especially grizzlies, but brown and black bears as well, in some situations. I am always concerned about grizzly or brown bears when I am outdoors in Alaska. I am less concerned about black bears, at least for my own personal safety, but black bears have killed (and often eaten) quite a few people in Alaska too.

I have not had any serious problems with bears anywhere, so my constant concern about grizzly bears and brown bears in Alaska feels like a good thing. I particularly enjoy hunting in places like Kodiak Island and the Alaska Peninsula because it feels to me like bears own those places and I'm just a guest or a visitor who must live by their rules. There are few other areas of the world where one can get that same feeling, except perhaps in parts of Africa with lions and other potentially dangerous animals. Grizzly bears, especially, add excitement and spice to my life in Alaska and when I visit areas of the Lower 48 states that don't have grizzlies, I feel that something is missing.

There is always a small chance of having a negative encounter with a bear almost anywhere in Alaska and if one spends a lifetime in the Alaskan outdoors, having a threatening or traumatic encounter with a bear is a virtual certainty. I feel lucky it hasn't happened to me (yet!), but I have many friends who have had scary encounters with bears, one who was severely mauled on Kodiak, and one who was killed by a problem brown bear in Kamchatka. One of the pilots I worked with had to shoot a bear at the ADF&G Driftwood field camp to protect himself and the biologist he was with. Two graduate students I either supervised in the field, or was associated with, had to shoot grizzlies to defend themselves. In one case, the student was alone in a caribou calving area and bears were actively hunting caribou calves and adults, so the bear may have thought the student was a caribou. In this case, a single bear walked toward the student in a snowstorm and the bear would not heed warning shots or shouting. At ten yards, the student decided to shoot because the bear showed no sign of stopping. The student felt very bad about shooting the bear and we gave him a lot of good-natured ribbing about it, partly to make him feel better, but none of us questioned his decision to shoot. Brown bears along fishing streams frequently come within ten yards of people, but it is usually clear they have no malicious intent. This Interior grizzly was different. If bear spray

Helicopter pilot Jonathan Larrivee with a grizzly bear killed by graduate student Frank Mörschel. Frank was alone during a snowstorm in a caribou calving area and had to shoot the bear after much shouting and warning shots because it would not stop advancing on him.

had been available, it might have saved the bear's life, but a single person alone in the wilderness trying to deter a bear with bear spray is taking a big chance. The best situation is to have at least two people, one with a rifle of at least .30 caliber or a 12-gauge shotgun with slugs and the other person with bear spray.

The other case where a graduate student had to shoot a bear was one of the most unusual bear situations I have ever heard about. The student was alone and staying in the old Naval Arctic Research Lab cabin at Noluck Lake. After he had been there a few days, a single grizzly showed up and started hanging around the cabin. The cabin had not been used recently and no food had been left there, except for the food the student brought with him. Over the next several days, the student had been prevented from returning to the cabin by the bear, or he had to wait inside the cabin for the bear to leave so he could go outside. Then, for a couple of days, the bear prevented the student from leaving the cabin altogether. The student used up most of his ammunition firing warning shots to try to scare the bear away. The bear paid no attention to the shots, which is not unusual. The student didn't have any bird shot with him either. This situation would have been a perfect opportunity to use bear spray or bird shot as a deterrent, but that was the mid-1970s, before bear spray was available. With only three slugs left for his shotgun, he had no other options but to shoot the bear. He opened the door one morning to find the bear looking up at him from the bottom step, so he shot it at point-blank range, even though the bear was not acting aggressive.

One of the reasons Audrey and I may have escaped some problems with bears, besides luck, was that we had a very good bear dog in the 1970s when we were often camping in bear country all summer long. He was a mongrel husky/collie mix Audrey picked out of a box of free puppies at the Wood Center on the University of Alaska Fairbanks campus in 1972. We named him Shublik (after a range of mountains and a spring in the Arctic National Wildlife Range). He stayed with us at the Driftwood field camp in northwest Alaska and kept a constant watch for bears. He lay on the top of the runway berm pile, with a good view of the surrounding area, ready to do battle with any bear that came by. He chased several bears out of camp, but one day, a large male grizzly came into camp looking for trouble and Shublik had met his match. He charged out barking. He never ran from it, even when it charged. He just darted around it in circles, barking. I first thought he'd be able to handle the situation himself but after a while it looked like he might need some help, so I went out and took off in my Cub to harass the bear from the air. With Shublik barking on the ground and the Cub diving on it from the air, the bear finally had enough and ran off. Dogs can be very good for bear protection, as long as

Audrey and Shublik. Shublik was fearless around bears and very good at defending our camps in the Brooks Range. Any self-confident dog can be a good bear dog. Audrey picked him out of a box of free puppies in 1972.

they don't chicken out and run back to their owners for help. It takes the right dog.

I have many friends and acquaintances in rural communities throughout the Interior who have shared their view of bears with me and it is almost universally negative. Bears cause an incredible amount of damge to cabins, fish camps, fuel caches, boats, and snowmachines, etc. In reality, most of the problems that people have with their cabins are human-caused. Bears are constantly on the lookout for food and if they find food in a cabin once, they will often come back repeatedly over many years.

Shadow Aviation pilot Andy Greenblatt stands in front of a cabin remodeled by grizzly bears on the Seward Peninsula. Once bears find something to eat around a cabin they can return for years, doing more damage each time.

Nuisance bears, both blacks and grizzlies, are frequently illegally snared on the Yukon Flats, and those bears are virtually never reported. In Dillingham, I was once casually talking to a local Native man about seeing a bear up the river. He said to me in an incredulous voice, "You didn't shoot at it? Bears are bad! You have to always shoot at them!"

I also saw one radio-collared dead grizzly bear that was probably shot from a passing boat and abandoned along the lower Colville River. In general, bears are widely feared and despised by most of the older Native people I have talked to in Interior Alaska. Once, when I was in Sleetmute, a large dead male grizzly was brought into

Interior view of the cabin in previous photo. Bears continue to cause damage long after any food items are gone. The Seward Peninsula seems to have more than its share of bear-destroyed cabins.

town and laid out on the airport apron. Most people in town came to see it. One man brought his mother, who was in her late 80s. She walked up cautiously to within about 40 feet of it but wouldn't come any closer. She looked at it furtively, with her hand mostly covering her eyes, and said, "Holy, holy. Those live around here?"

I have never been particularly interested in hunting bears myself and I have never shot a black bear, partly because of the concern for trichinosis in the meat, but also because Audrey and I prefer the meat of animals like moose, caribou, deer, sheep, and elk. The Native people I talked to around the state have quite a variety of views about bears as a meat animal. In the western Interior, black

Biologist Brad Wendling examines a grizzly bear probably shot and left along the Colville River. Many people in rural Alaska have a very low opinion of bears, especially grizzlies that damage cabins and raid fish camps.

bears are mostly considered a secondary meat animal to provide variety or fat in the diet, especially in the winter or spring when they have not been feeding on salmon, or in the fall when they are very fat and have been feeding on berries. In most of the rest of Interior Alaska, black bears are considered a backup food animal—potentially useful as food if moose or caribou are not available.

Grizzly bears are generally not thought of as a food animal by most people I know in Interior, Southeast, or Southwest Alaska, although some people think there is nothing wrong with the meat of grizzly bears that have not been feeding on fish. I worked briefly for the ADF&G in 2013 on a program to reduce bear predation on moose near the village of Sleetmute. We delivered the meat from bears that were shot to villages along the Kuskokwim River. We had trouble giving most of the grizzly bear meat away. People we asked said virtually the same thing, "Grizzly meat? That's just good for dog food." We finally found an older couple who wanted some in the village of Red Devil. The man was an 80-year-old, white miner from the Seward Peninsula and he was married to an Inupiaq woman who was also from there. When asked if they wanted any grizzly bear meat, the man said, "We'll take all the grizzly bear ribs you can deliver!" We made two trips with the Beaver and delivered about 100 pounds of grizzly bear ribs. They took them all. After that, we decided to use some grizzly bear ribs for camp meat, and they were delicious. We had a good cook in camp and he braised the ribs in the oven and served them with barbecue sauce.

In Southwest Alaska, moose were not present until after about 1950 and caribou numbers were low, except on the Alaska Peninsula. People lived on fish and brown bears. As soon as moose showed up, however, the interest in hunting brown bears for meat rapidly waned. They are no longer considered a food animal and are widely hated because of problems around fish camps. I am quite sure the reported harvest of brown/grizzly bears in Southwest Alaska greatly underestimates the true number of bears killed each year. That is probably true in some areas of the Interior as well, especially the Yukon Flats.

Besides my limited involvement with bears during my Master's thesis work north of Denali National Park in the mid-1970s and work in east central Alaska for the ADF&G during the 1980s, most of my experiences with bears occurred during a project to improve moose hunting in McGrath by moving most of the bears away from there.

Moving Bears

Planning

One of the highlights of my career with ADF&G was designing and starting the experimental program to see if we could improve moose hunting for people in an area surrounding the village of McGrath, a mixed Native/White community off the road system about 250 miles southwest of Fairbanks. In 1990, McGrath had a population of a little over 500 residents and the economy was based on a mix of mining, government employment, local services, and subsistence hunting and fishing. The Federal Aviation Administration closed the local Flight Service Stations, first in Farewell in the 1980s, and then in McGrath in the 1990s. Mining had also been in a long, protracted decline, and the population of the area was slowly declining as a result. Most people in McGrath and the three other villages in the region counted on getting a moose in the fall for their winter supply of red meat. Imported food, especially meat, was and is very expensive. People in McGrath had begun complaining about difficulties in getting moose starting in the late 1980s. Then, during the early 1990s, there were some very low salmon runs that resulted in disaster declarations, so substituting salmon for moose was no longer a real option. The ADF&G's Subsistence Division estimated that the town of McGrath needed about 130 moose per year to meet their needs and the average annual harvest was only about 90. Although black bears were abundant, people did not view their meat as a suitable substitute for moose meat and claimed a "traditional" aversion to eating bear meat because skinned black bears resembled humans.

In the late 1990s, Alaska's new Governor, Tony Knowles, who was a Democrat and owed some political favors, traveled to McGrath and agreed to help people improve their moose hunting. After the trip, he directed Commissioner of Fish and Game Frank Rue to work on the problem. Unfortunately, Knowles, unlike most previous Alaskan governors, was not an outdoorsman and had very little knowledge of wildlife biology. He had not done his homework and had no idea his offer to help the people of McGrath with their moose hunting problem would get him squarely entangled between two of the major constituencies who got him elected—Alaska's Native people and environmental groups. Many Native people rely on subsistence hunting for meat and have no problem killing a few wolves and bears if it leads to better moose hunting. Environmental groups were adamantly opposed to anything to do with predator control.

By the late 1990s, when Governor Knowles made his promise to the people of McGrath, the biological causes of low moose numbers and poor moose hunting success in Alaska were very clear and had been known for many years. The ADF&G spent millions of dollars and two decades figuring it out. During the 1970s, once technology companies designed small reliable radio-collars and biologists figured out how to make expandable collars that could be put on newborn animals, it became apparent in study after study that both black bears and grizzly bears are very effective predators. The dramatic effects of bear predation were first found by Mike Schlagel in an elk study in Idaho and then by Alaskan biologists in moose studies in central Alaska. In most areas of Interior and Southcentral Alaska, a majority of all the newborn moose calves that were radio-collared ended up being killed by bears within their first five or six weeks of life. Wolves killed very few. This new information presented a bit of a management dilemma because trying to improve moose calf survival would mean having to reduce bear predation on moose calves. No one had any idea whether reducing bear predation, or bear numbers, was either logistically feasible or politically acceptable.

Once Governor Knowles received the recommendation from the ADF&G that the only way to fix the poor moose hunting at McGrath was to reduce predation by bears and wolves, he did what most skilled politicians who find themselves in a political bind would do. He formed a planning group to study the matter and come up with a recommendation. That way, he could be viewed as doing something; the planning process would delay the inevitable controversy, and there might be a remote chance that environmental

Large male grizzly near McGrath on the carcass of a cow moose and both her twins. Large male grizzlies will often kill cow moose if they try too hard to defend their calves.

groups would reluctantly agree to allow the ADF&G to actually do something meaningful.

The planning group was called "The Adaptive Wildlife Management Team" and it included two people from environmental groups and two local people from McGrath. It also included the Director of the Division of Wildlife Conservation, Wayne Regelin, and the local ADF&G Area Biologist, Toby Boudreau. The group ground its way through meeting after meeting for several years and finally came up with a consensus recommendation (in March 2001) to reduce all causes of death of moose, including hunting by people (which was already closed), and predation by wolves and bears in a relatively small (750 square mile) "Experimental Micro Management Area", or EMMA, around McGrath and three other small villages (Nikolai, Telida, and Takotna). ADF&G agreed to write a management plan and a research plan. I was assigned the job of completing the research plan.

One of the problems that came up during the planning process was that ADF&G's estimates of moose numbers came under fire and the position of anti-management groups was strengthened as a result. The data on moose numbers had become an easy target for criticism because ADF&G started out by trying to determine how many moose there were in all of Game Management Unit (GMU) 19D East (a large area of about 5,000 square miles). It was a huge sampling problem, fraught with difficulties. The first three moose surveys indicated that moose numbers were crashing. I was skeptical. Our regional biometrician confirmed the numbers were statistically supported. Press releases were issued and advocates for predator control used the numbers to publicly defend their position. Then, the fourth survey showed that moose numbers miraculously recovered and were right back to where they had been in the first survey—a statistical probability, but a biological impossibility. This statistical SNAFU was dubbed, "The Miracle in McGrath." At that point, we realized that trying to get accurate estimates of a spottily-distributed moose population in such a large area was really not feasible without spending much more money, if it was even feasible at all. From then on, we focused on systematically counting almost every moose in the much smaller EMMA. The reality of the situation was that people in McGrath wanted help with their local moose hunting, and the arguments about how many moose there were way out there in remote and inaccessible portions of GMU 19D East were largely irrelevant.

Although environmental groups had two members on The Adaptive Wildlife Management Team who agreed with the recommended management approach, the environmental groups themselves suddenly backed away from the agreement after coming up with various reasons to object, including the unreliable moose numbers, the declining human population of McGrath, and the failure to get the most current moose count done because of weather. The environmental groups vowed to keep fighting any actions by ADF&G that would reduce bear and wolf numbers. These developments were not unexpected because it was not the first time something like that had happened. Lawsuits over the predator control programs continued for years until the environmental groups eventually lost their final appeal in the Alaska Supreme Court in 2009.

The Adaptive Management Team recommended a gradual, "phased-in" approach to reduce bear and wolf numbers, starting with expanding hunting and trapping seasons and eventually ending with aerial shooting of wolves and possible removal of bears. Expanding hunting and trapping wasn't controversial but ADF&G biologists already knew that approach wouldn't work. If the solution had been that simple, the problem would have been solved years before, and the whole complex planning approach would have been unnecessary. The "phased-in" approach was simply another stalling tactic that was required to get "consensus" within the planning group. Governor Knowles and Commissioner Rue supported the recommendations of their planning group, even though they eventually included predator control. They realized the real controversial actions would take place after they were out of office. From a political perspective, the planning process was a huge success. From a practical perspective, it was time-consuming and inefficient and was overtaken by unpredictable events. After the election in 2002, Frank Murkowski replaced Knowles as Governor and the whole situation changed. ADF&G immediately received the go ahead to do what biologists thought would make the most sense to help the people of McGrath.

However, the years of controversy, study, research, and planning actually did have a positive influence on the project. We originally planned a rather simple, management-oriented, trial and error approach, that would produce better moose hunting as quickly and inexpensively as possible, keeping in mind the whole controversy and the management program was based on the "need" for just 40 more moose! We had not planned a large research project because it would have doubled or tripled the cost. However, the delay caused by the planning process allowed ADF&G biologists to find out more about moose numbers and the difficulty involved in counting moose in a large, remote area. Even more importantly, we learned more about the movements of moose. It turned out that moose in the vicinity of the villages of Nikolai and Telida were mostly migratory while those around McGrath and Takotna were mostly resident. We would have figured out the moose movements, with or without the planning delay, but we would have had to adjust the management experiment after it had already begun.

Based on the new knowledge about moose movements, we eliminated the eastern end of the 750 square mile EMMA because it wouldn't have done much good to save calves there, only to have them migrate south to the Alaska Range, out of reach of the people along the Kuskokwim. Also, the village of Telida had become a ghost village after the number of school kids fell below ten (the minimum number required to receive state support) and the school closed down. After that, there were only three residents remaining in the far eastern part of the proposed management area. The new EMMA was now even more "micro," and the planned bear control portion of it was just the 528-square-mile area surrounding McGrath.

Because of the planning process and the recommendations that came from it, we had so much effort and manpower invested in planning the research around the management experiment that ADF&G leaders decided to make the project a model for how experimental predator control programs should be conducted. The project eventually turned into one of the largest, most expensive, and most thoroughly planned and reviewed management experiments conducted in Interior Alaska.

Another unexpected benefit of the expanded research project was that it accidentally started a 25,000-acre forest fire that created a very large area of great moose habitat (new young willows and aspens) right next to McGrath. The research crew had fired a cracker shell from a shotgun to scare away an aggressive cow moose while its calf was being collared. The cracker shell landed in dry grass and sparked a fire that quickly grew out of control. Part of the reason the fire escaped the initial attempt to control it was that a spring flood washed out the taxiway to the fire-retardant ramp at McGrath and the fire bombers had to come from Palmer, over an hour away. It was one more great example of how unpredictable events almost always change the most carefully laid "strategic" and "operational" plans, at least when it comes to wildlife management projects.

The very new and most difficult challenge in the McGrath project was coming up with a way to reduce predation on moose calves by the large population of black bears and the few grizzlies that lived in the EMMA. It would have been logistically easiest to simply shoot the black bears from a helicopter. Alaska has hundreds of thousands of black bears and tens of thousands of grizzlies spread over hundreds of thousands of square miles, so killing around 75 to 150 black bears and a dozen or so grizzlies in a 528-square-mile area would not have been a biological or a conservation issue. From an ethical standpoint though, we could not let the bear meat and bear hides go to waste, and that would have meant flying the meat far downriver to where there were more people. That could have been done relatively inexpensively, but it would have been one more logistical and political hurdle to overcome. It also would have involved taking the bear hides to Fairbanks to be prepared and sold at auction.

The plan I decided on was to move the bears away from McGrath far enough they were unlikely to come back, at least during the month of June, when the moose calves were still young and easy prey. We also got the Board of Game to allow local people to trap bears under permit—the first legal bear trapping allowed in Alaska since statehood in 1959. Once all the decisions had been made, I started planning and implementing the bear-moving project, with the assistance of Area Biologist Toby Boudreau and bear research biologist Harry Reynolds. Our recently hired Wildlife Veterinarian Kimberlee Beckmen, wildlife research biologist Mark Keech, and wildlife technician Danny Grangaard also played key roles in the project.

Before we began the McGrath bear-moving project, I reviewed the two previous bear-moving experiments that occurred in the Nelchina Basin in 1979 and in the Petersburg area in 1995. In the 1979 project, after 47 grizzly bears had been moved 87 to 160 miles away, moose calf survival improved greatly. However, most of the bears returned to the area within a couple of months, and the main boost in calf survival only lasted one year. Biologists had some pretty exciting times, too, because the main capture drug used on bears, Sernylan (also known as PCP) was banned for use in animals in 1978, the year before the project began. On short notice and with little time for testing, biologists and wildlife veterinarians had to come up with new combinations of drugs. Ketamine and Xylazine (also known as Rompun) were selected, but the combination was not ideal for bears because the Ketamine was metabolized much sooner than the Xylazine and some, apparently sleeping bears, suddenly woke up unexpectedly, especially if they were exposed to loud noises.

During the 1979 bear relocation program, biologists Bob Tobey and Lee Glenn were driving a sow with yearlings down the road toward Chitina to release them when Bob stopped to give the sow a supplemental dose of Ketamine. When he accidentally bumped the side of the truck, the sow woke up and swatted at him. Lee tried to help by banging on the driver's side of the truck and the sow then lunged for him and roared at the same time. Bob was able to jab the bear in the behind while it was distracted. In another case, Ted Spraker was chased around a pickup truck until he finally was able to scramble inside. After failing to catch his tormentor, the infuriated bear bit the tailgate, and the pickup was left with four canine holes punched through it before the bear finally staggered off into the brush. In a third instance, one of the relocated grizzlies that had been dropped off on the Petersville Road by Bob Tobey and Dennis McAllister chased their pickup and later tried to attack a miner who was walking his bulldozer along the road. He had to chase the bear around with the dozer and drop the blade on it before it got the message to move on. The miner was not happy and when he later found Bob and Dennis in a nearby roadhouse where they were having a hamburger, he unloaded on them.

In the Petersburg project in 1995, Area Biologist Ed Crain darted and moved 33 black bears to alleviate problems around the dump, which was going to be fenced. All but three of those bears were moved west to Kuiu Island, a distance of only about 50 miles. Unlike the Nelchina project, none of the bears returned to Petersburg, despite the relatively short distance they were moved. The difference was probably that those bears were moved in the fall just before denning, and they were taken to streams on Kuiu that were full of pink and chum salmon. Ed had done that deliberately. The three remaining bears were all cinnamon bears (brown in color) and they were taken to the mainland. None of those bears returned either, but surprisingly, one of them was taken by a hunter a couple of years later and it had turned black, with just the hair around its feet still brown in color.

In the McGrath program, I wanted to avoid the problems that had occurred in the Nelchina program, especially the problem of having most of the bears return to the area. We couldn't move them in the fall and provide them with a huge food distraction, as Ed had done, so I decided to move all of the bears at least 200 miles away. Although my supervisors were skeptical about whether moving all those bears was feasible, I told them it would be no problem, and it could be done for a reasonable cost by loading them in the ADF&G de Havilland Beaver and hauling them away to remote mining strips scattered around state land in the Interior. It would also be more efficient and faster than driving most of them, as they previously tried to do in 1979. Fortunately, ADF&G had some good leaders at the time, including Regional Supervisor David James and Director Wayne Regelin, and they were supportive of staff who were interested in getting things done, even if the ideas seemed a little unorthodox.

Expecting the next controversy was going to be about where we were planning to drop the bears—the NIMBY (not in my back yard) problem—I just told anyone who asked that we planned to drop them "on remote state land at least 200 miles from McGrath." That satisfied people for the time being but we eventually ran into some opposition when the bears were actually delivered.

The McGrath program also included wolf control on about 2,000 square miles, also a relatively small area compared with previous wolf control programs. We needed the wolf control because the goal was to improve moose calf survival and moose hunting, as quickly as possible. There wouldn't be any point saving the moose calves from bears only to have them eaten by wolves over the winter.

Some of the seven outside "experts" who reviewed the scientific merits of the program didn't like the idea of doing bear removal and wolf control at the same time and suggested doing one or the other first to see what happened. From a purely scientific or experimental design standpoint, those suggestions made sense, but the people of McGrath were more interested in getting their moose hunting back than in participating in a long, drawn-out, science project that would satisfy academics in universities. I could see both sides of the argument but I sided with the people of McGrath.

The Bears Leave McGrath

Around the first of May 2003, the bear-moving crew arrived in McGrath. We had one chartered Robinson R-44 helicopter, the ADF&G de Havilland Beaver, and a Bellanca Scout. We also chartered a local pilot and Super Cub. We set up an army surplus tent on the fire-retardant loading ramp at the southwest corner of the airport, farthest away from town. We also set up several other tents for the bear processing crew to get out of the weather. McGrath was a regional hub for the teams flying wildfires. They would normally have used the loading ramp where we were set up. We didn't have to worry about the big fire-retardant planes loading at the ramp that summer because the approach to it had been damaged in a flood the year before and the taxiway couldn't support the weight of heavily loaded large aircraft.

We had been working in McGrath for several years leading up to the bear move, doing calf mortality studies, radio-collaring moose, etc., so we made many friends in town and everyone was pretty excited to see ADF&G really trying to help with their moose hunting problem. People were intrigued by the idea of moving the bears and we always had an audience and we were never short of extra hands to help load bears into airplanes. Some of the women even brought food and baked cookies for us.

We wanted to get as much information as possible from each of the bears we processed, so we were prepared to weigh them all, draw a blood sample for disease screening and DNA samples, tattoo their lips, and put an ear tag in them. We also had 22 radio-collars to put on to track movements from their release sites.

Within just a few days of starting we had a pretty good routine going. The Scout and the Super Cub would take off about 8:00 am and go searching for bears. As soon as we found a bear, we radioed back to the apartment we rented and got the capture crew and the helicopter rolling. While the helicopter was on the way, we radioed the estimated weight of the bear and the crew prepared a dart with

Kimberlee Beckmen and Shelley Szepanski prepare a bear for transport while local helpers look on.

the correct drug dose. Most of the time it was a simple matter to wait until the bear ran across an opening and then swoop in with the helicopter, dart the bear, and back off and wait for it to go down. We had a few minor hiccups at the beginning of the project though. One was caused by me when I grossly overestimated the weight of the first black bear we darted. I radioed back to the helicopter that the bear was "a pretty big one, probably about 250 pounds." Well, it actually turned out to be a small sow weighing just 95 pounds. She received a heavy dose and ended up sleeping for about eight hours, plenty enough time to be slung back to McGrath, processed, kept standing by for a full Beaver load, and then flown two hours to her destination on the Yukon River west of Tanana. She never needed a second dose and did just fine, but I got a lot of ribbing, and my credibility over estimating bear weights took a hit.

The drug we used was Telazol, which is a combination of a tranquilizer and a dissociative anesthetic. It was (and still is) an

197

Black bear asleep on the shelf we built in the back of the Beaver. In 2003 and 2004, ADF&G transported about 130 bears away from McGrath to improve moose calf survival. We carried as many as five bears at a time in the Beaver, with the smallest bears riding on the shelf.

excellent drug for carnivores and acts rapidly to cause animals to calm down and lose coordination. It also has a wide dosage range. Telazol had become available in the mid-1980s and is a much more reliable drug for tranquilizing bears than anything that came before it. Sernylan had been used until 1978 and it was also pretty good compared to its predecessors, but it caused hallucinations in people and occasionally aggressive behavior in animals with less than a full dose. It also probably resulted in one of the very few injuries sustained by a biologist in Alaska while handling drugged bears. Harry Reynolds and his assistant, Ron Ball, were carrying a drugged bear to a helicopter on the north side of the western Brooks Range. They were moving the sow of a breeding pair with the intent for the sow to wake before the boar. Male bears sometimes kill sows and cubs so it is best to separate them after they are immobilized. When

Author with McGrath pilot Lucky Egrass and the second largest bear moved during the McGrath project. The bear weighed 625 pounds. We found it easier to transport the two very largest bears in a Cessna 206 because the cargo deck was closer to the ground than on the Beaver.

they were almost to the helicopter, the drugged sow's head came in contact with Harry's leg. Suddenly, the upside-down sow opened her jaws and clamped them on Harry's knee. It took a while to pry the bear's jaws loose with Harry writhing in pain, and he ended up with several painful canine punctures. It was quite a surprise, because Harry had handled several hundred bears by that time and had never had anything like that happen. Sernylan had been banned for human use in the 1960s because it had too many side effects, but it continued to be popular and it was known as "Angel Dust" for recreational use. The last straw came in 1978 when the TV News show "60 Minutes" did a special on it. From then on, it was banned for use in animals and its manufacture was severely restricted. Drugs are often metabolized very differently in animals than in humans, but once Sernylan lost the public relations battle, there was no getting it back.

We had very few problems tranquilizing the bears and keeping them down for several hours with Telazol—enough time to sling them to McGrath, weigh and measure them, load them in the Beaver, and take them on their 200+ mile, one-way ride to nowhere. Most bears required supplemental doses, usually half of the original dose required to knock them down. Of the 81 black bears and 9 grizzlies we moved in 2003, only one small black bear died. Although Telazol was a great drug, a problem we ran into at the end of the project was supply. We used all of the spare Telazol ADF&G had statewide and we also borrowed from several vets in Fairbanks. It turned out the manufacturer at the time only made the product once a year, with the quantity produced based on expected demand. They hadn't planned for the extra-large volume ADF&G needed for the bear project.

We were kept very busy during the first couple of weeks of the project. It was no problem finding bears in the beginning, and I averaged about eight of nine hours of flying per day. I would usually fly about three to five hours in the Scout during the morning, spotting bears for the helicopter, and then another three to five hours flying the bears away in the Beaver. After the first couple of Beaver loads, Mark Keech and I built a shelf in the back of the plane so we could stack the bears. The smaller bears were "shelf" bears and the larger ones were "floor" bears. We carried 1-6 bears per load but mostly carried 4 or 5. The nine grizzlies were considerably bigger than the black bears, so the loads that included grizzlies were smaller. Weight was not a problem for the Beaver. It could have carried about 1,750 pounds of bears per load, but floor space was limited. We had to keep the bears separated enough that we could watch their breathing and behavior in flight. If they started coming out from under the drug, the person flying "shotgun" in the right front seat had to get up and administer a supplemental dose of Telazol if the remaining flight was going to be longer than an hour, or Ketamine if it was going to be shorter. Our vet, Kimberlee Beckmen, usually had that duty and she was the right person for the job—we didn't lose a single bear in flight and never had to shoot one either. I carried my Charter Arms .44 special and Kimberlee had a Smith and Wesson .44 magnum, just in case.

Although we didn't have any serious troubles with bears in flight, towards the end of the project when we were running short of Telazol and some of the bears were lightly dosed. The only sow with cubs (a grizzly) that was transported growled for the whole two-hour flight. Fortunately, I didn't have to deal with them because I was back in Fairbanks for a couple of days taking care of some administrative duties and getting more food and supplies. Bruce Dale, the backup Beaver pilot, and Kimberlee bore the brunt of that situation, and Kimberlee certainly deserved her extra Moosehead ale at the end of that trip.

Finding places to drop the bears wasn't too difficult but required doing some homework ahead of time. The airstrips we took them to had to be on state land at least 200 miles from McGrath, they had to be unoccupied, and the surface had to be hard enough to support the weight of the loaded Beaver. Many of Alaska's unimproved airstrips are soft in the spring, with a layer of soft, wet mud over a layer of still-thawing ground. Before we started the project, I identified about a half-dozen suitable strips, including a couple we could get to without going through too much high terrain, in case the clouds were low. I didn't like the possibility of being airborne in bad weather with a load of bears and no place to land. If I didn't already know the strip well, I called around and checked with knowledgeable local people to see if there would be problems with the strips I had in mind.

One of the strips we ended up taking about 20 bears to was Grant Creek, about 15 miles downriver from Tanana on the north side of the Yukon River. Alex Tarnai, a local guide, pilot, and trapper, told me the strip had a good, hard gravel surface and he was pretty sure no one had been living there. It seemed like a very good choice because, in addition to being just over 200 miles from McGrath, it was on the north side of the Yukon, so the bears would have to swim about a mile of fast moving, ice-cold water if they wanted to head back to McGrath. Also, we could get there almost direct, even in bad weather, by only having to fly over a low part of the Kuskokwim Mountains.

I took three loads of black bears to that strip over the first couple of weeks of the project and we hadn't seen any sign of people living at the strip. However, when I left to take care of some administrative details in Fairbanks, Bruce Dale took over flying the Beaver, and he took another load of five bears to the strip. Just as the last of the five bears recovered and were disappearing into the willows along the runway, a man on a 4-wheeler came from the east end of the strip and drove up to the Beaver. He had been doing a bit of trapping and mining there and just moved to the strip a couple of years before. After a friendly greeting and some small talk, he asked, "Are you guys dropping bears off here?" Bruce, hoping the guy didn't know about the bear project, was a bit tongue-tied at first but finally said, "Yeah, we just let five go into the bushes." To which the man replied, "You know, there are plenty of bears around here and I don't really want any more. I have enough problems with the ones that live here now." After thinking for a few seconds, Bruce replied, "Well, one thing I can tell you for sure is they don't stick around once we release them. Most of them probably head back in the direction of McGrath, so they won't be bothering you for very long."

After promising not to drop off any more bears, Bruce and the crew departed in the Beaver. Shortly after takeoff, they decided to circle around and track the collars of the ten bears that had been radio-collared upon release at the strip over the previous several weeks. Contrary to what Bruce told the trapper, every one of the collared bears was still within a couple miles of the strip. That was good news for us but potentially bad news for the trapper. Good they weren't headed back to McGrath to start killing moose calves, but bad that the trapper might have to deal with a few more pesky bears than normal. About a month later, the trapper actually did have to kill a problem black bear that kept breaking into his cache and cabin. Surprisingly (or maybe not in this case), he reported the problem bear and turned the hide into ADF&G in Fairbanks. Usually, people in rural Alaska take care of their own bear problems and the bears just end up in the freezer (or dumped in the river if there is no freezer available), because the hunting season is open year-round on black bears with a bag limit of at least three bears per year. He was probably just trying to make the point about having to deal with the imported bears. As it turned out, however, the problem bear he shot didn't have a lip tattoo, so it wasn't one of our bears anyway.

The only other airstrip problem we had was near Tolovana Hot Springs. It was a newly built strip about 50 miles northwest of Fairbanks and about five miles south of the springs. The strip was actually in a great spot, but I had never landed there and I wasn't sure of the runway surface conditions in spring. I had not planned to use it and had been taking bears to old mining strips I knew well on the north side of the Alaska Range south of Fairbanks. However, Rod Boertje, an ADF&G moose biologist, was concerned that bringing bears to that area would alter the results of his long-term moose research project in Game Management Unit 20A. I told him if he didn't want me to take bears to the safe strips in the Alaska Range, he needed to give me an alternative. Rod contacted Tom DeLong, a local Fairbanksan who had the lease on Tolovana Hot Springs and built the strip. Tom had no problem with us dropping bears there.

When Kimberlee and I flew in with the first load of bears I carefully looked the strip over. It was plenty long and the approaches were good, but some parts still looked a bit wet even though it was already the 20th of May. I lined up and landed on the driest looking part of the strip and stopped OK. We unloaded the five drugged bears and sat around in the sun eating lunch while the bears came out of the drug and finally wobbled their way off into the brush. I then walked the part of the runway I planned to turn around on to taxi back to the south end. It was a bit soft, but since the plane was now lightly loaded, I hoped we wouldn't get stuck. As it turned out, I had been a bit too optimistic and halfway through the turn the outboard wheel sank in the soft ground. Full power wouldn't get the plane moving so I shut the engine down and got out a shovel, did some digging, and threw some sticks in front of the tire. At that point I was a little peeved at Rod for getting me into the situation in the first place, so I called him on my satellite phone and told him to get a crew together and bring out some two by four foot pieces of plywood. The worst of the soft ground was in a small area for about six or eight feet ahead of the left wheel. If we could just get the plane six feet further, we'd be back on hard ground.

While we waited for Rod and the rescue crew, I decided to give it one more try. I told Kimberlee if she would help push on the left gear leg of the plane, I might just be able to get us going enough to get to the hard ground. My last words to her were, "Watch out, it might get a little windy back there." Well, that turned out to be a classic understatement. When I brought the 450 horsepower Pratt and Whitney radial engine up to full power, Kimberlee was quickly blasted away and rolled over and over in the mud by the propwash. Whether her help contributed to the plane getting unstuck I wasn't sure, but the Beaver rolled forward just enough to get onto the harder ground. I shut down again after letting the engine cool and went to see if Kimberlee needed any help getting the worst of the mud and dirt off her clothes and out of her hair before getting back in the Beaver. I then called Rod and cancelled the rescue and we went on our way. Needless to say, that was the only load of bears we took to Tolovana Hot Springs.

I only had one occasion when I couldn't get a load of bears to the planned destination. I had taken off from McGrath on May 25th with a load of 4 bears under a cloud ceiling of about 1,000 feet. Not bad weather for flying in the flats, but too low to get over the Kuskokwim Mountains. Given the weather reporting and the forecast, I decided the best option was to head for the St. George Creek strip on the north side of the Alaska Range south of Fairbanks. Unfortunately, after passing Lake Minchumina, the cloud ceiling started coming down and it looked like we were running into a small weather front. I was hoping that by "scud running" near ground level I could get through it, but just after passing the Toklat River, the ceiling was down to about 400 feet and it was down to the ground in front of us. I knew of a recently built private strip at the east end of a small lake where I used to hunt moose before the Department of Natural Resources sold lots around the lakeshore. I headed for it as a last resort, and the weather was just good enough to land. I hoped no one would notice we unexpectedly dropped a load of bears at a private strip without permission. I knew that one of the owners was Chuck Gray, a veteran Alaska pilot whom I had known for many years, and I guessed that he probably wouldn't mind, under the circumstances. When I saw Chuck a few months later, the first thing he asked was if I'd dropped bears off at his strip. I hadn't told anybody, so I was quite impressed that he deduced from the wheel tracks that a Beaver had landed at his strip. Well, the only two Beavers on wheels in Fairbanks at the time were the ADF&G Beaver and the Civil Air Patrol Beaver, so he put two and two together. In hindsight, I wasn't too surprised he figured it out because Chuck is a sharp guy and he served as a military game warden in the 1950s. To make a good game warden you have to be both observant and suspicious. We both had a good laugh over it.

Bear Trapping

Although we used a helicopter to catch and move most of the bears, we also had a trapping crew running the Kuskokwim and Takotna rivers, setting bucket snares to catch bears that lived in the thick woods along the rivers that might be tough for us to get with the helicopter. Danny Grangaard, one of Alaska's most experienced and gifted trappers and an ADF&G technician, was in charge of the trapping effort. He was assisted by a local trapper from Takotna who we hired as a temporary employee. Bucket snares are a Canadian invention and a modification of the Aldrich Foot Snare that was invented in the 1950s by Jack Aldrich for controlling black bears in the private commercial forests of western Washington. Aldrich foot snares are widely used by biologists to live-capture bears, and if checked frequently, they seldom cause any damage to the bears' feet. The Canadian modification was to take the spring-loaded cable snare and adapt it for use in a 5-gallon plastic bucket. A bucket snare requires the bear to put its paw into the bucket to get bait wired into the bottom. Bucket snares are quite selective and almost never catch non-target species or bear cubs, so they were ideal for the bear trapping program at McGrath.

The bear trapping crew started out from McGrath every morning and checked their bucket snares daily. In the beginning it was a good-natured contest to see if the helicopter crew or the trapping crew would catch more bears. It was soon apparent there was no way the trapping crew could out-compete the helicopter crew, partly because the helicopter was quickly getting a lot of bears that might have eventually been caught by the trappers. The trappers did catch some key bears we might not have caught with the helicopter and they also had some exciting times.

Most of the younger black bears were quite docile and just cowered at the end of the snare cable, but some of the big males were aggressive and would charge as the trappers approached. We were most concerned about catching a cub and then having an enraged sow hiding in the bushes waiting for the trappers. Fortunately, the bucket snares proved to be so selective that no cubs were ever caught.

Author with a "bucket snare" used to live-capture bears in the McGrath project. Bucket snares proved to be very selective and no non-target animals or bear cubs were caught.

The crew did catch one grizzly though, and it caused some real excitement for Toby Boudreau. He was riding in the helicopter with Rick, en route to a bear that had been found by one of the spotter planes when they passed right by one of the bucket snare sets on the Takotna River. They looked at the set on their way by and it had a grizzly in it, caught by a front foot. The snare cable was about ten feet long and toggled to a small clump of four birch trees, each about four or five inches in diameter. The enraged bear had already chewed down a couple of the trees and had a 20-foot circle completely cleared of brush. Because the bear was under overhanging trees, they couldn't dart it from the helicopter so they had to land and walk in through thick brush to the opening where

Close-up of bucket snare in photo shown on previous page.

the bear was caught. Bears are incredibly strong and fast, so walking in on an enraged bear hoping the ¼-inch cable will hold is a brave act of faith.

Toby went ahead with the dart gun while Rick covered him with a shotgun. As soon as the raging, furious bear saw Toby coming, it charged from the far side of the 20-foot circle, but it hit the end of the cable and somersaulted well before it got to him. It takes some nerve to watch a grizzly coming at you at full speed, hoping the cable will hold! Toby made a good tranquillizer shot on the bear as soon as he could and then they backed off to wait for ten minutes for the bear to go down. The rest of the day was uneventful by comparison, but Toby got some good-natured ribbing that evening from Rick about being too cautious in approaching the snared bear. It's easy to talk when you are the guy second in line with the shotgun and not the guy first in line with just the dart gun and a sidearm!

Bear trapping by local residents of McGrath continued for several years, but it was a lot of work and required a considerable investment in fuel for boats, so interest eventually waned. The few people who continued to trap bears eventually tired of skinning and processing them and there was a very limited demand for the meat or pelts. In 2010, black bears were reclassified as both fur animals and big game animals so it became legal to sell black bear hides, skulls, meat, claws, and other parts, except gall bladders, everywhere in Alaska, not just in the bear control areas. The change in classification was mostly done at the request of Native people who wanted to make handicrafts from black bear products, not as a way to control black bear numbers.

One of the conclusions that came from the experimental public bear trapping programs was that despite liberalized hunting seasons for bears and legalized trapping in bear control areas, bear populations could not be reduced. Bears, both black bears and grizzly bears, proved to be so resilient to harvest and the access in most of Alaska so poor, it proved to be impossible to reduce bear numbers by hunting and trapping. Even where bears were reduced by darting and translocating them, their populations recovered within three years, despite continued liberalized hunting and trapping.

Did the Bears Return?

One of the first questions almost everyone asked of us about the McGrath bear project was whether the relocated bears returned to McGrath. In fact, most people just laughed and said, "I'll bet they came back, didn't they?" And they were partly right. Even though we moved the bears further than the 47 grizzlies were moved in the Nelchina Basin in 1979, about half of our 22 radio-collared bears returned. It took most of them at least six weeks to get back though, so most of the moose calves survived. It was too bad we didn't have all of the bears radio-collared but that would have greatly increased the cost, especially the cost of tracking them down. Besides the radio-collared bears that returned, quite a few of the black bears that were trapped and shot around McGrath over the next several years had lip tattoos, indicating they had been moved away but returned. In 2004, after I had retired, 34 more black bears and one more grizzly were removed. None of them were radio-collared but all received ear tags and lip tattoos.

The movements of the translocated bears that didn't return to McGrath were also interesting. As near as we could tell from the limited amount of monitoring we did of the 22 radio-collared bears, almost all of them started out in the direction of McGrath after they were released. Some stalled out part way back and settled down to new lives in new areas. A few others went in apparently random directions and seemed to not care or not know the direction to McGrath. The amazing thing about animals, other than humans, is they almost all seem to have a built-in sense of direction.

We expected the bear population in the EMMA would quickly return to pre-removal levels because the surrounding area had lots of bears and the largely bear-free EMMA would just fill in. It actually took until 2007 (about three years) for the bear population to return to its previous level. The reduced mortality on moose calves actually continued longer than that, and for several years, the moose calf-to-cow ratio in the EMMA was considerably higher than it had been before the bears were moved.

Over the next several years, moose numbers doubled around McGrath, and because of the 25,000-acre Vinasale Fire that was accidentally started by the ADF&G crew in 2002, the growing moose population had some very good habitat to move into. A construction project to remodel and repave the McGrath airport in the late 1990s also helped people take advantage of the expanding moose population. To get rock for the project, the construction company built a ten-mile road to a rock outcrop southeast of town. The road provided access to the part of the moose population that started using the new burn.

One of the really fun things about wildlife management is that projects often arise and then change because of unforeseen events. In the McGrath project, good political connections led to a promise by the Governor to do something. Opposition from environmental groups led to one of the best research projects done on wildlife in Interior Alaska, and an accidental fire started by the research crew created some of the best moose habitat McGrath has ever had. The people of McGrath had their moose hunting problem solved, and now there are just as many wolves and bears around as there were at the start of the project. And all of that was because people in McGrath needed just 40 more moose per year.

Lucky's Bear

One of the best stories that came out of the McGrath bear project is the story of the bear we called "Lucky's Bear." Of the nine grizzlies we captured and moved during the project, two were exceptional in size for Interior bears. The first big one weighed 625 pounds. The second one was even bigger. When I first saw him, I didn't fully appreciate his size, and I had no idea how involved his story would become.

We were in the final week of the program in 2003 and very few bears were left to move. One evening, three of us were flying in an R-44 helicopter about 15 miles south of McGrath trying to find the few remaining bears in the 528-square-mile EMMA bear control area. The project was running out of capture drugs and we had enough drug for just a few more bears. We had two Super Cubs in the air for spotters, but we were also searching along the gravel bars of the Kuskokwim with the helicopter.

At about 10:00 pm we found the tracks of a pair of bears in the sand and silt along the river. The tracks were big, and still wet where the bears had just swum the river, so we knew they were close. After about five minutes of searching, we found a large grizzly in tall willows and called in one of the Super Cubs for support. When the Cub arrived, we hazed the bear into the open. The darts we loaded were for average-sized black bears and we only had two. Ted Spraker, a former ADF&G biologist from Soldotna and newly appointed member of the Board of Game, was in the shooter's position in the left front seat. I was riding in the back, ready to pass the second dart up to Ted. Rick Swisher was flying. The only way to get the bear down was to hit him with both darts and Ted did not disappoint us. He made two perfect shots and the bear reluctantly went down after about 15 minutes.

The Super Cub crew landed on the gravel bar and the five of us walked into the willows to find the sleeping bear. I was first in line carrying a 12-gauge shotgun loaded with slugs. The bear was in open willows with good visibility and I first saw him at about 40 feet. He was sleeping lightly and making occasional low snoring growls, but his size was astounding. I had plenty of experience around Interior black bears and grizzlies, but I'd never been around coastal brown bears and I'd certainly never seen a bear this big up close. After "oohing" and "aahing" and taking a few pictures, we all realized that we were faced with a bear we were not equipped to deal with. The largest bear we immobilized and translocated in the project so far was the 625-pound male. It had been just barely possible for the R-44 to sling that bear. This guy was obviously bigger and the R-44 we were using didn't even have a cargo hook. It seemed we had two choices; let the bear go, or shoot him while he slept. Although it was a "non-lethal" control program, we did have approval to euthanize key bears if the circumstances made translocation impossible. We had translocated about 85 bears and had not killed one yet. The decision was up to me because I was the project leader and I floated the suggestion that we euthanize the big grizzly. I glanced around at the four other crew members, all experienced hunters who usually had no qualms about shooting animals if the circumstances were right. I could tell right away that shooting this magnificent, sleeping bear was just not going to happen.

We needed a "Plan B" and all eyes turned to technician Danny Grangaard—a guy never at a loss for good ideas. Danny had been hunting and trapping in Alaska since the 1960s and he had been working for ADF&G since the late 1970s. If Danny couldn't come up with an idea, we were going to let the big bear go.

After thinking about it for a minute, Danny said, "How about we take a bucket snare cable, duct tape a moose calf transmitter to it, then cable clamp it around the bear's neck? Then we can track him down in the morning, dart him from the R-44, and sling him to McGrath with Forestry's Bell 212." It was a brilliant idea and we couldn't think of any reason it wouldn't work, unless the Forestry guys were not willing to give up their helicopter for a couple of hours, or we ran out of capture drugs. So, after collaring the bear with the moose calf collar taped to the foot snare cable, we headed back to McGrath. At worst, if the big helicopter wasn't available, we would just have to come out and take the makeshift collar off the bear.

Toby called the Forestry guys first thing in the morning, and they were game to let their helicopter go for a couple of hours to sling the bear. I took off in the state Scout followed by Rick, Toby, and Ted Spraker in the R-44. The Bell 212 followed about 15 minutes later. I heard the big male bear's signal beeping in the general area where we left him sleeping the previous evening. When I was about a mile out though, I unexpectedly flew right over another smaller grizzly, probably the female that the big male had been with the previous evening. This was an unexpected bonus, so I called Rick on the radio and he flew over to dart the female—the collared male could wait. The female went down as planned, but she fell in a very swampy area. The big Bell 212 landed OK, but the pilot had to hold power to prevent the helicopter from sinking into the swamp. I landed the Scout on a nearby gravel bar and Rick picked me up to go help lift the female grizzly into the back of the 212. She only weighed about 300 pounds, but it took four of us to load her up, and she was growling the whole time. The 212 pilots didn't like the idea of loading the growling bear, dripping with swamp muck, into their helicopter but there was a high bulkhead between them and the bear and I assured them she was probably "all growl and no bite." They lifted off with her and landed on the nearby gravel bar while Rick and Toby darted the big male. Darting the male was no problem, but he went down in 30-foot tall willows. The 212 crew prepared a big cargo net, lowered it through the willows, and we rolled the male into it. We were all impressed with the power of the Bell. With the two big pilots, the 300-pound sow in the back seat, the 700-pound male (which we weighed later in McGrath) slung underneath, the 100-pound cargo net, and over two hours of fuel, the 212 powered straight up for 100 feet and then headed for McGrath.

The next challenge was weighing the big bear (which we did with the Bell 212), loading him in an airplane, and then giving him the required 200-mile one way ride before he woke up or we ran out of capture drugs. By the time we were ready to load the bears, a crowd of local spectators gathered to get a look at him. Most local people know those big bears are around, but they have huge home ranges and few people ever see more than their tracks on gravel bars. They are an almost mythical creature, and next to impossible to hunt. I think that many people in the Interior don't realize the biggest Interior grizzlies are only about half the size of the largest coastal brown bears but they are impressive beasts nevertheless.

Although we had the ADF&G de Havilland Beaver for transporting bears, the 700-pound bear would have been very difficult to load onto the high floor of the Beaver without heavy equipment. We opted to load it into a chartered Cessna 206 instead. A local pilot, Lucky Egrass, agreed to fly it. By pushing the tail down to the ground, we were able to roll the bear into the back through the cargo doors. We had two people pulling from inside the plane and four people

From left: Biologist Toby Boudreau, pilot Lucky Egrass, author, and pilot/ biologist Mark Keech with "Lucky's Bear", the largest bear moved during the McGrath Project in 2003. The diaper helped contain "accidental discharges" from sleeping bears.

pushing from outside. When we finally got the bear inside, he filled up the whole cargo space behind the two front seats. The center of gravity was too far back for the nose wheel to come back down, but Lucky didn't think it would be a problem. He had flown awkward loads of mining equipment before and said that when he got into the pilot's seat and started the engine, the nose wheel would come back down and it would fly fine. He was right, and off he went. I flew the 300-pound sow in the Beaver with Kimberlee. We decided to take the bears to the Upper St. George Creek airstrip about 60 miles south of Fairbanks on state land in Game Management Unit 20A about 220 miles from McGrath. It is an old mining strip that sits up on a ridgetop with no people living nearby. After a two-hour flight and having to give the bears an extra dose of precious drug, we both arrived at the airstrip and unloaded them. Kimberly was very relieved to get on the ground and get the female out of the Beaver. During the flight she must have asked me at least six times "How much farther do we have to go." Every time I just answered, "Oh, it's not too far now." I could see she was pretty nervous and I was, once again, having a little fun at her expense. She couldn't see the GPS very well from where she was sitting and she had been focused on watching the sow and hoping our meager supply of drugs would keep her down. Lucky was pretty blasé about flying with the big male and acted like it was all in a day's work. We had given him a couple of syringes with extra drug and told him if the bear started moving too much to just give him a jab.

Getting the big bear out of the Cessna 206 was a lot easier than getting him in. We had already tattooed the lips and put tags in the ears of both bears back in McGrath, so we just had to wait to make sure the sow got away first, and then we left for McGrath. The big bear's lip tattoo was #201. We expected that was the last we would see of him. We radio-collared the sow, though, and about a week later I tracked her down with the ADF&G Cessna 185. She was right near the top of Chitsia Mountain in the northern Kantishna Hills, just inside the Denali National Park boundary. She was headed in the direction of McGrath but she had about 150 miles to go. I had Tim Mowry with me on that flight. He was the outdoor editor for the Fairbanks Daily News-Miner and was doing a story on the project.

I retired from ADF&G in June 2003, shortly after the last of the bears were moved. Mark Keech took over the research project, but I did continue to fly for ADF&G as a private contractor, and some of the work was in McGrath. In November 2008, I was helping with a moose survey and heard that Lucky Egrass had shot a big grizzly bear the previous spring. Anytime someone in McGrath shoots a big grizzly it's a rare and noteworthy event. I found Lucky and he told me the story.

In May 2007, he and his nephew decided to go spring bear hunting. They went down river in a little flat-bottomed john boat and were floating the river in the vicinity of Vinasale Mountain when they spotted a dark object in the water leaving a wake behind it. They went to investigate and it turned out to be the head of a very big bear. By the time they got to within shooting range, the bear had climbed out of the river and was going up a high cutbank. Lucky shot it in the back with his .458 Winchester magnum and the bear fell growling and tumbling down the bank into the deep water of the river. Lucky had his nephew drive the boat up to the thrashing bear while he grabbed it by the ears and held on. It seemed like a very brave and reckless thing to do, but Lucky said he thought the bear was probably dying and he didn't want it to sink (bears don't float very well in the spring when they have used up most of their fat during hibernation). Fortunately, the bear gave up the fight and died in his hands.

With Lucky still holding it by the ears, they boated across the river to the gravel bar side where the water was shallow. By tipping the boat sideways, they were able to load the bear into the boat and then bail the boat and get it floating. The load was so heavy they only had about four inches of freeboard and couldn't get on step, so it was a long, slow trip back to McGrath. Another boat almost sank them with its wake before realizing what was going on. When they arrived in McGrath, they loaded the bear into the bucket of a front-end loader and took it to Lucky's house. Word got around, and practically the whole town came by to watch Lucky skin and butcher the big bear. The story got even better when the ADF&G Area Biologist let everyone know the bear lip tattoo #201 was the same one Lucky had flown over 200 miles away four years before!

Altogether, it was quite a story, especially because Lucky had been the one who flew the bear away from McGrath in the first place, and then (living up to his nickname), he ended up being the hunter who shot the unusual bear four years later, in nearly the same place it had originally been captured. When I was passing through McGrath in 2014, I went to see Lucky again to catch up on McGrath news. I just happened to ask him what he had done with the bear's skull. He said he had it in a 5-gallon plastic bucket out behind his house. I asked him if the skull was still in good shape. He thought it was.

The next morning, I suggested I take the skull to Fairbanks and clean it up and have it measured for the Boone and Crockett records. (I long ago discovered that the Boone and Crockett and Roland Ward records contain a wealth of information and I used them in my caribou research to compare the size of caribou antlers in Alaska's 33 caribou herds). Lucky was agreeable and I took the bucket with the green, mossy skull back to Fairbanks. Amazingly, all the teeth were in the bottom of the bucket and after some soaking in Oxyclean and hydrogen peroxide, I had the skull looking pretty good. I glued in all the teeth and took it to Bob Boutang in Fairbanks and we measured it for Boone and Crocket. It measured 26 ⁵⁄₁₆ inches total, and would be tied for number 32 if it is ever officially entered in the records.

Throughout the drainages of the Kantishna, Koyukuk, Kuskokwim, Porcupine, Tanana, and Yukon Rivers, there are widely scattered spawning areas for chum, silver, and king salmon. Some grizzly bears know about those areas and the ones that do can grow much bigger than the average Interior grizzly. These big bears also hunt moose calves in the spring and kill plenty of calves and their mothers too. They also look for rut-wounded bull moose in the fall. The combination of moose cows and calves in the spring and salmon, berries, and the occasional bull moose in the fall is a winning recipe for huge bears. Some of these bears have run-ins with people frequently enough they sometimes acquire nicknames, such as "The Salcha Slasher," a bear that marauded cabins along the Salcha River and Shaw Creek for many years in 1980s and early 1990s. By sheer chance, the career of the Salcha Slasher ended when he walked under the tree stand of a moose hunter at Blair Lakes. The bear must have been very old by that time.

There is a rich lore about these big, widely-wandering Interior grizzlies, especially ones that are still active after freeze-up. I had several Native elders tell me stories about these bears in the 1970s and 1980s. According to the stories, because they stay out late to take advantage of the late fall salmon runs well after freeze-up, they are often coated with ice. Legend has it that these "ice" bears are bullet proof and very dangerous. There is probably a good deal of

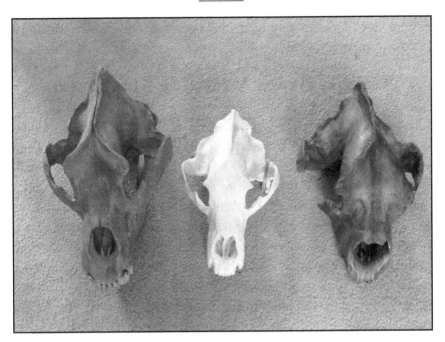

*Skull of 700-pound "Lucky's Bear" (center) compared with Pleistocene short-faced bear (*Arctodus spp.-*right) and Pleistocene brown bear (*Ursus arctos priscus-*left). Humans are very recent arrivals in Alaska compared with bears.*

truth in these stories because in the old days, the small, black powder cartridges with soft lead bullets that were widely used would have been marginal for big bears anyway. Even in the 1970s, the .30-30 Winchester was by far the most common rifle used in Bush Alaska. A good coating of ice may very well have made a big bear tough to kill.

Some winter grizzlies probably just get old and are in such poor shape they can't hibernate. If there are cabins around, they break in and help themselves in their desperation to survive. One such bear was reported to Daily News-Miner reporter Kelly Bostian in 1995. It had come by Frank Gurtler's cabin on the north fork of the Innoko River in mid-January. The bear tried to get into the cabin when Frank was inside. He shot it through a window pane with his .357 magnum revolver. By the time the battle was over, Frank had shot the bear seven times with his .357 and three or four times with slugs from a .410 shotgun. The bear had almost no front teeth, was in its twenties, and very skinny.

Grizzly Bears Attacking Muskoxen

One of the most unexpected situations with grizzly bears in Alaska began on the North Slope during the 1990s. Muskoxen had been reintroduced there in the late 1960s after an absence of about 60-70 years. Two groups of muskoxen were relocated from Nunivak Island; one group to Barter Island (51 in 1969) and the other group to Kavik (13 in 1970). During the next 20 years, there was essentially no documented predation on the introduced animals by either bears or wolves. Then, in the late 1990s, grizzly bears began to kill muskoxen with increasing frequency in the Arctic National Wildlife Refuge. For many years, most known causes of death of radio-collared muskoxen were bear predation. By the early 2000s, muskoxen had been completely killed off throughout their traditional range along the coastal plain of the entire Arctic National Wildlife Refuge. The only exceptions were occasional groups that came from state land to the west and a couple of groups that were seen south of the Brooks Range.

On state land to the west of the refuge, predation by grizzly bears on muskoxen began after 2000. Observations by biologists and survey pilots indicated most of the predation involved a few individual bears. It appeared some bears were becoming real specialists at killing muskoxen and the tradition was likely being passed on to young bears by their mothers. Some of the observations were remarkable and enlightening. When the bears came out of hibernation in April, some of them were traveling to where they found groups of muskoxen. Then they would hang around and harass the group, often for days at a time. Harassment by the bears was causing the muskoxen to form defensive circles much of the time and preventing them from feeding. The bears were mostly after the muskox calves, but they killed adults too. Muskoxen are usually sedentary in winter and they conserve energy by not moving. Pilots and biologists had several observations of repeated attacks on muskox groups by individual bears or sows with cubs that resulted in several dead muskoxen and then the group running nearly 40 miles to get away from the bear. The combination of intimidation, harassment, and direct attacks by bears was more than the muskox population could tolerate.

By 2009, it appeared the muskoxen in the central North Slope might also be headed for extinction too. I was serving as Deputy Commissioner for Wildlife then. I listened to all the arguments and counter arguments about whether removing some of the most predatory bears was justified. We didn't really know why the muskoxen had suddenly become so vulnerable to bear predation, but if they went extinct, like they had in the Arctic Wildlife Refuge, we would never know. I decided to encourage the ADF&G staff to come up with an experimental approach to remove up to ten of the most predatory bears and get hunters to take some too by providing the general locations of the predatory bears. After planning for a couple of years, in 2012, Board of Game approved a plan for the recovery of muskoxen in the central North Slope.

Over the next several years, seven bears were killed by ADF&G staff and several more of the most predatory bears were taken by hunters. The decline in the muskoxen stopped. However, in the winter of 2012-13 a whole group of 20 muskox fell through thin ice on a lake west of Nuiqsut, and at least for that year, the progress made by removing the predatory bears was negated by those accidental deaths. The muskox population has stabilized, but the whole situation remains something of a mystery and has never been adequately funded, studied, or documented in writing. A similar situation has also developed on the southern Seward Peninsula, where grizzly bears are abundant and have learned to kill muskox calves. Bears are long-lived and seem to have good memories, so once they learn where to find food, they try the same strategies year after year. Whether it is raiding cabins or harassing groups of muskox, bears will continue to do it as long as there is some possibility of reward.

Some surprising and unexpected situations where predators learn to specialize on unusual prey have come to light in recent years in other parts of Alaska and the U.S., and in Africa too. Cougars have learned how to make a living by killing wild horses in Nevada, killer whales have learned to kill sea otters in the Aleutians, lions have learned to kill elephants in Botswana, and wolves are hunting black bears in Southeast Alaska. The situation with grizzly bears and muskox on the North Slope and the Seward Peninsula appears similar and probably demonstrates how the learned behavior of a few individual predators can be passed on and become "cultural." If muskoxen are gone from the coastal plain of the Arctic National Wildlife Refuge for long enough, bears may lose the tradition of hunting them and the muskoxen may once again become reestablished as long as a source population exists.

Chapter 5

Wolves

In the first parts of this chapter, I relate facts, stories, and my observations about wolves as a species and as a predator. In the latter parts I focus on wolves as individuals. Most wildlife biologists are trained to view species of wild animals collectively and unless they spend many years in the field, they fail to appreciate that populations are made up of individuals and that individuals are unpredictable. I view this as a growing problem, and it has become much worse in the computer age.

A current fad among modern wildlife research biologists is to use their powerful computers to "model" everything, assuming their assumptions are correct and their model predictions are real. "Modeling" is a widely used word among scientists today and generally refers to any structured thinking and analysis. Without specifically using the term "modeling", scientists have been creating mental and graphic models for thousands of years. In my criticism of modeling, I'm referring specifically to predictive computer models. Predictive computer models are a good tool for formulating ideas and hypothesis, but they are an inappropriate tool for testing hypotheses and finding out if original ideas prove to be correct. Wildlife biologists are much too quick to assume their computer models are automatically correct and that they will fit a wide variety of situations when they actually don't fit any situations. In extreme cases, biologists even insist on believing their predictions while ignoring actual observations to the contrary. It is now easy to get complex, quantitative modeling papers published, even if they have no applicability in the real world.

Computer modeling of wolf populations and the effects of wolves on prey have been widely published. On the other hand, many of the real stories and observations about wolves and other animals remain unpublished or have been published in scientific literature but are largely unknown to most people. This chapter is my small attempt to correct some of that with regard to wolves, and also just to tell some stories about wolves that will appeal to almost everyone with an interest in animals.

I had always been intrigued by wolves, and the thought of living in an area that had a more or less natural wolf population was one of the idealistic attractions Alaska had for me. As a student at the University of Maine, I traveled twice to the nearest wolf population in Algonquin Park Ontario to hear and hopefully see wolves. Once I got to Alaska in 1972, wolves became an important part of my life as a biologist and as a trapper.

Wolves are widespread throughout Alaska and, unlike the Lower 48 states, their distribution has been essentially unaffected by people. Wolves occur essentially everywhere, except in the core areas of the biggest cities, the ice fields where there are no prey animals, and on some of the islands off Alaska's coast. Wolves are reasonably good swimmers, not as good as bears, deer, or moose but certainly better than wolverines or mountain goats. They were able to recolonize all of the near-shore islands after the last ice age in Alaska, including Unimak and even Zarembo and Prince of Wales islands, but other islands like Admiralty, Baranof, and Chichagof were apparently too far to swim or perhaps wolves were unable to compete with the brown bears there. Afognak and Kodiak islands were likely too far for wolves to swim too also, but even if wolves had made it there, they would have found little to eat, except for brown bears and salmon. Normal prey animals like mountain goats, deer, and beavers were all introduced to Kodiak and/or Afognak in the twentieth century.

There is a wealth of good information published in scientific journals about wolves in Alaska and also available on the ADF&G website and E-library. The ADF&G Management Reports that have been periodically written by Area Biologists since statehood in 1959 are a particularly valuable source of information. These Management Reports are often an overlooked source of information and they contain data that were routinely collected over long periods of time. There are also lots of untold stories that for one reason or another have never been published. These stories are usually just related by biologists, hunters, trappers, and guides in bars, around camp fires, hunting camps, and in other informal settings. Sometimes one has to sort the wheat from the chaff, but these are the most intriguing of all Alaskan wolf stories and it is some of these that I want to retell in this book. Most of the experiences and stories in this chapter happened to me personally, or I was around when they happened to other biologists and pilots and I got the stories firsthand. A few of them were told to me by reliable trappers, Native people, and wildlife survey pilots. The information in the final section in this chapter on how dangerous wolves are to people came from a variety of sources, including published and unpublished reports, Russian biologists, Native people in Alaska, and two helicopter pilots I worked with in Interior Alaska.

There are two subspecies of wolves in Alaska, and they are quite different genetically and in the size. Wolves in Interior Alaska are essentially the same as those in Interior British Columbia and Alberta. The wolves on the islands of Southeast Alaska and British Columbia and the coastal fringe of Alaska and northern British Columbia are about 20% smaller than Interior wolves and probably similar in size to the wolves that originally inhabited the Great Plains and the Rocky Mountains south of Canada. The wolves reintroduced to Idaho and Yellowstone Park in the 1990s were the larger subspecies from interior British Columbia and Alberta. Unfortunately, the guesses about the weights of the original Great Plains and Rocky Mountain wolves are based on their skull sizes because too few of the original Great Plains and southern Rocky Mountain wolves were actually weighed.

The average skull size of wolves in an area is a reasonably good predictor of the average weights of wolves in the area if the sample size is over about 30, after the weights and measurements are separated by sex and wolves are at least six months old. However, the skull size of an individual wolf will not provide an accurate indication of that individual's weight. Like humans, some wolves are stocky and heavy, while other wolves are lanky. If wolves have had an easy time catching prey animals, they can put on a considerable amount of fat and that can affect their weight. Wolves are also adapted to gorging and then going for long periods (many days or even a couple of weeks) with little food. A stomach full of meat can be over 15% of a wolf's total body weight. ADF&G biologists in Fairbanks have looked at, and weighed the stomach contents of thousands of wolves and it is not uncommon for a wolf to have 10 to 15 pounds of meat in its stomach. The heaviest weight of stomach contents I have ever seen in the records was 22 pounds.

Data from hundreds of male wolves older than six months from all over the state (except Southeast Alaska) indicate the largest male wolves are around 140 pounds. On average, these males weigh about 95 to 102 pounds. From similar records, the largest female recorded in Interior Alaska so far has been 108 pounds, and females have averaged 79 to 82 pounds.

In Southeast Alaska, I worked with Area Biologist Rich Lowell in Petersburg to obtain data on wolf weights. I paid trappers $50 for each wolf skull they brought in as long as it was accompanied by the animal's weight from a calibrated, accurate scale. We obtained 45 skulls with accurate weights that way. We also had access to records from wolves captured on Prince of Wales Island during the 1990s and early 2000s, and from wolves weighed by ADF&G biologists and technicians in the Petersburg area during the 1960s and 1970s. The heaviest males recorded were 114 pounds, with an average of 83 pounds. The heaviest female ever recorded there was 95 pounds and females averaged about 69 pounds.

Any reports about wolves in Alaska (or anywhere in North America) that weigh over 140 pounds should be verified with accurate scales and witnesses. I once shot a male wolf in Interior Alaska that weighed 132 pounds and it had 6 pounds of moose meat in its stomach. So that animal would have weighed about 126 pounds with an empty stomach. If that wolf had a completely full stomach with about 20 pounds of meat in it, it would have weighed 146 pounds. So, one can get an idea of the theoretical maximum weight for male wolves in Interior Alaska of somewhere around 150 pounds. I have never heard of a verified record of a wolf that heavy, but it is within the realm of possibility.

Wolf Behavior, and Wolves as Hunters and Predators

Wolves, like dogs, exhibit a wide variety of behaviors with each other, ranging from aggressive to playful to affectionate. But, above all, they are a large, powerful wild dog, with a very well-developed instinct to hunt and kill. Like all predators in the wild, many of the behavior patterns of wolves are unconscious and reactive, triggered automatically by circumstances, or the behavior of other animals, including humans. That is the main reason why wolves rarely make good pets, and why the state of Alaska has made it illegal to own wolves or wolf/dog hybrids. Even domestic dogs sometimes exhibit some triggered behaviors, occasionally resulting in unexpected attacks on children, domestic animals, or other pets. Some breeds of dogs are worse than others, but wolves and wolf/dog hybrids are particularly bad.

I was once the target of reactive or triggered behavior from a wolf and it was quite startling and potentially dangerous, although it was my own fault. In the early 1970s, the Institute of Arctic Biology obtained two female wolf pups. They were originally kept indoors in the animal quarters but were later moved to a large outdoor pen. Audrey had been studying the development of their behavior as they grew older and named them Brushes and Piper. Brushes was more outgoing and had become reasonably accepting of people, although never really friendly. Piper was always shy and standoffish and wouldn't generally allow people within about 30 feet. One day, several of us entered the pen and brought our young husky pup in to play with the wolves. Both wolves were friendly toward the pup. After about ten minutes, I decided to liven things up by pretending to be aggressive with the husky pup and flipped him over on his back. The pup didn't even squeal or whimper, but in a flash, Piper (the usually shy wolf) darted in behind me and clamped her jaws on my lower right leg. She bit me really hard and then darted away just as quickly. Fortunately, I was wearing tall mukluks with ½-inch felt liners that protected my lower legs. Over the next couple of days, the calf of my right leg turned black and blue. If I had been alone in the pen and fallen down, who knows what would have happened. I was much more cautious around those wolves from then on and I had a healthy regard for the power of their jaws.

Besides their normal prey animals like moose, caribou, deer, sheep, goats, and black bears, wolves will readily kill any other animals that inhabit their home ranges, including birds, squirrels, marmots, foxes, coyotes, wolverines, and grizzly bears. Sometimes they will eat those animals and sometimes they won't. They will almost invariably chase any animals that try to run from them, including in some cases, humans. The instinct to chase is so strong that once, when I was chasing a wolf, trying to dart it from a helicopter, a ground squirrel ran across the wolf's path and the wolf momentarily forgot all about the helicopter and chased after the squirrel. It made such an abrupt turn to chase the squirrel we couldn't follow it with the helicopter and had to circle to make another pass.

The pack mentality of wolves is also very strong. They often function as a hunting unit and key off each other's behavior. For example, if a pack of wolves is lying and resting and one wolf looks intently in a certain direction, other wolves will also look that way. This kind of positive feedback also applies to hunting. If one wolf decides to give chase, most of the other wolves in the pack will too.

The pack mentality and the instinct to chase fleeing animals plays a part in wolf wars between packs. I call them wars but a better word would be skirmishes, and in areas where wolves are common, skirmishes between packs are common. On the Tanana Flats south of Fairbanks when two packs of about seven wolves each met and fought, three wolves were killed and several others were seriously wounded. We were able to follow the blood trails leaving the area.

In another case, I watched a pack of 14 wolves we called the Tata Pack meet a pack of 10 wolves we called the Gold King Pack in the benches of the northern foothills of the Alaska Range south of Fairbanks. At first there was a standoff, then one wolf in the Tata Pack started running toward the Gold King Pack. Almost immediately, several other wolves in the Tata Pack started running too. The Gold King Pack appeared to lose their nerve and started running away. The chase went on for over two miles when some of the members of the Tata Pack started tiring of it or losing interest and began lagging behind. The original leader that started the chase got so far ahead of the others and so close to the tail-end wolves in the Gold King Pack it suddenly realized it was alone, and stopped. The Gold King Pack appeared to notice the tables had turned and one of them did a one-eighty and started chasing the now lone wolf of the Tata Pack. Several others quickly took up the chase, obviously cueing off the first wolf. After about a half mile, the members of the Gold King Pack that were now doing the chasing started seeing more members of the Tata Pack, and stopped. After a bunch of sniffing, peeing, and tail wagging, both packs went their separate ways.

Skirmishes between wolves don't always seem to lead to bloodshed, but in many studies where wolves are not heavily hunted or trapped, the leading cause of death of wolves is attacks by other wolves. Some of this is from skirmishes between packs and very often it is the dominant adults that are killed. Subordinate wolves can have a very difficult time too, especially young dispersers trying to carve out a territory of their own, or members of packs that are never quite given accepted status. Although the Tata Pack was basically a pack of 14, a single wolf consistently followed behind them, sometimes being allowed within a hundred yards or so. For several weeks this single wolf was tolerated by the pack as it followed them around, cleaning up the remains of their kills. We had a good opportunity to observe this because we were intensively following four packs of wolves twice a day for a month. We were tracking them with radio-collars and from their tracks in the snow. We were doing a "kill rate" study, trying to determine how many moose, caribou, and sheep were being killed by the wolves.

One morning, we had just come in to look at the carcass of a moose killed by the Tata Pack when we noticed wolf fur in the willows around the carcass. We then noticed a dead wolf covered with frost and frozen saliva. The snow was fresh enough to put the story together. The lone wolf had apparently taken too many liberties with the Tata Pack, or she got too hungry, or she had been a bit too eager to clean up the scraps of the kill. The Tata Pack decided enough was enough, and killed her. She was small, thin, and badly mauled, but essentially whole and uneaten.

Trappers in Alaska who have had much experience with trapping wolves commonly report having trapped or snared wolves killed and sometimes eaten by other wolves. During the 1990s, because of controversy over aerial shooting, ADF&G was forced into using trapping and snaring to reduce wolf numbers in GMU 20A south of Fairbanks. During that program, 99 wolves were killed by ADF&G biologists and technicians. About 85 of those were trapped or snared and 10 of the 85 were killed by other wolves while they were in snares or traps.

There are several theories about what leads to wolves killing other pack members caught in traps and snares. One is that an adult may be caught and killed and then the partly grown pups in the pack eat the adult because they are hungry. Another theory is that when a trapped or snared wolf panics, it triggers "mob" behavior in the rest of the pack. Once the target animal is dead, perhaps the normally intense pack competition for food takes over. That kind of "mob" behavior has been documented in many animals, including in humans (except the eating). I suspect the latter explanation is most likely, but no one really knows.

Wolves

During the 1990s, Audrey and I, along with UAF graduate students and volunteers, had some great opportunities to observe wolf behavior and feeding at a den site in the Alaska Range. Over the course of several weeks, we got to see how much food wolves need (or will eat) and how they interact with other species, like grizzly bears, around their den. We were doing calf mortality studies on caribou, and lamb mortality studies on Dall sheep. One of the experiments we decided to try was "diversionary feeding" to reduce the number of caribou calves that were being killed by wolves. The main calving area of the Delta Caribou Herd was in Wells Creek, north of the Denali Highway. That year, the main pack of wolves in the area numbered 8 wolves and they denned about 4 miles from the caribou calving area. We radio-collared 50 newborn caribou calves in 1995, and found that wolves and grizzly bears were killing many calves. We put a GPS collar on the dominant male wolf in the pack in 1995 and followed his movements during the caribou calving season. We also had people watching the wolf den 24 hours a day from a high ridge during May and early June. The male and his pack members went to the calving area several times a week to hunt caribou, targeting young caribou calves.

In 1996, our idea was to try to keep the wolves at the den by giving them free food in the form of caribou carcasses from bull caribou we shot and delivered to them and meat from road-killed moose. We were careful not to touch any of the carcasses we brought into the den with our bare hands because some wolves are reluctant to eat meat that has human scent on it. It was quite a job keeping the pack happy and fed. Beginning on 14 May and continuing through about 15 June, we delivered the carcasses of 10 bull caribou, one road-killed yearling moose, and one adult cow moose to the vicinity of the den. In the beginning, the carcasses were not placed close enough to the den and the wolves started hunting calves on the caribou calving area. They found the first caribou carcass near the den on 18 May and from then until 9 June, when the caribou left the calving area, the wolves mostly stayed near the den. We estimated the diversionary feeding probably "saved" about 150 to 250 caribou calves, compared with the previous year.

Graduate student Frank Mörschel and helicopter pilot Jonathan Larrivee with the remains of caribou calves killed by wolves on the calving area of the Delta Caribou Herd in 1995.

We tried the diversionary feeding experiment again in 1997. To avoid having to shoot so many bull caribou, that year I bought about 100 beaver carcasses from trappers and stored them frozen in sawdust until we needed them in early May. The first load we gave the wolves was about 40 beavers. Beaver is like candy to most carnivores so we figured the wolves would welcome them and dive right in, even though we couldn't avoid getting human scent on them. Surprisingly, they didn't. They were certainly interested, and they would approach to within a few feet of the pile of beavers, but for three days they just watched. On day four, a big male grizzly showed up and he went straight for the beaver carcasses. The wolves tried chasing him away and were obviously not happy having him so close to the den. However, he was a big, experienced bear, and he wasn't

Skinned carcass of a caribou calf killed and abandoned by wolves on the Delta Herd calving area in 1995. Wolves seem to get caught up in the thrill of the chase and kill many calves on caribou calving areas. Some, like this one, appear fine on the outside but are extensively bruised and bitten by wolves.

very intimidated, even with five or six wolves circling him and trying to run in from behind and bite him in the butt. He just ambled up to the pile of dead beavers and started gorging himself. After about an hour of slurping down the free beavers he wandered off about a half mile to take a nap. As soon as he left, the wolves dove in to the pile of beavers and had a good feed. A little competition was all it took to overcome their fear of the human scent. Audrey and I had seen a similar situation in the Brooks Range in 1972 when ADF&G biologists dropped off a dead caribou for us to watch. In that case, a wolf found it first but just hung around for a day watching it. During the second day, a grizzly bear showed up and was headed for the carcass. As soon as the wolf saw the bear coming, it ran to the carcass and started feeding.

A whole caribou calf cached under the snow by a wolf. If they are hungry, wolves will eat the whole calf, but if they are not, they either cache calves for later use (or not) or simply abandon them and move on.

During the second year of the diversionary feeding experiment (1997), the results were similar to the first year, even though we provided food to the wolves starting earlier in May. We were successful at keeping the wolves away from the caribou calving area from 15 May until about 27 May. Then, on the 28th, the wolves ate a whole bull caribou, rested for a couple of hours, and headed for the caribou calving area. They ended up killing several radio-collared calves and many other uncollared calves as well. They certainly could not have been hungry. They did it either because they just had the urge to hunt or were tired of lying around, or they felt they needed to patrol their territory and their hunting areas to make sure no other wolves were encroaching. Over the two years, calf survival was probably slightly better than it had been without the diversionary feeding but the results weren't spectacular. The caribou ranged more widely that summer and were available to more packs of wolves than in 1996. So, even though we may have "saved" about the same number of calves, by the time we did the caribou composition counts in early October, there was no difference in the calf to cow ratio between 1997 and 1995 (the year before we tried diversionary feeding). Unfortunately, we never were able to compare the movements of the GPS-collared alpha male during the first diversionary feeding year with the previous year without diversionary feeding. The GPS box came loose from the collar and when we recaptured the wolf it was missing, but the remains of the antenna were still in the collar band. I flew at low level all over the wolf's range but never did hear the signal. All of the movement data was stored in the missing box. All of those kinds of unpredictable small problems and unexpected changes in caribou movements illustrate why experiments in wildlife management are relatively "sloppy" compared with lab studies.

There has been much written in the popular and scientific literature on the subject of whether wolves only take the weak, sick, or unfit prey animals and thus serve as a "healthy" force in nature. The truth is that wolves catch whatever they can. Very often it is young animals that are perfectly healthy, but sometimes it is also unlucky animals that are caught by surprise. Moose are big enough and dangerous enough that wolves typically don't kill prime-aged animals between about 2 and 7 years of age, but in any attack or chase, anything is possible. I once watched a pack of wolves attack a cow moose and her calf in late winter. When it was over, the cow was dead and the calf escaped. In other cases, I watched or saw where wolves attacked and wounded moose and then left and never came back. In one case, the moose died but was never fed on by wolves. In general, when weather conditions (usually deep snow in Alaska) make it easy for wolves to kill animals, wolves do well and produce and support lots of pups. In shallow snow winters or when most prey animals are generally young and healthy, wolves aren't as successful at hunting and fewer pups survive to become adults. The importance of age and vulnerability of prey animals makes general predictions about how wolves affect prey species virtually impossible. Those factors change all the time, and the changes are often unpredictable. All the computer modeling in the world could never adequately predict the outcome.

A good example of the unpredictable nature of wolf predation is a situation that was spotted by a pilot from Glennallen and investigated by ADF&G Area Biologist Bob Tobey on 9 November 1988. A pack of at least five wolves trapped a group of 20 Dall sheep rams while they were crossing a gully near the Dadina River. The wolves managed to kill all 20 of the rams. The snow in the gully was fresh and around 30 inches deep. The snow on the nearby ridge where the wolves were traveling when they spotted the sheep was about 15 inches deep. Although it is just one example, it illustrates how weather conditions, luck, and learning by predators can play a large role in determining the outcome of predation and why predictions about the effects of wolf predation are difficult to make with accuracy.

One aspect of wolf predation that some people either try to deny, overemphasize, or ignore, depending on their point of view, is how "cruel" wolves are. "Cruelty" is a human value that has no parallel in nature. Jim Davis and I once watched a pack of 11 wolves attack a group of caribou and bring down two females at the same time. One of the caribou died very quickly but the wolves fed on the other one for ten minutes before she died. The second caribou tried to regain its feet twice while the wolves were tearing great chunks of meat off its back legs. The caribou was able to get up on its front legs twice and both times a wolf threw it back to the ground and continued feeding. The caribou finally died when a wolf started tearing at its flanks and probably ruptured the diaphragm.

Surplus killing (killing more prey animals than they need for food) is also common, particularly on caribou calving areas where wolves often encounter numbers of young calves that can't run fast enough to escape. Wolves run around and bite calves in the excitement of the hunt. Some of the wounded calves survive for many days before they die. Surplus killing also occurs when snow is deep, especially where wolves are hunting deer or caribou. During my first year working for

ADF&G, I was sent to investigate mostly intact carcasses of caribou near Norutak Lake west of Bettles. It turned out that the snow was very deep there and all the caribou had been killed by wolves and only lightly fed on. On three of the caribou, the wolves had eaten only the tongues (by tearing out the tongue from under the throat). I was reluctant to tell very many people about that because I was afraid most people wouldn't believe me. I never saw a situation like that again, but it was clear wolves were having such an easy time killing caribou in deep snow they were only eating the choice parts. Those kinds of behaviors by carnivores have been going on for millions of years. They are just a fact of life (and death).

Predation by wolves on caribou calving areas can have a very large influence on caribou, especially in small caribou herds that number less than about 10,000. On the southern Alaska Peninsula in the early 2000s, the caribou calf to cow ratio reached almost zero because of heavy predation by just two packs of wolves. When 14 wolves were removed, the fall calf to cow ratio jumped from 0.5 to 45 calves per 100 cows and the herd began to recover rapidly. Within a couple of years, the herd had doubled in size from about 300 to more than 700. Without intervention by ADF&G, the Southern Alaska Peninsula Herd would have been virtually wiped out by wolf predation and it would likely have taken many years for caribou to reoccupy the area.

The Mysteries of Wolf Breeding Behavior Solved

The breeding behavior of wolves is quite complex, and the details of breeding activities in wild wolves have not been fully understood until recently. During the 1960s and early 1970s, a very large collection of wolf carcasses was studied cooperatively by ADF&G in Alaska and by the Yukon Game Branch next door in the Yukon Territory. One of the key findings was that over 70% of all females over the age of two were pregnant. This information was at odds with information from penned studies of wolves, where only the dominant females in captive packs were pregnant each year. Much more information collected by ADF&G from wolf carcasses in Alaska during the 1980s and 1990s supported the original findings that most adult female wolves are pregnant every year.

During the 1990s and early 2000s, Mark McNay, a biologist with ADF&G in Fairbanks, finally collected information from radio-collared packs of wolves in the central Alaska Range that explained the previous conflicting information from the penned studies and studies of carcasses of wild wolves. Mark had all the females in several packs radio-collared and he caught them and scanned their bellies with a portable ultrasound machine every year for several years a few weeks after the breeding season. As in the previous studies of wolf carcasses, Mark found most females over two years of age were pregnant every year. He also found that packs would usually only support the pups of the dominant female. The subordinate females either had their pups in satellite dens and lost them, or they dispersed away from the pack and had their pups far away with no support from other wolves. One young pregnant female wolf traveled several hundred miles before denning alone and losing her pups in the western Yukon Territory. He also found that if a dominant female is killed between the breeding season and the denning season, the pack will support the pups of one of the other subordinate females. This helps explain why wolves can increase very rapidly in number and why they are so resilient to heavy hunting and trapping, even late in the winter.

In penned situations, the dominant wolves in a pack can prevent subordinate wolves from breeding. In the wild, the subordinate females can get away from the dominant adults and almost always find a male to breed with. When food is really abundant, sometimes the pups of subordinate females are supported but it probably depends on the personalities of the wolves involved and is not very predictable. During the early 1990s in the Alaska Range, we saw a pack go from 11 wolves one year to 32 wolves the next year. We didn't have enough of the wolves radio-collared to know for sure, but I suspected that pack of 11 had multiple litters. Moose were abundant, the caribou herd reached a record high level, and the winter had been severe, making it much easier for the wolves to hunt.

Pack Size

The pack of 32 wolves we saw in the early 1990s was the largest pack I had ever seen or heard about in Alaska at the time. I have recently heard a reliable report of a pack of 34. There are documented reports of packs of around 40 wolves in northeastern British Columbia. That is an exceptional area though—the abundance and variety of big game animals is astounding. Some areas have moose, Stone sheep, caribou, mountain goats, bison, elk, mule deer, and white-tailed deer.

In Alaska, most packs of wolves number around 7 to 10; anything over 15 is exceptional, and I think packs over 20 are usually quite unstable and short-lived. A whole adult moose won't even feed 20 wolves, so unless moose are really abundant and vulnerable to predation, it is unlikely those very large pack sizes will persist. In Alaska, if they have a choice, most packs seem to feed predominately on moose. Very small packs or singles and pairs will almost certainly feed on caribou or a combination of caribou and sheep if those animals are available. Lone wolves are usually scavengers and don't typically remain alone very long. Lone wolves are also usually dispersers looking for a pack to join or a mate to link up with. In Alaska they live a precarious existence and are often killed by other wolves.

How Many Prey Animals Do Wolves Kill?

The number of game animals that are required to feed wolves each year is a subject that comes up in the context of how wolves compete with people for game like deer, caribou, elk, moose, sheep, and goats. The subject has been well studied in both captive and wild wolves. Captive adult wolves require about five pounds of meat per day. Wild wolves that are traveling and exercising most of time probably require at least ten pounds of meat per day. In the 1960s, the Canadian Wildlife Service studied the number of caribou required to sustain a wolf and they estimated that if a wolf is living exclusively on caribou, it would require an average of about 25 caribou per year. There have been several more recent "kill rate" studies in Alaska. Biologists followed radio-collared wolves several times a day and then backtracked them to previous locations to determine how many large prey animals the wolves killed. These studies have all been done in winter because they require following wolves by both radio-tracking and snow-tracking.

In the one study in the central Alaska Range that Jim Davis and I did from 6 March through 4 April, 1989, we radio-tracked and snow-tracked four packs of wolves two or three times daily and tried to determine exactly how many animals they killed. We also flew to almost every kill site with a helicopter and determined the condition of the animals and how much meat remained after the wolves were finished feeding. The largest pack had 14 wolves in it and one lone wolf followed along behind, cleaning up the scraps. Over the 30-day period, they killed six moose, six caribou, one Dall sheep, and one wolf (the 15th wolf that tagged along behind). The second largest pack (eight wolves), killed eight moose and two caribou. The third largest pack (four wolves), killed two moose, three caribou, and several snowshoe hares, and the smallest pack (two wolves), killed seven caribou and one Dall sheep.

After watching the pack of 14 wolves kill and eat a whole Dall sheep in about five to ten minutes while we circled in the airplane, and then going in with the helicopter within an hour of the kill and looking at the remains, we realized we could easily have missed sheep kills during our 30-day study. The 14 wolves had torn the sheep to pieces so quickly and completely there was very little evidence left at the kill site, just some blood, hair, and stomach contents. A light dusting of snow would have made all the evidence invisible from the air or from the ground.

Wolves probably kill more animals in late winter, both because they require more food in cold weather and because their ungulate prey animals are not as fat and are more vulnerable to predation as snow gets deeper, so late winter kill rate studies may overestimate the number of animals killed annually. Also, in summer, wolves "snack" on things like bird eggs, baby birds, mice, ground squirrels, and the newborn young of caribou, deer, sheep, and goats. With all these kinds of considerations in mind, it is difficult to say exactly how many large animals are needed to feed a single wolf for a year. A good guess would be something like 25 caribou, or seven to nine moose. Recent kill rate studies of wolves in Yellowstone Park by biologist Doug Smith and others found that wolves make about two kills of large game animals (mostly elk) per wolf per month, or about 24 elk per wolf per year. Almost half of the elk killed were calves. In western North America, wolves typically don't feed exclusively on a single species of large prey animal, except in Interior Alaska, where only moose occur. Also, they don't appear to be able to consistently live on sheep or goats. ADF&G biologists in Southeast Alaska have recently found that black bears, sea otters, and moose are important prey animals for wolves on some islands.

Wolves require so much meat to survive they cannot live for long on small islands in Southeast Alaska. In 1960, there were about 500 deer living on wolf-free Coronation Island (about 28 square miles in area) when ADF&G biologists Harry Merriam and Dave Klein introduced two male and two female wolf pups. In 1963, they brought one additional adult female to the island. In three more years, the wolves increased to at least 11 and the deer were almost eliminated. By 1970, deer were down to just a few individuals and there was likely only one wolf left. By the late 1970s, wolves were gone from Coronation Island and deer recovered, but many local people were still angry about the wolf introduction experiment because Coronation had been a popular deer hunting area for people with large boats. On the larger islands that have wolves, wolves can have a tremendous impact on deer, especially during and after bad winters, and recovery of deer can be very slow.

Another example of how influential wolf predation can be comes from northwest Alaska in the 1970s. The Western Arctic Caribou Herd was estimated to be about 242,000 in 1970, but bad winters starting in the late 1960s provided easy pickings for wolves and resulted in a high wolf population. In the mid-1970s, ADF&G biologists estimated there were about 1,000 wolves on the southern winter range of the caribou herd and these wolves were killing around 20,000 caribou per year. In addition, people in northwestern Alaska were also killing between 15,000-25,000 caribou per year, depending on where the caribou wintered—a level of harvest that had been sustained for many years. By 1975, the caribou herd declined below 100,000 and it was in a rapid decline because of hunting and wolf predation. In the winter of 1975-76, ADF&G biologists estimated that either wolf predation or hunting alone would cause the caribou herd to continue declining and there was little hope the decline could be stopped. They proposed a drastic reduction in hunting and a wolf control program. Although the wolf control program was effectively blocked by lawsuits from environmental groups, local wolf hunters were able to kill hundreds of wolves by land-and-shoot hunting with aircraft, and hunting with snowmachines. I knew one pilot in Kotzebue who killed 50 to 75 each winter during 1975-76 and 1976-77. With the reduced wolf numbers and fewer caribou harvested, the decline of the caribou herd was stopped at about 75,000, and the herd then began a rapid recovery.

One surprising thing about wolves as predators is that they are cautious about taking on animals they are not familiar with, especially big animals. There are many examples of cattle disappearing into the Superior National Forest in northern Minnesota—an area with a large wolf population—and returning a month later without a scratch. Another example is the fact that when bison were introduced into the Farewell area in Alaska, it was about 20 years before wolves killed the first bison calf, even though they routinely hunt bison in Wood Buffalo National Park. Hunger causes them to take greater risks in testing new prey animals, as can be seen in the last part of this chapter.

Wolves as Individuals

Several of the best Alaskan wolf stories are about individuals. Some of these stories are about how tough wolves can be and some are just about the varying personalities of the individuals; some are about both. Over my 49 years in Alaska, I encountered a few individual wolves that really impressed me.

Playful Wolf

Like the young of most animals, wolf pups are very playful and frolicking is an important part of learning how to be a wolf. Adults are usually too busy or too tired to play but sometimes they provide interesting surprises. In 1973, Audrey and I were working on her Master's thesis project on the Marsh Fork of the Canning River in the eastern Brooks Range. Audrey was studying scavenging activity in arctic mammals and we spent most of our time watching from vantage points on the side of mountains along the river. One day we spotted a wolf trotting up the riverbank. We knew of no den nearby, so the wolf had probably been traveling for a while, and it appeared tired. As it came opposite us, it decided to cross the river to a gravel bar on the other side. The current was swift at that spot and the wolf hesitated, watching the water. Suddenly, it jumped into the river, swam to the middle, grabbed something, and then continued swimming across to the other side. When it got out, we could clearly see in the spotting scope that it had a stick in its mouth! It cavorted around on the bank with the stick for a few seconds, then stood there, dropped the stick, and continued trotting on its way. For a minute or two it looked just like a dog fetching a stick for its owner.

Friendly Wolf Goes for a Ride

During the 1990s there was pressure from people in Alaska and the Yukon to bring back the Fortymile Caribou Herd to a level where it would provide more meat for hunters, including subsistence hunters. The only way to reasonably accomplish that was to reduce predation by wolves, but there were several animal rights and animal welfare groups who were opposed to wolf control and they had the ear of then governor, Tony Knowles. As a result, biologists with ADF&G were tasked with conducting a so-called "non-lethal" experimental wolf control program in east-central Alaska. The idea was to capture as many members as possible from about 15 packs of wolves, sterilize and release the dominant pair, and then translocate all the remaining wolves at least 250 miles away, so they would be unlikely to return. I was enlisted to help with the project by flying the ADF&G de Havilland Beaver to drop off several loads of undrugged wolves in dog kennels. I also sometimes used one of the ADF&G Bellanca Scouts to transport drugged wolves two at a time without restraint in the back of the plane.

One day in early April, I departed Fairbanks with two wolves in the back of the Scout and headed northwest. Rod Boertje, another ADF&G biologist, was in another ADF&G Scout with one drugged wolf onboard. We were headed for the vicinity of village of Atqasuk on the North Slope, but we had to stop in Bettles for fuel. Just before the fuel stop, I glanced at my two passengers and noticed the small female in the back had her head up and was looking at me. She didn't seem agitated in any way, just lying there peacefully, enjoying the ride, but looking at me whenever I turned around to look at her. I got on the radio and told Rod about the wolf. He radioed back while laughing, and said, "I think she needs another dose!" Another pilot, Marty Webb, was also flying a load of wolves to the southwest of us. He also heard me and also came back on the radio laughing, with a similar comment.

While on a long final approach to the runway at Bettles, I looked at my passengers once more. The wolf nearest me, a big male, was starting to move a bit so I broke off the approach, made a wide circle, and gave the big guy a jab of 250 milligrams of Telazol. The little female in the back was definitely awake, but she was very calm, so I just decided to keep watching her. I landed, so did Rod, we fueled up and departed again. It was two more hours to our destination. The big male continued sleeping and the little female just lay there, looking at me. We couldn't quite get to our destination near Atqasuk because of fog, so we turned around and backtracked for about 30 miles before I found a suitable lake to land on. After landing, I grabbed the sleeping male, pulled him out by the scruff of the neck and the rump, and laid him out in the snow. He was just starting to move a bit. I opened the rear baggage door and looked at the female. She was looking at me calmly, so I just reached in, grabbed her gently by the scruff, and pulled her partly out with my left hand. As her rear end came out, I grabbed her rump with my right hand and set her gently on all four legs and let go. She walked away about ten feet and then turned around and looked at me, as if to say, "Thanks for the ride," and trotted off toward the edge of the lake. Rod landed as she was leaving. I told him what happened and he looked at the trotting wolf, shook his head laughing, and said, "You're crazy!" Maybe I was, but I felt like the wolf and I developed an understanding during the two-hour ride from Bettles. I was a little sad to hear the next winter that she had been caught by a trapper near Wiseman, about two hundred miles southeast of where I dropped her off.

Wolves are Tough

Compared with humans and our four-legged canine best friends, wolves certainly are tough. During Interior Alaska winters, they are constantly on the go in temperatures of -40F and lower; traveling, killing moose, chewing on frozen meat, and fighting with neighboring packs to hold their territories. They are tough in other ways too. During necropsies of thousands of wolf carcasses performed by biologists during the 1970s, 1980s, and 1990s we saw some amazing injuries that wolves sustained and recovered from. Fractured ribs were common, probably mostly received in fights with moose. We also saw healed, fractured skulls and long bones. Probably the most unusual injury I ever saw a wolf sustain was actually the result of being darted by a biologist.

The particular wolf with this dart injury turned up on the necropsy table after having been trapped by a man in Tok. It was about three years after the "non-lethal" Fortymile wolf control program was over. The carcass of the wolf appeared perfectly normal externally and internally. Just as the necropsy was about over and we had done all the usual weights and measurements, including weighing the stomach contents and assessing the amount of internal fat, someone noticed an abnormal looking lump on the heart. While slitting the pericardial sac to investigate the lump, the scalpel clinked against a metal object. The object turned out to be a 3cc Palmer Cap-Chur dart about three inches long with the ¾-inch barbed needle and wool tail piece still attached. On checking the data associated with the sealing certificate, it turned out the wolf had been radio-collared and was a dominant male from the "non-lethal" control program. It had received a vasectomy and then been released about 30 miles north of Tok. Tok Area Biologist Craig Gardner remembered having darted a wolf in that area and mentioning to the veterinarians who performed the vasectomy that although he had seen the dart flying toward the wolf during the chase, he never saw the dart again, even though the wolf went down. He thought the dart had either bounced out or penetrated too far. The two vets thoroughly inspected the wolf and looked for signs of a dart injury. Not finding anything, they cleared the wolf for release after the vasectomy. The dart had indeed penetrated too far, completely through the skin, in between two ribs, and through the pericardium, before being stopped by the heart itself. It had become lodged between the heart muscle and the pericardial sac. It completely healed and the wolf lived a normal life and maintained a territory for over three years with the dart stuck in its heart.

Another tough wolf was the alpha male in the Wells Creek Pack, the pack we had done the diversionary feeding experiment on in the Alaska Range. He kept his dominant status through all three years of the study. Although it eventually became apparent he was a very tough wolf, in the beginning I had my doubts. Despite his weight and large size (he weighed about 125 pounds), he was very sensitive to the capture drug Telazol. The first time I darted him, he slept for five hours, instead of the normal 60 to 90 minutes, and he didn't fully recover from the drug for two days. The second time I darted him, he slept for over three hours with half the dose I had given him the year before.

In the fall of 1997, he was apparently shot and wounded just above and between the eyes by a hunter. When I recollared him in late September, I could see about two inches of his exposed brain. Despite that impressive wound, he was acting quite normal and was still the dominant male in the pack. The next year when I recollared him again, the wound had healed and the remaining, finger-deep groove from the bullet wound was completely fur covered. If I had not seen the fresh wound the year before, I would not have known what caused the groove. He was eventually shot by a hunter near Cantwell a few years later.

Trappers have told me some amazing stories about wolves that were paralyzed with broken backs during fights with moose. One of those survived for over a month, dragging its rear legs around while scrounging for food from old kills. By the end of the month, the wolf's back legs were so atrophied from disuse there was little muscle tissue left. Surprisingly, the wolf's pelt was in good condition and the trapper received full price for it from the fur buyer.

Goldstream Blackie

ADF&G conducted a wolf control program in GMU 20B from 1984 to 1986. It was designed to increase moose numbers and hunting success in Minto Flats and surrounding areas. Although I was a regional management biologist specializing in caribou at the time, because I was a pilot, I was assigned to the 20B wolf control program full-time in winter for those two years. Mostly, I worked together with ADF&G technician Ed Crain. We flew in the state Bellanca Scout every decent day in winter setting and checking snares around wolf kills and shooting wolves from the air. It was challenging and exciting work and kept us out of the office. Much of the area surrounding Minto Flats is heavily wooded so it was no simple matter trying to reduce wolf numbers in those areas. Even on the more open flats, the main wolf packs traveled widely and we were lucky to find them in the open.

At the end of the first year of the program, after having pretty good success reducing wolf numbers on the flats, we decided to try putting radio-collars on some of the adult wolves in the more wooded surrounding areas and use them as "Judas" wolves (to find the packs and remove pack members without collars). We were still using turbine helicopters (Jet Rangers and Hughes 500s) in those days instead of the more efficient Robinson gas-powered helicopters and helicopter time was expensive (about $500/hour in 1985 dollars).

One November day in 1984, Ed and I tracked down a pack of about eight wolves in Goldstream Valley and found them in a good spot for darting near the Alaska Railroad tracks around Old Saulich. While we circled the wolves at high altitude, we relayed a message to the ADF&G office through the Flight Service Station and scrambled a darting crew. About an hour later, the helicopter arrived with caribou research biologist Ken Whitten and Management Coordinator Bud Burris. As the helicopter came in, we identified a large black wolf as a likely adult and directed the helicopter after it. With a little practice, it's not too difficult to make an educated guess about which wolves are likely to be adults and pups and even to guess their sex, based on size and speed. The adults are typically more nervous around aircraft and run for thick cover when a helicopter shows up. Adult males are typically larger and slower than adult females. Females also tend to be lighter-colored wolves. We were pretty sure the wolf we put the helicopter on was an adult male. Ken made a good, quick dart shot in a difficult chase and within about 10 minutes the wolf was down and Ed and I went on our way to find other wolf packs. We didn't realize it at the time but we were in for some remarkable experiences with that collared black wolf. We soon named him "Goldstream Blackie."

When we got back to the office later in the day, I asked Ken about the black wolf. He confirmed the wolf was a male and was likely the dominant adult and an older wolf. He had a grey muzzle, a scattering of gray hairs throughout the body, and worn teeth. But, the most noteworthy thing about him was that he had probably been trapped in the distant past and his right-hind foot healed with an extra joint in it. From the air we hadn't noticed anything strange about how he ran.

We gave the pack a couple of days to get back together and relax and then began tracking them with the radio-collar to try to find them in a good spot to remove the uncollared members of the pack.

Wolves

Within a week all seven uncollared wolves had been removed and Goldstream Blackie was alone for several weeks.

Although the western GMU 20B wolf control program was not particularly controversial within Alaska, it nevertheless was opposed by several national animal rights and environmental groups. One group found a lawyer who figured out that ADF&G did not have approval from the Federal Communications Commission to use the frequencies we were using with our radio-collars. The group filed suit to have the collars removed from the Judas wolves in the 20B wolf control program. The only approved frequency range for radio-collars on wildlife at the time was a narrow band of VHF frequencies called the Forestry-Wildlife Band. Most of the collars ADF&G had on moose, caribou, bears, and other wildlife were also technically illegal but the lawsuit only asked for the removal of collars on wolves. It was pretty obvious the lawsuit was primarily just a form of harassment. Although its effect was small because we only had two collars on wolves in Unit 20B and we could still trap and shoot wolves from the air, catching Blackie to remove his collar presented a real challenge. He was an experienced wolf with a Ph.D. in helicopter and aircraft evasion because he had been darted once and all of his pack members had been shot out twice. There was almost no chance of darting him again with the helicopter. Every time he heard a helicopter, or an airplane, he high-tailed it straight for the nearest spruce thicket. Using steel traps for live-capturing wolves is commonly done but the weather has to be above freezing to prevent foot damage. That really only left the snaring option. We designed a live snare by taking a No. 4 Thompson snare (⅛-inch diameter steel cable) and putting a stop in the loop at 18 inches to prevent the snare from closing down all the way. We then boiled up a dozen of the modified snares and kept them in the plane in a plastic bag with a couple of clean pairs of gloves ready to go in case we found Blackie near a kill where we could land.

After about a week of checking on him every day we found Blackie on a calf moose he had just killed about a mile from a lake near Dunbar on the Alaska Railroad tracks. The snow was shallow enough to walk without snowshoes so we carefully walked to the kill, avoiding walking in any of the wolf trails. We set six snares on Blackie's trails going to and from the kill, making sure to set the snares from the side of the trail where he passed through brushy spots. We left by stepping in our incoming tracks to minimize the amount of human sign left behind.

As soon as it was light enough to fly the next day, we took off from Chena Marina and went straight to the sets we made for Blackie. As we approached the dead moose, we saw Blackie immediately. He was caught in one of the snares and had chewed down a circle of small trees and brush and was looking up at the plane. We landed, grabbed a jab-stick and some immobilizing drug, and ran for the captured wolf. From about 20 feet away we could see he had fought the snare pretty hard and only a few strands of cable remained. He was obviously pretty angry about being caught (again!) and if looks could kill, we would have died right there. Despite being pretty hot and excited, Blackie responded well to the Xylazine (immobilizing drug) and was peacefully sleeping within five minutes. We replaced his collar with one with an approved frequency and looked him over. He was very gray around the muzzle and his teeth were very worn, but they didn't seem to have any recent damage from the cable snare. He was in pretty good shape, but his fur was covered with frost and frozen saliva. The extra joint in his right hind foot was completely covered with fur and didn't appear to be a problem at all. There was no evidence of swelling or breaks in the skin there. The snare we used to catch him had worn away some hair around his neck but there was no skin damage. He appeared none the worse for the experience.

I do not remember radio-tracking Blackie over the summer of 1985, but after freeze-up in October, we found him around Dunbar with what appeared to be a light-colored female and four or five pups. We soon eliminated the female and pups and Blackie was back to being alone again. We then only tracked him about every two weeks for the next three months but almost every time we found him, he was on or near a moose he had recently killed. Even alone, he was obviously a proficient moose hunter and hadn't turned into a scavenger like many lone wolves. Most of the moose he was killing appeared to be calves or yearlings which wasn't too surprising because very few prime-aged moose between two and seven years of age are killed by wolves anyway. What was surprising was the regularity and apparent ease with which he continued to kill moose, even as a loner with well-worn teeth.

We located Blackie about once a week through December and January and frequently found him alone on new kills. During the breeding season in February, he paired up with a female. The two of them together didn't seem to be killing any more moose than he had been killing alone, but we decided to remove his mate to prevent the pack from having pups and expanding over the summer. He was still alone in April when we located him for the last time that winter.

We started locating Blackie again in October, 1986, and were surprised to see he traveled with three other wolves and was still using the same territory in Goldstream Valley that he had used for the previous two years. We found him often enough to guess the pack was still killing a moose a week, not much different than when he was living alone. Nevertheless, we decided to remove his pack mates, and by late November he was a lone wolf once more. By this time, the wolf control program and private trappers had removed most of the wolves from Minto Flats and just a few packs remained on the periphery of the flats. We couldn't justify spending much more time working on the western 20B wolf control program, but the fact that Blackie was still killing a moose a week in Goldstream Valley, whether or not he was with other wolves, made us reconsider the strategy of leaving him alone as a Judas wolf.

In early November we reluctantly decided that Blackie had to go. He had certainly gained our respect, especially considering his age, the tough life he had lived, and the fact he had been darted once, trapped once, and snared once. We decided to try to shoot him from the Scout the next time we found him in a good spot. Within a few days we found him in the bottom of Goldstream Creek where there was some open muskeg nearby. We tried to get him to go out onto the open muskeg but he was smart enough to just run back and forth in the bottom of the creek. After about 30 minutes without success, we decided to leave him for a couple of hours and check some snares in Minto Flats and then try him again. When we returned, Blackie was in the same spot but we decided to try to get him to make a mistake one more time before we headed back to Chena Marina. Much to my surprise, on our first pass Blackie bolted up the creek bank and headed straight across the only small frozen lake in the whole area. I yelled, "GET READY" at Ed, opened the right window to the blast of cold air, and set the plane up in a forward slip about 50 feet above and behind Blackie. The approach was perfect and Blackie had no way to escape. We finally had him! I held the plane in position as long as I could, expecting to hear a bang from the 12-gauge and see the black wolf crumple. After what seemed like forever without hearing a report from the shotgun, I pulled the plane up, but not before the right wing hit the top of a spruce tree at the edge of the lake. It sounded like a pretty good whack, and after I closed the window, I leaned forward to look at the leading edge of the right wing. It looked like someone had hit the leading edge with a baseball bat. I turned around and gave Ed's still-masked face a questioning and very dirty look. We didn't use intercoms in those days so I just assumed it must have been some kind of operator error and didn't ask about the details. It turned out the shotgun, a Browning A-5, had not been properly cleaned of oil to prepare it for the -20F temperatures we were flying in. The firing pin struck the primer too slowly to set it off. Anyway, we were done for the day and I headed back to Chena Marina to assess the damage to the plane.

About a week later I had brand new Fairbanks Area Biologist Mark McNay in the back seat of the Scout. He had never shot from the air so I ran him through some basics and we headed out via Goldstream Valley for the Minto Flats to do a little practice shooting. On the way we decided to check on Blackie just to see where he was hanging out and whether he had any new wolves with him. We got his signal almost right away and found him looking pretty dejected, sitting with his right front foot in someone's trap about a mile down a snowmachine trail from the Standard Creek woodcutting trail. I thought about trying to get Mark to shoot Blackie from the air to put a quick end to his latest misfortune but we decided to just let the trapper deal with him.

We expected Blackie's radio-collar to be brought in to the office before long so it was a couple of weeks before we tried listening for him while flying around in western GMU 20B. When we finally did try to find him, we were very surprised to hear his signal coming from COD Lake in northeastern Minto Flats. Ed and I tracked in on the signal and found Blackie alive and well and not even limping. He had apparently broken out of the trap and got away, but he was done with Goldstream Valley. I couldn't blame him.

We tracked him one more time that spring when the snow was almost gone and the wolf control program was over. He was with two other wolves and still living around COD Lake. Before long, the batteries in his collar died, but he must have been well along in years by that time. As far as I know, he was never trapped again and probably died of natural causes, but he sure was a survivor and we both actually felt pretty good to see his story end that way.

Romeo

During 2009 and 2010, when I served as Deputy Commissioner of ADF&G in Juneau, "Romeo" was the talk of the town. He had shown up in 2003 at Mendenhall Lake. Stories differed, as many do, but supposedly, one of the first encounters with Romeo was by the owner of a pug, who was taking her dog for a walk near the lake. A black wolf appeared, grabbed the pug and vanished. The pug was never seen again. The pug owner, and community of pug owners in Juneau were on the war path against the black wolf. Six years later, in late 2009, I talked to a woman who worked in the Department of Administration, and also owned a pug, and she was still upset and still hoping to see the black wolf gone. However, she was by that time, among a small minority of Romeo haters. Most of Juneau loved Romeo. He had won everyone else over with his charming and friendly behavior.

After the pug incident in 2003, no more dogs were ever attacked near

Mendenhall Glacier. Instead, the black wolf adapted to a solitary lifestyle, mostly staying around Mendenhall Lake, but occasionally disappearing for weeks at a time. When he was at Mendenhall Lake, he regularly played with dogs that people brought there for exercise. I always wondered how Romeo was making a living, but there was no evidence people were feeding him, so he was apparently at least making an "honest" living.

After Romeo first showed up in 2003, ADF&G staff in the Douglas regional office were rightly concerned the pug incident with the overly habituated black wolf at Mendenhall Lake was the beginning of problems to come. They first tried "aversive conditioning." That is, they drove a state pickup to the lake and shot cracker shells at the wolf and let him know people and their dogs were not to be messed with. The result was that Romeo quickly figured out that state pickups and the people associated with them were bad, but everyone else was friendly. The situation went on for several years. Romeo played with dogs and was generally accepting of most people, but avoided state pickups. In early 2009, two other wolves showed up and briefly associated with Romeo. This was a big red flag. One wolf alone, acting friendly, was one thing, three wolves getting habituated to people was likely going to be a real problem. However, after the initial sighting of Romeo with the two other wolves, Romeo was never seen with them again. It was almost as if he considered the options; return to the wild and take his chances with other wild wolves, or continue his lifestyle of being single and playing with people and their dogs. He had chosen the latter.

Unfortunately, Romeo was illegally shot north of Mendenhall Lake in the fall of 2009 in an area closed to hunting. Private sleuthing by concerned fans of Romeo led to the conviction of the perpetrators. Just before I left Juneau in December 2010, fans of Romeo held a memorial and put up a plaque in honor of this most unusual wolf. Author Nick Jans subsequently wrote a book called *A Wolf Named Romeo*. It is well worth reading.

Problems with Wolves

People in Alaska have probably always had conflicts with wolves, whether it was wolves competing with them for food, wolves killing their dogs, or wolves (including rabid wolves) occasionally attacking people themselves. When I first arrived in Interior Alaska in 1972, it was a very different place than it is today. Fairbanks was a small, compact city of about 30,000 with very little sprawl, although subdivisions were beginning to spread out. The winters of 1970-71 and 1971-72 had been severe, with heavy snow falls interspersed with extreme cold temperatures. Moose, caribou, and sheep populations crashed to very low levels by 1974. Wolf numbers increased to high levels during the early 1970s because of the hard winters and the abundant but declining moose and caribou. In contrast, snowshoe hares were at a cyclic high level. Hares were everywhere. Squashed hares were commonly seen along the roads, willows and aspens were girdled, lynx, great-horned owls, red foxes, and goshawks were commonly seen hunting hares.

As "poor, starving graduate students," Audrey and I lived on snowshoe hares, hunting them after classes and on weekends. We cooked them every way we could think of and we even made hare sausage. Like us, other large predators, including wolves and wolverines, that normally didn't live on snowshoe hares, were eating a lot of them. I chopped open the frozen stomachs of several wolves and wolverines that had been caught by Percy Duyck at Knight's Roadhouse near the Toklat Springs in March, 1974 and they were all packed full of snowshoe hares. When the hares started crashing in 1974, the already stressed wolf population faced starvation.

In November 1974, reports of wolves killing dogs in the Fairbanks area started to trickle in to ADF&G. There had always been occasional reports of wolves killing dogs in winter, especially in the villages, but this seemed different. At first, people just assumed the wolf on dog problem was an aberration that would resolve itself and be over quickly. But by mid-winter, the toll of dogs began to really add up, and other domestic animals, like goats and sheep, were being killed too. People started really paying attention and most people were becoming a lot more concerned. By the end of January, at least 20 dogs had been killed and reported to ADF&G but two or three times that number probably went unreported. Some of the stories were quite dramatic. There began to be a public clamor to have ADF&G hunt down the wolves with a helicopter. On the other side, people were defending the wolves and arguing they were just being wolves and people should be more careful with their dogs and livestock. There were two petitions, side by side, on the bulletin board at Ivory Jack's store in Goldstream Valley. One advocated having ADF&G hunt down the wolves, the other asking ADF&G to leave the wolves alone. By the end of the winter, there were more people on the petition to not have ADF&G intervene. Some people were just pro-wolf, but I'm sure most people were just independent-thinking Alaskans who wanted to deal with their own problems and not waste government money. Over the course of the two winters, I remember one official tally of dead dogs being 66 with many more missing. However, Bob Stephenson, then a wolf biologist with ADF&G, documented only 29 with at least 10 reported missing. Bob did say that most dog losses were never reported and he estimated around 200 dogs were lost to wolves. The total number of dead and missing dogs was a subject of debate and there were really no accurate records kept. No aggression toward people was ever documented, but some of the individual stories that I have related below were quite scary and dramatic.

Ted Dixon, manager of a sporting goods store and a renowned Fairbanks gunsmith, had been out taking his two Labrador retrievers for a walk in Goldstream Valley when wolves attacked one of the dogs. It was dark but he could hear growling, snarling, and yelping. He had no choice but to retreat with his remaining dog. When he came back in the daylight with a rifle, there was just blood and hair in the snow.

John Henshaw, a biologist working on his Ph.D. at the University of Alaska, lived in Goldstream Valley, where he was proving up on an old homestead. He had a beagle he let out every morning first thing, to pee. John, like practically everyone else in Goldstream Valley, was aware of the wolf problems and he had a loaded rifle ready next to his bedroom window. One morning, he let the beagle out and went upstairs to get dressed. He heard the beagle yelping and looked outside to see two wolves chasing the beagle down the driveway toward the house. Before he could grab his rifle and open the window, the wolves grabbed the dog, tore it in two, and ran off. He said he just stood there looking in disbelief and never had a chance to shoot. When he came into the University that morning, he told us the story and he was quite philosophical about it by that time. He concluded the story with a wry smile and said, "It may have been a dear beagle to us, but it was just a bagel to those wolves." The fact that he was British and said it with a strong accent made it seem all the more humorous. Humor at the expense of the poor beagle.

Another friend of mine, Patty Dyer, had a similar problem. She lived a couple of miles out Murphy Dome Road with her two huskies. She worked at the University and often left the huskies at home, tied up in the back yard. It was early in the winter 1974 and the wolf problems were just starting, so people had not yet begun to take the problem seriously. Patty came home from work one day and found one of her huskies cowering in its dog house instead of barking and eagerly greeting her. At the other dog run, there was just a loose chain with a collar, a big patch of bloody snow, the tail of the husky, one back leg, and a kidney lying in the snow. Patty was understandably quite upset, but she picked up the remains of the dog and put them on her back porch before going to the neighbor for help, a gun, and moral support. When Patty arrived back at her house with the neighbor, the back leg of the dog and the kidney were missing from the porch. They never saw the wolves, but it was dark.

Sverre Pedersen was a student at the University at the time, and he was also a dog musher who owned 16 sled dogs. He lost three of them to wolves during the fall and early winter of 1974-75. Sverre was very interested in wolves and he did his Master's thesis on skull sizes of wolves in Alaska. He was quite philosophical about the wolves killing dogs in Fairbanks, although he did have a scary experience that he mentioned in an interview with *Fairbanks Daily News-Miner* reporter Tim Mowry in 2007. While mushing with eight or nine dogs in the team during the winter of 1974-75, he was closely followed by a pack of wolves in the dark. He said they came up to within 15 or 20 feet of him. He wasn't carrying a gun and it was quite alarming.

Most of the animals killed by the wolves were sled dogs tied out on chains but there were exceptions, like John Henshaw's beagle and

Ted Dixon's Labrador. The sled dogs of that era were not like sled dogs today. Many of them were large and aggressive, weighing up to 140 pounds. Some were also real fighters and fights among sled dogs were a major problem mushers had to contend with. Adult wolves are expert fighters and killers and even those tough old sled dogs didn't have much of a chance against a pack of wolves. The more modern, smaller, less aggressive sled dogs of today would be a real pushover for any wolf.

As the winter of 1974-75 dragged on and the wolf attacks on dogs and other animals continued, more and more people were driving around armed and ready, especially in Goldstream Valley. Most of the reports of dead and missing dogs were from Goldstream Valley, but there were also attacks around the Steese Highway, along the Chena Hot Springs Road, and a few on Farmer's Loop Road. By the end of the winter, it was pretty clear that only one pack of wolves was involved and they numbered around 14. The wolves made enough mistakes that they started getting picked off, one by one. Two friends of mine, Jim Curatolo and Tim Smith, were headed out trapping on Murphy Dome Road when a wolf crossed in front of them. One of them jumped out and shot the wolf. A similar thing happened to Gerry Kelly, a local photographer. He had been driving around all winter with a rifle in his car, just in case. One morning on the way to work he had his chance. He saw a wolf at the junction of Murphy Dome Road and Sheep Creek Road, jumped out, and shot it. By the end of March 1975, at least 13 wolves had been shot or trapped in the area and the problem stopped as spring arrived. The wolf excitement caused some collateral damage. Several people who had eagerly set out traps for the wolves ended up catching neighbors' dogs. I never heard of dogs being shot by mistake but it likely happened. Everyone agreed there were definitely fewer stray and loose dogs around after the winter of 1974-75. There were just a few reports of wolves killing dogs around Fairbanks in the fall of 1975 but the problem was largely over.

Since the 1970s, attacks on dogs in Bush Alaska have continued at their normal, low level. In winter 2007-08, there were again attacks along the Chena Hot Springs Road and three dogs were killed, but trappers quickly caught the offending wolves.

The Danger of Wolves to Humans

During the 1970s, wolves were absent from the Lower 48 states, except for Minnesota. In the U.S., sympathy for wolves was becoming widespread after a century of persecution, and many biologists, conservationists, and environmentalists were trying to portray wolves in a positive light. The subject of how dangerous wolves were to humans was revisited in several popular articles by prominent biologists in Canada and the U.S. The prevailing view was that wolves had historically been a danger to humans in Europe, primarily because rabies had been prevalent, but there was no credible history of wolf attacks by non-rabid wolves. In North America, most experts believed there were no clearly verified cases of wolves attacking humans. A commonly quoted statement was, "There has never been a verified attack by a wild wolf that resulted in a death or serious injury to a human in North America." That view was prevalent until the 1990s. Then, dissenting voices began to emerge.

The dissenting voices, including prominent biologist Dr. Valerius Geist in British Columbia, began to notice a pattern. As wolves were repopulating areas of their former range in North America, the new tolerance that people were showing towards wolves was resulting in wolves taking liberties with people and their pets and testing the limits of people's tolerance. In some cases, wolves were becoming dangerously habituated to humans. Geist himself had seen habituated wolves near his home on Vancouver Island in 1999 and talked to others whose dogs had been killed there. At the same time, rapidly improving information technology made old reports of wolf attacks in North America more readily available to researchers. In addition, the collapse of the Soviet Union and the era of Glasnost made much more of the Russian information available.

In Alaska, ADF&G wolf research biologist Mark McNay made the first concerted recent scientific effort to gather verified reports about wolf attacks on people throughout North America. He published an article in the Wildlife Society Bulletin in 2002, in which he reported that between 1900 and 1969 there was only one verified instance of an unprovoked attack by a wolf on a human in North America. From 1969 to 2000, there had been 18 unprovoked attacks, most of them caused by wolves getting habituated to people. McNay also reviewed information about the Native American experience with wolves which had not been well-documented. From his thorough review of the interactions of wolves and humans in North America prior to 2001, he concluded that prior to about 1870 wolves had been more aggressive toward humans but that extermination programs and constant negative interactions caused wolves to become less numerous and less aggressive.

A separate review of wolf attacks on humans was also done in 2002 by Dr. John Linnell and other biologists at the Norwegian Institute for Nature Research. Linnell found several other cases of wolf attacks in North America that McNay had not found, including two separate cases where men had been killed by rabid wolves during the 1940s in northwestern Alaska.

In Russia there is a much longer written record covering a much larger wolf population. Not surprisingly, there are many more documented cases of wolf attacks on humans, both from rabid and non-rabid wolves. Rabid wolves aside, the Russian record clearly shows that wolves are always on the lookout for food and if they can take advantage of humans to obtain food, they will. The most famous example, which existed only in hearsay and rumor until the early 1980s, came from World War II. I discovered it because I decided to learn Russian to have access to the Russian scientific literature on wild reindeer. I had also become acquainted with some biologists in Russia and I had been able to get money from the International Science Foundation to pay for their travel to come over for a couple of North American Caribou Workshops.

During the late 1990s, I was given a book in Russian by Dr. Leonid Baskin of the Russian Academy of Sciences in Moscow. The book was titled *The Wolf* by Michael P. Pavlov and it was first published in Russian in 1982. Pavlov had the equivalent of a Master's degree and he had been a management biologist who had taken a strong interest in wolves in Russia, both from an economic perspective and from a human-interest perspective. One chapter really caught my attention. It was titled The Danger of Wolves to Humans and I laboriously worked at translating it, both to learn to read Russian and to find out about the Russian wolf experiences. The more I translated, the more fascinated I became. The Russian wolf experiences were so different from anything I had heard about in North America that they stretched credibility.

A few months after I had very roughly translated the chapter, Dr. Baskin was in Alaska again so I asked him about Pavlov and whether Pavlov was a credible source. Baskin said yes, he knew of Pavlov, and Pavlov had a very good reputation among field biologists in Russia; he was a member of the Russian Academy of Sciences, and there was no reason to doubt what he had written. He thought Pavlov was probably in his 80s and likely still living in Moscow. I said I would like to pay Dr. Baskin and his wife Valentina to translate the chapter of the book and that I would make it available in English somehow. I also gave Baskin $200 to give to Pavlov, as compensation for allowing the chapter of the book to be published in the United States. Baskin accepted the offer and the money for Pavlov.

About three months later, Baskin emailed me and said the translation of the chapter was going well and he had also found Pavlov in an apartment in Moscow. Pavlov was flattered that he was offered $200 in exchange for the rights to publish the chapter in English and he was very glad someone in the U.S. discovered his work. However, he said he was satisfied with his life in old age and that he was too old to really use the money, so he declined to accept it. Knowing how difficult things were in Russia at the time, I was rather impressed that he refused the money. The translated chapter was finally published as an appendix in Will Graves 2007 book, *Wolves in Russia—anxiety through the ages*. The problem with many translations of Russian scientific works is that, unless they are done by professional scientific translators, the language used by Russian biologists often seems "quaint" or unprofessional to Western biologists. When we translated the chapter, I wanted to leave as much of Pavlov's original wording intact and avoided "smoothing" it into professional scientific-sounding English during the final editing. Some wolf advocates will likely use that as an excuse to cast doubt on it.

The gist of the translated chapter was that Russian experiences with wolves have been very different from those of people in North America. This was partly because Russia is so big, it stretches across seven time zones, and partly because rabies occurs over huge areas. In contrast, in northern North America, at least within the range of the wolf during the twentieth century, rabies was largely confined to coastal areas. That is also true in Alaska today. Wild rabies is enzootic in arctic foxes, it is not particularly virulent or transmissible to people, and only occurs along the coastal fringes of the state. In addition, Russians have never had the easy access to firearms that North Americans take for granted. Russian peasants were very poor and then Russian governments instituted gun control very early on, first by the Czars and then by the Communists. A third reason is the two world wars in the twentieth century were much more devastating and life-changing events in Russia than they were in North America. The single most startling thing to me about Pavlov's translated chapter was what happened in the Kirov Oblast (province) during and after World War II.

When Germany invaded Russia in June 1941, most of the men and all of the available firearms were sent west to fight the invading German army. It took several years, but wolves in Kirov Oblast learned that humans were no longer protected and they became increasingly habituated to people in many remote villages. They first began preying on small livestock and then started living in towns, even curling up and sleeping in town squares. In 1944, they started attacking and eating people, particularly children. At first, it was probably just one pack of wolves, but eventually many packs were involved in a large area of the oblast. It took until 1954 for the Russian government to completely eliminate the wolf attacks on people. The information on wolf attacks had been suppressed for many years by the Communist regimes. But in the 1960s and 1970s, Pavlov found several people who had survived the wolf attacks and he interviewed them. The chapter makes fascinating reading and demonstrates just how adaptable and determined wolves can be if given the chance. The wolves in Russia are no different than wolves in North America, it is just that they have had quite different opportunities to test humans and to take advantage of them. The wolf attacks on dogs and livestock in Fairbanks in 1974-75 were an indication of what wolves are capable of. If people in Fairbanks had not had access to firearms and modern steel traps and people had been living in a more rural setting, it is not hard to imagine how much more serious the problem could have become.

Since 1990, there have been four documented cases of provoked aggressive attacks by wolves on helicopters during darting operations in Alaska. In addition, there have been many other unprovoked attacks on humans in North America, including two fatal attacks, since 2000. One of the fatal attacks was in Saskatchewan in 2005 and the other was in Alaska in 2010. The apparent increasing level of aggression by wolves in North America probably results from an increase in wolf numbers and their expanding range, but the less aggressive attitude of many people towards wolves is also a factor. Also, with digital technology, old newspaper articles that had escaped notice previously suggest there have been as many as a dozen fatal wolf attacks in North America, mostly during the late 1800s and early 1900s. These include two recorded fatal attacks by rabid wolves in northwest Alaska during the 1940s. Many of the reported nonfatal attacks could easily have been fatal if circumstances had been a little different.

The first documented attack by a wolf on a helicopter in Alaska occurred during the 1990s. Tim Osborne was darting wolves near Galena and was pursuing a large black male wolf in a Bell 206 (Jet Ranger). The pilot hovered the helicopter across the trail in front of the wolf that was running toward tall spruce trees. Rather than veering around the helicopter or running away from it, the wolf charged and leaped up with snapping jaws and came within two feet of Tim who was sitting in the back seat with the door off and his feet on the cargo rack.

I witnessed an attack by a wolf on a helicopter one day in February during the late 1990s and it was quite a surprise to me. I was flying the state Bellanca Scout as a spotter during the "nonlethal" wolf control program. I tracked down a new pair of wolves in the Seventymile drainage southwest of the village of Eagle in east-central Alaska. I circled while waiting for the Robinson R-22 helicopter to arrive. The biologists running the program wanted to radio-collar the female and then watch the pair for a few days to see if there were other wolves in the pack. As the helicopter came in to dart the female, it flew low over the male because the female was running in the lead. As the helicopter flew over, the male leaped up and tried to grab it. I yelled over the radio, "Hey, did you guys see that? The male just tried to bring you down." They hadn't seen that because they were focused on darting the female. They probably thought I was exaggerating. They successfully darted the female and then backed off while I circled with the wolves in sight, waiting for the female to go down. She went down as expected after the normal five to ten minutes. What was not expected was that the male stayed with her. Usually, the other wolves in a pack will head for the nearest thick cover or high mountains as soon as the helicopter shows up. The R-22 crew came in and landed about 150 feet from the wolves. After just a few seconds, the male charged the helicopter. The door was off on the left side and there was nothing protecting the darter. Fortunately, Larry Larrivee, the pilot, was watching the male closely and had not reduced power. Just before the wolf arrived at the helicopter, he lifted off again and the wolf leaped for the helicopter a second time. Larry then tried to herd the male away but he kept returning to the female. Finally, they darted the male so they could collar the female.

After that, there was one other case of a male wolf attacking the darting helicopter in a different pack northwest of Tok. Then, in the early 2000s a wolf leaped into the air at a Robinson R-44 helicopter flown by pilot Troy Cambier while he was darting wolves in Denali National Park. This time, the wolf actually grabbed hold of the right skid and held on for a few seconds. I photographed the skid of the helicopter after its return to Fairbanks. The wolf's teeth made large scratches along it. If it had been a small two-place R-22, instead of the larger R-44, a hundred plus pound wolf unexpectedly hanging on the skid might have caused a crash.

I was serving as Deputy Commissioner of ADF&G in March 2010 when the first contemporary fatal wolf attack occurred in Alaska and made international news. A pack of wolves killed and partially ate a young woman near Chignik Lake on the Alaska Peninsula. I arranged for two experienced trappers (Danny Grangaard and Chuck McMahan) to go to Chignik Lake and try to shoot or trap the offending wolves. They were eventually successful after about ten days of trying. DNA evidence confirmed they had found some of the wolves responsible for the attack.

The situation in Chignik Lake went a long way to explain why the unexpected wolf attack occurred there. People in Chignik Lake had become accustomed to having wolves around and no one in the village trapped anymore. There were two packs of wolves that were frequently seen in the vicinity of the village. People no longer viewed wolves as a valuable furbearer, but more as a commonly seen part of the local fauna, like bears, or eagles. Even though the wolf hunting season was open all winter and many people in the village were hunters and hunted moose and caribou for food, people no longer hunted wolves. It was a rather surprising discovery for me. In most villages in other parts of Alaska, there is usually someone who still traps, or certainly, a few people who are willing to handle their own wildlife problems without having to call on government employees for help. People had apparently become rather blasé about the presence of the wolves around town. The two trappers I sent out to Chignik Lake did find two local men who were willing to learn how to trap wolves in case they had problems in the future. They also found that, although people had been tolerating the presence of wolves and the wolves were likely habituated to the presence of humans, there was no evidence wolves had been fed, or were stealing dog food or garbage. There must have been some advantage to them in hanging around the village, but whatever it was, it wasn't obvious.

It appeared the unfortunate young woman at Chignik Lake had been jogging and surprised a pack of wolves that were lingering around a road intersection about two miles from the village. She had then tried to run away from the wolves, probably triggering a predatory chase and attack. There had been fresh snow, so it was possible to piece the story together from tracks, but all of the exact details will never be known for sure. Running away from any threatening wild animal, especially large predators, is never a good idea unless you are sure you can beat your pursuer to safety. Most often, if you turn and run, you will either trigger a predatory chase or you will trip and fall, or both. A person standing up on two feet has a much greater chance of facing down an attack, or dodging out of the way of a charge, than a person lying on the ground. Biologists with ADF&G wrote a very detailed report about this case, and it is available on the ADF&G website.

After the Chignik Lake incident came to light, I began thinking about a similar situation that Audrey and I had seen in Canada while we were doing wolverine surveys. We were on a long transect that passed over the village of English River in southwestern Ontario in March 2004. We flew right over the village landfill and I glanced down to see what was going on. I did a double take and said to Audrey, "Did you see that?" I looked around and she was intently looking too. I circled up higher and we watched for a while. In addition to the usual cloud of ravens and whisps of smoke from burning trash, there was a pack of 12, mostly black, wolves feeding at the dump. Two men were standing next to a pickup truck nearby, calmly smoking and watching the wolves from about 50 feet away. It was an illustration of how much times have changed in northern Canada. Just twenty years before, people would have viewed wolves as a valuable furbearer and any wolves that started hanging around the dump would have ended up on a stretching board. According to older First Nations people and Bush pilots we talked to in Manitoba and Ontario, the economy in rural northern Canada was largely based on trapping and fishing until around 1980, when it changed rather abruptly to a mostly welfare and services-based economy. The kind of habituation we saw with the wolves at the English River dump is likely going on all over northern Canada, and apparently also in some places in Alaska. It is quite clear now that wolves should not be taken for granted, especially habituated wolves. They are not as likely to attack or kill people as bears, but in the right circumstances, wolves can be dangerous.

Followed by Wolves

In the 1990s, when I was trapping wolves on the Tanana Flats near

Wolves

Blair Lakes, I had my own rather frightening experience with a pack of wolves. If I had known what I know now about wolves, I would have been even more frightened. In those years, I had been trapping wolves by using my Super Cub to fly around and look for kills. Wolf pelts were worth about $300 average, and it was an exciting way to get exercise and a bit of sunlight and to see all the things there are to see in Interior Alaska in the winter time.

I had just found a fresh kill, but it was late on a Sunday in January. Because I had to work the next day, I decided to set the kill immediately, rather than wait and come back with more daylight. The closest I could land was about a mile and a half away on the south side of a lake. It was about -20F when I landed, so I put on the engine cover before I grabbed my snowshoes and my pack with two wolf traps and a dozen snares in a bag with some clean gloves. I headed for the kill as fast as I could but I had to break trail in about 24 inches of snow and I was sinking about 12 inches with each step. It took me about 45 minutes to get to the kill, including stopping to cut down a 4-inch diameter green birch to make two drags for my traps.

When I got within about a quarter mile of the kill, I ran into the first set of fresh wolf tracks. At the kill site, there were fresh wolf tracks everywhere but the moose was mostly eaten and I hadn't seen or heard any wolves. I suspected the wolves had eaten their fill and gone on their way and they might not be back for a week or so. That would be a good thing, because I had learned that it was best to let a set "age" and get some hoar rost or light snow on the trails, trap locations, and snares or the wolves would detect them more easily. As I approached the kill and opened my pack, I realized I had forgotten my trapping revolver, a Ruger Single Six .22 Long Rifle that had been a gift from my former boss, Jim Davis. It was a great little revolver I usually carried in my pack or on my belt, but I had been in a hurry and left it lying on the floor in the back of the Cub. I wasn't too concerned about not having it, just a little annoyed at myself for being forgetful.

I first set a couple of Manning No. 9 traps (now called Alaska No. 9) in the open, on wolf trails about 10 feet away from the kill. That was

Tooth marks of a wolf on the skid of a helicopter. Between 1990 and 2015, there were four documented cases where wolves attacked helicopters during darting operations.

closer than I normally liked to set, but I had the pan tension at about 15 pounds to avoid catching foxes or ravens. Setting the traps took a while, because I was trying to be careful and not make too much of a mess. I then circled the kill and set ten modified No. 3 Thompson snares (with No. 9 wire attached) on all the wolf trails that came near or through any brush within 50-100 yards from the kill. I also saved a couple of snares and left them on my snowshoes to set on my snowshoe trail on the way back. I left my snowshoes about 150 yards from the kill to avoid making too much of a disturbance in the snow and thus alerting the wolves to my presence. Wolves will sometimes shy away from human tracks in the snow, so the more you can make your tracks look like moose tracks, the better. Once the wolves start getting suspicious, they spend more time sniffing around and will sometimes clear out and never come back. You can probably never completely eliminate human scent, but it seems to improve trapping success to be as inconspicuous as possible.

I was sinking most of the way to ground as I walked around without snowshoes, and it was slow going. It took much longer to make the set than I planned, and by the time I was done, with my pack and snowshoes back on, it was getting quite dark. I would rather have flown home with some daylight, but it is usually light enough to fly at night in the winter in Interior Alaska unless it is snowing. That is especially true on the Tanana Flats south of Fairbanks, because the lights of town provide a visual reference and with a high overcast, they bounce off the clouds above and the snow below.

My snowshoe trail had not quite had enough time to set up, so the trip back to the parked plane was not as fast as it would have been on a hard trail, but I thought I was making pretty good time. I wasn't in a particular hurry anymore, because it wasn't going to get any darker, so I stopped to snare up my snowshoe trail. Just as I started off again, I heard the first wolf howl. It was behind me and to the south of my trail, but quite loud. I didn't think too much about it, except that I had been thinking the wolves had left the area. Obviously, they were still around, so it might be worth checking my set the next day if I could get off work, rather than waiting for the next weekend. I'd heard lots of wolves howling while running traps and hunting in Alaska, so I wasn't particularly alarmed. I even thought maybe I might catch the wolf in the snare I just set. However, about five minutes later, I heard another howl. It was a lot louder and to the north of my trail. Either the same wolf was following me and crossed the trail behind me, or another wolf was coming in from a different direction. With the faint glow of the lights from Fairbanks and the white snow background, I should have been able to see a wolf if it had been moving in the open birch forest within a couple of hundred feet or more.

I didn't want to spend too much time looking because my mind was already becoming unsettled and I wanted to get back to the plane. After a few minutes more of fast shuffling on my snowshoes, my mind really started working. What if there were two wolves and they were both following me on purpose? I was trying to talk myself out of being alarmed, but I kept coming back to same thought, "I know wolves don't eat people, but if they were going to eat someone, this might be just the kind of situation when it would "happen." At that point, I really regretted leaving my .22 revolver behind. At least I'd be able to make noise with it and a muzzle flash to scare them if they got too close. By the time I reached the plane, I had been snowshoeing as fast as I could go, without running, for about 15 minutes and I was dripping with sweat, despite the cold. I was sure the wolves were following me quite closely and there were at least three of them. They howled several more times, probably just out of alarm at having a human near their kill, and maybe also to keep track of each other, but it was unnerving because I was alone and it was dark. I was very relieved to get to the plane and I resolved to never leave my trapping revolver behind again.

Chapter 6

Trapping

T rapping was a big part of my life from the early 1970s until the late 1990s. Since then, my interest in it has waned, partly because I no longer enjoy extreme cold weather and partly because fur prices have declined to all-time low levels. I expect I will always be interested in trapping, it's in my blood. I just won't do it as much as I used to. I was so excited about trapping in the 1970s and 1980s that I couldn't imagine my life without it. I was never a full-time trapper, except when I was on seasonal leave from ADF&G for two or three months a year during the late 1970s and 1980s. I thought about trapping all the time in winter and read as much as I could about it. It was such an interesting and educational challenge that I used to lie awake at night thinking about how animals would react to my latest sets.

I learned a great deal about animals from trapping, especially running a trapline on the Minto Flats about 40 miles west of Fairbanks from 1977 to about 1995. There is no other way to learn some things about animals without being a trapper, and I always believed the biologists I worked with at ADF&G and federal agencies who trapped had an edge in practical knowledge over those who didn't. Those very few biologists I worked with who neither hunted nor trapped were at significant disadvantage in both biological and practical knowledge. I believe that is even more true today, especially now that an even higher proportion of professors and students in the field of wildlife management and conservation are from urban or suburban areas. Besides learning a lot about animals and about operating aircraft, snowmachines, and other machinery in severe cold, I also had some very exciting and fun times.

First Traplines

Pelts of wolverines, wolves, red foxes, and beaver taken during my seasonal leave from ADF&G in 1988. I tried to make as much money trapping during my seasonal leave as I would have if I had been working. I often did better, even counting the expenses for the airplane.

When I arrived in Alaska in 1972, I had never trapped before, except for protecting quail that I raised in New York from marauding skunks. Snowshoe hares were at the peak of their 11-year cycle over a large part of Interior Alaska. I first started seeing lots of hares in the western Yukon on my drive north in my Volkswagen bus. By the time I got to Fairbanks, I had seen hundreds and hundreds of dead hares along the highway. In one stretch between Delta and Fairbanks there was a dead hare every few hundred yards. On the University of Alaska Fairbanks campus, there was a stand of young one- or two-inch aspens between the upper dorms and the University Observatory and all of them were girdled by hares. The trees survived but you can still see the scars on the few raining trees there from the hare population high of the early 1970s.

Lynx were also numerous and prices had begun to climb. People were talking about $300 lynx. To someone with no job, no income, and a total of $1,200 in a savings account, a $300 lynx was a real incentive to learn how to trap. I got together with two fellow students who didn't know how to trap either, and we set out our first 'line. It was on Alder Creek, off the old Fairbanks-Nenana Highway (now the Old Nenana Highway). We ran the 'line on weekends and picked up about five lynx and a couple of foxes that first winter. It wasn't much of a catch for three trappers but the only expenses we had were for a few traps and gas for my Volkswagen.

After the first winter, we decided to go bigger and trap Spinach Creek off the Murphy Dome Road. The road had just been built and paved to the bottom of the climb to the Murphy Dome radar site. Until the road was completed in the early 1970s, Murphy Dome was considered a "remote" site for pay purposes and the access was over a narrow, remote pioneer road along the ridge west from Cleary Summit. The site was still manned by a contingent of 200 people and a full-bird Colonel named Caphammer. He would give us grief about parking anywhere near the site, supposedly because it was a restricted area. After about the third time of him giving us grief about parking, we nicknamed him "Colonel Hammerhead," but we took the hint and moved the start of our trapline east to where the old and the new roads met. We parked one car at the Spinach Creek Bridge and one car at the road junction on top so we could walk the 'line downhill between the two cars. During my second winter trapping (1973-74), the hares and lynx populations were still high and lynx prices were even higher. Our catch was not greatly improved over the Alder Creek 'line but there was more variety. We picked up a couple more foxes and two or three marten. I remember we got over $400 for one of the lynx. That was equivalent to a over a month's salary with our teaching and research assistantships at the university. The bit of extra money I was making and the excitement and anticipation of catching valuable lynx, fox, and marten really gave me the trapping "bug."

Finding Frank Glaser's Trapline

Trapping

My next adventure with trapping in Alaska was quite unexpected. During the summers of 1974 and 1975, I was fully focused on completing my field work on grizzly bears in the proposed northern extensions to Mt. McKinley National Park. The work involved hiking around with pack dogs north of the park looking for grizzly bear sign, measuring tracks, looking at scats, and otherwise trying to determine roughly how many bears might be using the area within about 15 miles of the existing park boundary. I also joined the Civil Air Patrol so I could occasionally use their aircraft on my project. The cost to rent the CAP Cub was $15.00/hour, less than half of what I would have to pay to charter a Cub.

Audrey and I spent quite a bit of time in the Kantishna Hills during those two years. The area had a rich history of mining and prospecting, but was largely free of people by then. There was no lack of old remains of cabins, shovels, picks, wheel barrows, buckboard wagons, and other abandoned mining artifacts. At one old cabin in the hills above the Stampede Mine, I found a rusty old model 1895 Winchester rifle stuck in the corner of a collapsing cabin. I tried to resurrect the rifle but it was far too rusty to work.

As part of my research into the history of the area, I read Charles Sheldon's book *The Wilderness of Denali*. The book contained a wealth of good information about the history of the people and wildlife in the Kantishna Hills. Besides looking for sign of the abundant grizzly bears, I was also interested in finding out if any Dall sheep had returned to Kantishna Hills after they were eliminated by market hunters in the early 1900s. It has now been over 100 years since sheep lived there and they have still not returned.

Although the Kantishna Hills were mostly known for their history of gold mining, trappers had also been active there as they had been in virtually all other areas of Alaska. We found a few old traps hanging here and there but didn't think much about them. Then, in July 1975, we decided to hike down the west side of the Savage River and climb up into the hills north of the Stampede Road, an area locally called the "Outer Outer Range" by some. We had not hiked the area during 1974 and were looking forward to exploring the new area. Just before starting the climb, I found a Prince Albert tobacco can attached to a mining claim stake. In the can was the claim paperwork that had been filed in Fairbanks and dated in the early 1900s. A pretty neat find. We left it as we had found it.

After climbing to the top of the ridge on the west side of the Savage River, we headed west. The ridge was easy walking, mostly lichen-covered gravel with patches of *Dryas* (a low-growing tundra plant) and sparse grass and sedge. After walking a hundred yards or so along the ridge, we noticed a prominent grass tussock, much larger, and different-looking than any of the other clumps of grass. Knowing animals will often scent mark at places like that, we went over to look at it. It was obviously a wolf and fox scent post. There was one old wolf scat and several red fox scats of different ages. We also found an old trap, and it was still set. I picked it up. It was wired to a 10- or 12-inch spike that easily came out of the gravel. It was a 21½ single long-spring Newhouse with cast jaws. I recognized it as a fairly old trap, and I had a couple somewhat like it but larger. I had been scrounging and bying any old traps I could find around Fairbanks over the previous couple of years. I tested the springs of my new find and they seemed a little weak from having been set for many years, but I thought they would still be strong enough to hold a fox or marten, so I put the trap in my pack thinking it would come in handy on our trapline.

We continued on along the ridge and about a quarter mile further saw another big clump of strange-looking grass. It was similar to the first one, with several fox scats and another trap (this one sprung) next to it. It was another 21½ Newhouse. The springs on it were stronger. Another trapping bonus, so into the pack it went and we continued on. This happened several more times, and by the time we dropped off the ridge we found seven traps, some still set, all wired with 10- or 12-inch spikes. I didn't think much more about the traps, but I used most of them on my trapline at Murphy Dome the next winter and then for a few years at Minto. A couple of them had weak enough springs that I retired them and threw them in a box of old junk that I had in my garage.

Trapping

Many years later, I was reading one of Jim Rearden's relatively new books, *Alaska's Wolf Man*, published in 1998. It was about Frank Glaser, a truly amazing outdoorsman and hunter/trapper who was active in Alaska from about 1915 until 1955 as a market hunter, lodge manager at Black Rapids, trapper, and wolf hunter in the Fortymile Country and the Seward Peninsula. I was thoroughly enjoying the book as my bedtime reading. In the 1920s, Glaser made lots of money fox trapping and he once received $800 for a single cross fox and about the same for a single silver fox. Eight hundred dollars was about the annual wage a laborer could expect while working on the gold mines around Fairbanks at the time. Glaser had made so much money trapping foxes he kept a room year-round at the Nordale Hotel in Fairbanks. The Nordale burned down the year before I came to Fairbanks but I had seen the remains of it and knew it had been the most prominent hotel in town for many years.

One evening, as I continued reading about Glaser's exploits, I got to the part about his last trapline for foxes at Savage River. Fortunately, Glaser kept a journal which Jim Rearden used to write the book, and Rearden included lots of detail, including how Glaser made his fox sets and what types of traps he used. He also mentioned that Glaser dug up tussocks in the valley bottoms which he carried up and transplanted to ridges. He wired the traps to 10- or 12-inch spikes to secure them in the frozen ground. When he mentioned transplanting the tussocks, the light bulb went on and I exclaimed to Audrey, who was half asleep, "Hey, you remember those traps we found while we were hiking around the Savage River in 1975? That was Frank Glaser's old trapline and those were his traps." She barely remembered, but I sure did. The next morning, I went to the garage and dug through my box of old, retired traps. I found three still wired to the 10- or 12-inch spikes and saw they were 2 1/2 Newhouse traps, exactly the traps Reardon described. Glaser abandoned the Savage River 'line in 1930 in mid-season, after fur prices crashed with the Great Depression. He walked away, with all his traps still set, and never returned. In recent years, National Park Service historians and archaeologists investigated Glaser's old cabin along the Savage River.

One of about six number 21½ Newhouse traps that I found in 1975. The traps had belonged to Frank Glaser (see Alaska's Wolf Man *by Jim Rearden). The traps were abandoned in 1929 when the fur market crashed during the Great Depression.*

I subsequently donated two of Frank's old traps to the Alaska Trappers Association auction as fund-raising items at their annual Trappers Fling. The second time I donated one of the traps, Jim Reardon also attended the Fling and we auctioned off one of the traps along with a signed copy of *Alaska's Wolf Man*. I still have two of the traps at home.

Trapping at Minto

My main trapping experience in Alaska has been at Minto Lakes west of Fairbanks. My first boss at ADF&G, Jim Davis, had been trapping there for two years when his partner moved to Anchorage. He asked if I wanted to trap with him. I was all in. The trapline had been a traditional 'line trapped by Chief Peter John in his younger years, before Minto village had been moved in 1968 because of flooding. After the village moved, Peter John's son trapped there briefly before tragically dying of alcohol poisoning. After that, Al Wright trapped beaver there on occasion but gave Jim and his former partner permission to trap there. At that time, Ken Fanning trapped on the east edge of the flats and along Goldstream to the north, a 'line that Jim Masek later took over.

During the years I trapped at Minto (1977-95), we rarely saw snowmachine tracks that were not made by us and we didn't have any conflicts with other trappers. Once we found a group of older men from Minto who were trapping beavers to make some money to go to the Fur Rendezvous in Anchorage. They told us about some of the old portage trails and, in exchange, I brought them some spark plugs which they needed from Fairbanks.

Since we were the only ones using our trail, we were able to set trail sets for wolves right in the trail. However, on one occasion I encountered a dog musher who was out exploring. He found my trail at the southwest end of Big Minto Lake and started running on the trail when his lead dog stepped in a Manning No. 9 (a large wolf trap). By sheer luck, I came along just as it happened. The musher turned out to be a colleague I had worked with in northwest Alaska doing vegetation mapping a couple of years before. We had no trouble releasing the dog and the musher went on his way across Minto Flats.

When I started trapping with Jim on weekends at Minto, it was mostly for red fox and mink in winter, and then beavers and a few muskrats in the spring. Otters were common but difficult to trap and we seldom set specifically for them. We made general sets at beaver houses for lynx and anything else that might come by and we caught two or three otters per year at those. There were very few moose and no wolves on the eastern part of the flats in the late 1970s and early 1980s. The winters of 1970-71 and 1971-72 had been very severe. The severe winters and over-hunting of cow moose in the early 1970s caused a moose decline. The few remaining moose stayed in the hills to the east of Minto in winter. Jim and his partner had just caught the end of the lynx cycle in 1975, but by the time I started trapping there in 1977 lynx were essentially gone. It was several more years before we caught a single lynx there. Al Wright told Jim that mink and marten would be the main furbearers, which surprised us, because we didn't catch a marten during the first eight years we trapped there.

Trapping was an important part of my education about wildlife in Alaska. For almost 20 years, Jim Davis, Rod Boertje, and I ran a trapline on the Minto Flats west of Fairbanks.

Minto is a complex and productive system of lakes and sloughs with constantly changing water levels, methane upwellings, and slowly moving currents. In summer, depending on water levels in the Tanana River, water can either flow from the Tanana into the lake system, backing up the clearwater rivers coming in from the north, or flow out of the lake system into the Tanana. During winter, a whole separate world exists under the ice, a world dominated by otters, mink, beaver, ermine, mice, blackfish, wintering pike, and whitefish. From the surface one gets only a few tantalizing glimpses of what is happening in that underworld.

Mink were the bread and butter of Minto trapping. We had two main methods of catching them. We made plywood boxes, open on one end with a small cutout that would hold a #110 or #120 Conibear (body-gripping kill trap). We used fermented duck remains for bait. These we placed along the banks of Goldstream Creek and the other sloughs south and west of Big Minto. Our other main way of catching mink was to find natural holes where they go in and out of beaver houses. Most carnivores will check out beaver houses, so they are excellent places to set traps. Finding a mink hole in a beaver house almost always resulted in a catch, and in some of those holes we caught five or six mink in the course of a season. There are occasionally nice, big male mink at Minto, but nothing like the huge, well-fed mink from the Yukon Delta. Prices of wild mink were very good in the mid-1980s. A mink rancher in Washington recently told me that during those years some of the ranchers would take their domestically-produced pelts and deliberately mishandle them and stretch them on amateur-looking stretching boards to make them look like wild-caught mink. That will probably never happen again. Mink ranchers worldwide have made tremendous strides in developing large, high-quality mink in huge numbers. Some of the genetic stock for those big, ranch mink came from Southeast Alaska and the Yukon Delta. High-quality ranched mink, produced in huge quantities in countries like Denmark and China, have probably done more than anything else to keep wild fur prices low in recent years. The exception being a few special purpose furs that have occasionally still been quite valuable, like bobcat, marten, and coyotes.

Running the same trails over a period of many years makes a person realize how much things change in the Alaskan wilderness over relatively short periods. Very little stays the same. Mink numbers seemed similar over the 18 years we trapped at Minto, but they were about the only thing that did. Fox numbers changed dramatically over relatively short periods and so did the color of the foxes. In some years, reds were most prevalent but in other years cross foxes were far more abundant than reds. Silver foxes were always rare and I only remember catching one, which I kept it for myself and did not sell. It was a small female but had beautiful fur. I still have it in my house today.

In the mid-1980s, we finally started seeing some moose sign on the trapline. Moose can be a problem on a trapline when they stomp all over trail sets and potentially get caught in fox or wolf snares, etc. We were very careful in setting snares for wolves and we never mistakenly killed a moose in a trap or a snare at Minto. We used leaning poles to divert moose around wolf snares and also used break-away devices as soon as they became available, so if a moose did get caught in a wolf snare it would be able to free itself by pulling harder than a wolf could pull. Once moose started wintering on the trapline, wolves were not far behind. From 1985 to 1995, wolves were also present and we spent a lot of time trying to catch them.

Another major change in wildlife abundance at Minto was an influx of marten that started in the late 1980s. I was amazed to catch the first one in a mink box around 1988. From then on, they became more regular, and during the last five years we trapped, we caught as many marten in the mink boxes as we did mink. In our best years we caught about 30 mink and 30 marten. Muskrats were up and down, but just when we hoped they'd start getting really abundant, they'd crash again. Apparently, the last period of real abundance for muskrats at Minto was in the 1950s. There has been much speculation about why muskrats have never again become abundant at Minto but it is a big mystery. Muskrats have continued to cycle, with periods of abundance and scarcity on the Yukon Flats and around Northway, but not at Minto.

Lynx never did become abundant while we trapped at Minto. The hare cycle of the early 1980s was virtually a complete bust and the early-mid 1990s cycle was not much better. It was quite disappointing because the lynx prices remained consistently high, sometimes up to $800 for large males with spotted bellies.

The final change in the mid-1990s was the appearance of coyotes. Coyotes have occurred in Interior Alaska for at least a century, but they were always restricted to a few areas of the Interior, like Delta Junction, the Delta River, the Healy area, the Tanana River, and along the Wood River. My theory was that they could only exist in areas that are windblown, because in soft snow, wolves can easily catch them. I don't know why I never expected to see coyotes at Minto, because it can be very windblown, especially in late winter. We could have missed their tracks because they can be nearly impossible to tell from fox tracks, but I did not catch my first one until 1995 when I was trapping with my son Toby.

Trapping

There were some particularly exciting things that happened on our trapline at Minto, some of which were pleasant surprises, some that were unpleasant, and some that were just plain surprises. We had constant problems with overflow and thin ice. In flat country, overflow happens when the weight of new snowfalls causes the ice to sink a bit. The resulting hydraulic pressure forces water up on top of the ice, under the snow, where it stays liquid because of the insulating snow cover. It seems hard to believe that water can remain liquid while sitting on top of the ice with the temperature well below zero.

Overflow can sometimes be very difficult to see. We used low-powered Ski Doo Elan snowmachines that had rounded half-inch paddles. They couldn't deal with overflow more than about six inches deep. If we found serious overflow, we had to find a way around it. Thin ice was as much of a problem, but more dangerous and also difficult to see. One day Jim and I were walking across our base camp lake side-by-side going to check a beaver set and he went straight down through the ice right next to me. I just heard, "Help!" and whipped my head around, and there he was up to his chest in a hole in the ice out in the middle of the lake. Another time he was following behind me on his Elan and then he wasn't. I turned around and went back down the trail and there he was with the skis of the machine sticking straight up and the back end of the machine submerged. He had been running right behind me in the same trail. I probably cracked the ice and he was a bit heavier than I was.

One year, we had so much trouble with thin ice I decided to wear a life jacket while riding my Elan. The first day I tried doing that I rode around all day uneventfully and then decided to stop and take a short break at a beaver house. I took off my life jacket, laid it on the seat of the snowmachine and started pulling out my tea thermos when I noticed a faint otter track on the back side of the beaver house. I climbed the beaver house to take a closer look and took one step too many. Without warning the whole snow drift on the back side of the beaver lodge collapsed into a large area of hidden open water. Adrenaline takes over in situations like that and I wasn't even aware of how, but I vaulted and rolled out of the hole and was standing, dripping wet, next to my Elan. It was about -10F and I didn't feel cold, so I just kept going, checking the rest of my traps on the 'line back towards our wall tent. It took me about an hour to get back, stopping to check every set. When I got off the machine next to the tent, I still wasn't cold but I was like a knight in shining armor. My coveralls were coated with ice, except around my knees and elbows where movement had kept those joints free. I could relate to the Tin Man in Wizard of Oz. I fired up the wood stove and then tried to get out of my frozen coveralls. It took a while for the zippers to thaw.

One other aspect of the thin ice on Minto Flats is that it can create natural moose traps. Rotten Slough is particularly bad, hence the name. Once moose started using the flats in winter, one to three moose would get trapped every year. If a moose falls through the ice and doesn't get out right away, all the struggling and splashing makes it impossible for the moose to escape because sloping ice builds up in a ring around the hole. We did not set traps close to the drowned moose because it was illegal at the time to use moose meat for trap bait.

Once, we were at our base camp just about ready to start checking the 'line, when a blue and white Fish and Wildlife Protection Super Cub flew over, circled, and landed. The officer, who we both knew but whose name I will not mention, had received a report about someone on Minto Flats setting traps around dead moose. We put two and two together and carefully explained the situation with the thin ice. He seemed satisfied but we suspected he would want to go and check the situation out for himself, "trust but verify!" As he walked out of our camp, I emphasized to him the reason the moose fall through and get trapped is because the ice is THIN, and cautioned him not to taxi too close to any moose carcasses in the sloughs. He didn't listen well, apparently, because he put one ski through the thin ice next to a drowned moose. The result was a bent prop and damaged a wing tip. The troopers decided to rescue the Cub with a helicopter, but it started swinging too much on the way to Nenana and the helicopter pilot jettisoned the load. That was the end of one very expensive state Super Cub.

We also had several adventures with wolves, but the two I remember best were catching my first wolf, and one that got away. Jim had a few

#114 Newhouse traps (large traps originally designed for trapping cougars) and one #4½ Newhouse and I had an odd assortment of big traps. One day, I saw where a wolf came out of the willows, stepped on a small shelf midway down the bank of Goldstream, and then trotted down the creek. I made a set with one of Jim's #114s on the shelf, hoping the wolf would do that again. It was what I called a "hope" set. Not likely to work, but you could always hope. There was 10 feet of chain on the trap and a two-prong grapple drag. The area was surrounded by thick willows so I figured there was no way a trapped wolf would get the chain and drag very far.

When I came by a week later, the "hope" set was gone and there were wolf tracks and drag marks leading away down the slough. The wolf had quickly headed up the bank into the thick willows. At first, it was easy to follow the sign. There were areas where lots of willows were chewed down, but the wolf had always gotten the drag loose and kept going. I followed the trail out of the willows onto windblown Wooden Canoe Lake. Luckily, the trap and drag left occasional scratch marks on the icy surface and by going very slowly and carefully, I finally found the wolf over a mile away with the drag hooked to a single old stump, frozen in the ice. It was a large, light gray, old female. I didn't really notice at first, but it had a hair condition called *follicular dysplasia*, which leaves the top hair looking normal but the sides of the wolf woolly and practically devoid of guard hairs, sometimes referred to by trappers as a "Mohawk" wolf. It actually looked pretty good to me, and it was my first wolf, so I was very proud of it and I still have the tanned pelt hanging in my living room.

The wolf that got away was one we caught in a trail set made with the #4½ Newhouse, a very large trap that is not ideal for trail sets, unless some snow falls to cover the set well. One of the odd things about the trap was they originally came with just three feet of chain and a short, poorly designed grapple drag. We had not added more chain or a better drag but wired it to a five-foot-long piece of four-inch diameter green birch. The wolf had been caught out in the open in a trail set made right in the snowmachine trail. It had then taken the trap and drag straight into the nearby willows where it got hung up. It hadn't stayed there very long before getting out of the first patch of willows. Rod Boertje was with me that day and we waded through the snow on foot into the next patch of willows, expecting to find it there. It had hung up again but then broken the wire holding the green birch log to the chain and taken off across big Minto Lake. We tried following it with our snowmobiles but it was hopeless. The lake surface was so hard that even with the big trap and remaining chain and drag it wasn't leaving a scratch. We went back to my Piper Cub and took off and flew around the edge of Big Minto. On the far east side of the lake, we found where the wolf left the hard ice and got back into soft snow where it was once again leaving tracks. We landed and continued the pursuit on snowshoes. At that point I thought the chance of finding the wolf was less than fifty-fifty, but it had Jim's trap that was worth about $100 at the time. We followed the wolf toward the Dunbar Trail for about a mile and it occasionally hung up, but not for long. We were at the point of giving up when I saw the trap lying in the trail ahead of us. The drag hung up on a one-inch spruce tree and it had one toe in it! One missing toe would not have slowed the wolf down a bit, but I certainly was impressed by the strength of a wolf toe!

From about 1985 on, there was at least one pack of wolves running around our trapline at Minto and we had to be prepared for them even when they might be absent for several weeks. One problem was that we were setting trail sets for foxes in our snowmobile trails and then the wolves would come by unexpectedly and get caught in a fox trap. It wasn't a problem for the wolves; they would just break the trap and get away, but it was frustrating for us. We finally welded up all the weak points of the fox traps so at least they had a chance of holding a wolf. It was a lot work and it may have resulted in one more wolf being caught, but we really never overcame the problem entirely. We did find though, that if we trapped out a pack and several weeks or even a few months went by when wolves were absent, the next pack to show up would use all of the same trails the previous pack had used. So even if there weren't any wolves around, we made sure all the old favorite setting places had snares or traps in them.

Wolverines were the one animal we did not find on Minto Flats. It is odd because they occur virtually everywhere else in Interior

Alaska that I know of, except the Fairbanks bowl. Jim trapped one in 1976 and I landed and shot one about ten miles to the west of our trapline in 1985, but those were the only two wolverines I heard of on that part of the Flats from 1975 until 1995. Later, when ADF&G biologist Craig Gardner conducted a widespread wolverine survey in Interior Alaska north of the crest of the Alaska Range, Minto Flats was the only area where wolverines were found to be absent.

Marten Trapping at -55F

Besides running the trapline at Minto, when I had my two-month seasonal leave from ADF&G, I tried to make up for my missing two months of salary by trapping. In December 1979, a few months after I bought my first airplane, I decided to take advantage of the increasing fur prices and get some return on my investment in the airplane. I certainly needed money and so did my good friend and neighbor Ed Crain. There were rumors of marten prices approaching $50.

Ed was trying to buy some land in Fairbanks and was desperately short of cash. The plane had cost me $10,000—all the money I saved during my first seven years in Alaska. To make matters with the airplane even more pressing, after the first 60 hours of flying, the engine needed an overhaul, which set me back another $1,800 (about 2 month's salary at the time). I was so short of cash I even tried selling my Winchester Model 94 .30-30 to Jim Davis. He wouldn't buy it, but he loaned me $150 instead, with the understanding I'd pay it back when the fur check arrived from Seattle Fur Exchange.

The winter of 1979-80 started out warmer than normal in Interior Alaska, with a good freeze-up and below normal snow in November, and temperatures pretty steady around +10F to -20F. While working for ADF&G on Western Arctic caribou during the previous two years, I was beginning to get familiar with northwestern Alaska and figured out there was some decent marten country between Bettles and the upper Kobuk that wasn't being trapped. Hoping to keep the logistics simple and costs down, Ed and I planned on setting up a comfortable wall tent not too far west of Bettles, parking the airplane for the duration, and running our 'lines on snowshoes and skis. I had most of the equipment we needed, including the wall tent and airtight stove, snowshoes, skis, a good sleeping bag, and a box of fermented duck carcasses for bait. I also had a few #110 Conibears, #1 Victor long-springs, and #1 Victor jump traps. Ed had a few traps also, and we borrowed some #0 Victor jump traps and some #120 Conibears from Jim. The #0 Victor jumps were muskrat traps (now a collector's item) and a little bit small for marten, but I figured they'd work on marten pole sets.

After a few days of running around getting the rest of the kit together, Ed and I were ready for the challenge. About the tenth of January we dropped three apple boxes full of food at Frontier Flying Service for delivery on the mail plane to Bettles and then started packing my 90 hp Piper Cub with everything else. It took quite a creative packing job to get everything aboard, including 100 traps (most packed into the wood stove), wall tent, stovepipe, two pairs of skis and ski boots, two pairs of snowshoes, scoop shovel, .30-30 rifle, backpacks, plastic sled, caribou hide sleeping pads, sleeping bags and the engine cover for the plane. Several items were tied on the wing struts, including the stovepipe, skis, snowshoes, and scoop shovel. The following morning, we gassed up my plane at Bachner's, and departed from Phillips Field. The weather was cloudy and calm, about 0F at altitude, and the two-hour flight to Bettles was uneventful. The bulky external load on the wing struts slowed us down by about five mph, so our cruise speed was only about 75 mph and it took us about two and a half hours to get to Bettles.

Instead of landing right at Bettles, we flew on and planned to do about an hour of recon, looking for marten tracks and evidence of other trappers. Right away, we ran into some spectacular marten sign along the lower Malamute Fork of the John River about 15 minutes out of Bettles. It was like nothing I had ever seen before or since. The area burned in the mid-1970s and apparently now had an abundance of rodents. Marten tracks were everywhere and there were even pathways that were so heavily used they could, at first glance, be mistaken for rabbit trails. The area of really abundant sign was probably no more than ten miles east to west and five miles north to south, but for our purposes that was plenty big enough. There was also a small lake just long enough to land on and it was surrounded by burned spruce trees and sheltered from the wind. At that point, there was no sense in continuing the recon. We also wanted to limit our fuel consumption and hoped to not have to buy fuel in Bettles. Inflation and a recent surge in gas prices had driven the cost of 80/87 octane avgas up from the long-term standard Bush price of $1.00/gallon to over $2.00/gallon (about $6.00/gallon in 2020 dollars). At that time, we were paying about $1.00/gallon in Fairbanks.

Rather than landing then and there in the middle of that abundance of marten, we decide to fly back to Bettles, talk to locals about whether anyone else was trapping along the Malamute Fork, and check on our boxes of food. In Bettles, we ran into to John Hanke who I knew trapped north of town. He said he didn't get that far west but he had heard a rumor that Steve Alleman, who lived on Timber Creek between Bettles and Crevice Creek, was planning to trap west of the John that year. It was already almost mid-January and neither Ed nor I thought it likely anyone was really going to trap where we had seen all the marten sign, but there was no place to land near Steve and Cathy's cabin, so rather than risk any trapline conflicts, we decided to head further west to Norutak Lake. We added one apple box of food to our load and arranged with Andy Greenblatt to bring the other two boxes the next day in his Citabria.

The weather deteriorated as the day went on. When we launched for Norutak, it was down to about three miles visibility with light snow and only two hours of daylight remaining. By the time we reached Norutak an hour later, the visibility was down to a mile and Ed was getting pretty claustrophobic. With the extra apple box in his lap, gear packed all around him, and the plastic sled tied overhead, he could hardly move or see out. All he could see out of the one side window was snow. We had also run into light rime icing just west of Bettles and I changed our heading several times to try to avoid the worst of it. Ed told me later he was convinced we were lost, which was not an unreasonable thought in those days, especially while flying in marginal weather and short daylight with a only a vague idea of

Trapping

the country and a sectional map and compass for guidance. As we approached Norutak Lake, I heard Ed yelling about something, but I couldn't hear what he was saying, so I just made a quick circle around the north end of the lake and landed. He had been trying to ask me if I knew where we were. He hadn't a clue we were already at the lake and he thought we must be badly lost. We were both glad to be on the ground and out of the icing and poor visibility.

I parked next to a stand of birch in an otherwise continuous forest of stunted black spruce. I wanted to camp in the birch because there would be more light, more chance of finding rabbits, and the green birch would make good, long-lasting firewood to keep the stove going at night. At the northeast corner of the lake, there was on old cabin and dog houses that belonged to Guy Moyer from Kobuk. He and an Eskimo partner headed out from Fairbanks to prospect for gold in the Brooks Range in the 1930s in a Stinson Reliant, but the pilot was new to the country and didn't like the weather, so he had turned around and started heading back to Fairbanks. Guy then persuaded the pilot to just drop them at Norutak Lake instead. They tried prospecting and trapping there for a few years, but eventually abandoned the place and mushed down to Kobuk, where Guy still ran the village store. Ed and I rented a cabin in Kobuk from Guy while we were trying to count the caribou crossing the river for the ADF&G in the fall of 1977. Guy was full of tales of the old days in Alaska and told us how he had agreed to marry his partner's wife Minnie in the event his partner died young. This in fact happened not long after they made the deal. Guy and Minnie spent the rest of their years in Kobuk. I would like to have heard her side of the story, but Minnie didn't speak much English. Guy mentioned the old cabin at Norutak Lake and that someone told him the roof had fallen in. The area around the old cabin was exposed and the old cabin would have been hard to heat even if we could have put a roof on it.

The snow at Norutak was about two feet deep, fairly shallow for the area and time of year, but perfect for trapping and camping. It was not so deep as to be a problem for the airplane, even with my small Landis 1500 skis. In short order, we put the plane to bed by digging down to the ice and blocking up the skis. The 90 hp Cub was a great trapping airplane because it only weighed 945 pounds on skis. With two people, it was an easy matter to lift the skis off the ice one at a time. In the 1970s before plastic bottoms, we put epoxy on the ski bottoms but frost accumulation and snow sticking was still a real problem. Once ski bottoms frosted over or the plane was left for more than a day in cold weather sitting on the snow, the plane had to be jacked up and the frost and snow removed by melting or scraping. Even with modern plastic ski bottoms, when skis are left in contact with the snow for more than a few days, frosted ski bottoms are still a problem.

We picked a spot for the tent about 30 yards into the trees and then shoveled out a place for the big airtight, sheet metal wood stove and built a spruce pole and snow sleeping bench in the back of the 8 x 10 tent area. We then set the tent up over the spot. Once the tent was up, we shoveled snow over the sod flaps and then piled up more snow against the walls for insulation. The addition of a white plastic tarp over the whole thing finished the job and helped insulate the roof a little. We were in no particular hurry because we figured the marten weren't going anywhere. We spent the next day getting in more firewood with the Swede saw and packing a runway near the plane so Andy would have a nice take-off spot when he brought in the remaining food. We were done with camp chores and getting our trapping gear ready, talking about how much money we were going to make and musing about the lack of game sign besides marten, when we heard Andy's Citabria approaching. At the time, Andy was an eager young pilot in his early twenties. He left home and moved up to the Brooks Range when he was 15 and he had just bought his first airplane at age 20. "Building hours" is a priority for any new pilot, especially if someone else was willing to pay for the fuel. Andy had our two boxes of food and some news about the weather getting colder. We weren't too concerned about the cold since we weren't planning to use the plane and had a nice warm tent with at least three weeks food.

That night we made a trapping plan. We were each going to run three 'lines of about ten miles, and each 'line would take a day to check. Once we had a good trail, we were confident that we could do 10 miles a day. I took the east and north side of the lake and Ed took the northwest and west. The area to the north of the lake had been closed to all hunting and trapping by President Jimmy Carter in December 1978 under the Antiquities Act, but we were prepared to ignore that because our 'lines would barely cross that very arbitrary boundary and nobody seemed to be taking those closures seriously. We planned to make the 'lines relatively straight without too many sharp turns so once we had them laid out with snowshoes we could switch to skis for faster traveling and less effort on the checks. We discussed whether to take two days to set out each 'line but decided it would be better to just push really hard the first three days and get all the 'lines out, then start checking and maybe improving each line based on the sign we saw. After that, it would be a simple matter to run each 'line on skis in an easy day and we might even have time for skinning any marten that weren't too frozen. It was an ambitious plan, but we were both in our late twenties, so the thought of having to take a day off to recuperate after breaking 30 miles of trail in three days never even crossed our minds. Our goal was to get 100 marten or an average of one marten per set and then head home by the end of January when we either ran out of food or ran out of marten to trap.

The next morning, we awoke to clear skies and sharply colder temperatures. The thermometer on the airplane read -30F. We both shrugged it off and headed out, in the dark, sinking in about 12 inches with each step on our big, military surplus wood and rawhide snowshoes. I'd run a marten line near Fairbanks for a few years and caught about 20 marten with pole sets. I had the pole set method down and planned on making one about every half mile or so. The fermented duck baits had some odor, even at these cold temperatures, and the wing attractors were daubed with Mapleine and glycerol and I had also put some on the end of the pole. I figured I could average a little over one mile per hour breaking trail and making sets and it would take about nine or ten hours to get back to the tent. We both left the tent at about 8:00 am and figured to be back about 5:00 pm. Although we were about 20 miles north of the Arctic Circle, with the clear skies there was more than two hours of semi-daylight before the sun came up at about 10:30 am, and another good two hours after the sun went down at about 2:00 pm. If things didn't work out for some reason, or it got too dark to find our way, we figured we could always turn around, head back on the broken trail and make good time back to the tent. I considered making my 'lines straight out and back, but I didn't like that idea because we needed to hit the territories of as many male marten as we could and the extra work of making a loop trail might result in a few more catches. Ed agreed and did the same with his 'lines.

During that first day of breaking trail in the extremely cold temperatures, I ran into an immediate problem. I needed to pace myself, mostly to avoid sweating even though I was dressed fairly lightly. After about four hours, when I took my lunch break and made a small fire, I guessed I had only gone about three miles. Some sweet, lukewarm tea from the Nalgene bottle I kept in my pack wrapped in my insulated overpants and parka perked me up and I picked up the pace after lunch. I was acclimating to the cold and getting used to the pace. I was also walking more efficiently on the snowshoes, and the terrain was a little flatter. Over-heating wasn't as much of a problem in the afternoon. After several hours it began to get dark enough that making sets was getting to be difficult, so I just concentrated on making a nice straight line heading back toward the tent. The darker it got, the less sure I was that I was even headed in the right direction. In the black spruce forest, I couldn't see any distinguishing landmarks. I was beginning to see some stars though and I had a compass with me so I wasn't too worried about getting lost. Even if I went a little wrong, I would eventually hit the lake, or my out-going trail if I was headed too far south. My main worry was heading too far north and missing the tent altogether, but there was a hill about half a mile north of the lake that would be hard to miss. As it turned out, my heading was just right and I intersected my trail about 200 yards from where I left the lake in the morning. It was pretty much as dark as it was going to get by the time I reached the tent at about 5:00 pm. I checked the thermometer on the plane on the way past and it was -35F.

Trapping

Ed was already back, with hot water going and dinner started. About a quart of warm Tang later, I dug into the main course—Trio sliced dried potatoes with soup mix and chopped up dried moose meat. That evening, we discussed what we had seen as we prepared our traps and bait for the next day. The first time on a new 'line is always really fun and I had thoroughly enjoyed myself and seen just enough marten sign to be optimistic about catching a few. There was nowhere near the sign we had seen on the lower Malemute Fork and our goal of getting 100 marten was starting to look a little optimistic, but we were committed now and resigned to make the most of it. With the temperature at -35F, I wasn't keen on trying to get the plane going anyway.

Life in a wall tent at those cold temperatures requires unusual dress. We had our bunny boots, wool pants, and wool long underwear on, but were stripped down to our T-shirts on top and the air temperature at head level when we stood up was probably 80 degrees. I learned early on the key to making a wall tent comfortable in the extreme cold is to have an "L-shaped" sitting/sleeping bench at least two feet off the floor with the stove dug down to solid ground right inside one of the door flaps. That door flap is then permanently closed. At night, we put one six-inch diameter dry spruce log in the stove next to one six-inch diameter green birch. When the stove was stoked that way, it put out just a little heat most of the night, but by morning it was pretty much ambient temperature in the tent. We breathed through the wolf ruffs of our parka hoods and within a few hours there was a breathing tunnel of frost. Getting up at night was to be avoided and we drank just enough in the evenings to stay somewhere between dehydrated and having to pee. I was closest to the stove so it was my job to light the fire in the morning. The great thing about wall tents is that they heat up really fast.

The second day was much like the first, but the temperature had again dropped and it was -40F when I headed north to set out my second 'line. I was dressed the same as the previous day—canvas mukluks, wool long underwear, wool pants, T-shirt, turtle neck, flannel shirt, sweater, canvas anorak (pullover) with hood, and my wool hat. On my hands I had Monkey Face cotton work gloves with Air Force mitts over them. For reserve, in my pack I had quilted overpants from Alaska Sleeping Bag Company, my Eddie Bauer parka, and my muskrat hat. With the colder temperature, I also needed a scarf over my mouth and nose to keep from getting frostbite. My second 'line mostly followed a ridge north of the lake, so I got some relief from the cold because of a slight inversion. Everything went according to plan and I was back at the tent at 5:30 pm, just in time to hear the creaking of Ed's snowshoes along the north shore of the lake in the dark. The temperature was obviously still dropping and all I could see of Ed's face when he arrived at the tent were his eyes through the holes in his facemask. I checked the thermometer on the plane and it was -45F.

That night, the birch trees around the tent were popping and cracking and by morning it was -55F. I had seen -65F before in Fairbanks but I never worked outside or trapped in those temperatures. I had read all the Jack London stories, especially *To Build a Fire*, so I thought I knew how quickly things could go bad with any sort of mishap at those temperatures. A tent fire was our main concern, so we spent a little time piling up a big mound of snow. In an emergency, we could dig a snow cave into the pile once it set up. Snow caves are relatively warm and are great for survival but not so great for trapping because it is impossible to dry out clothes inside one.

Because of the cold, we lingered a little longer in the tent that morning, and the subject of food came up. We were still in good shape with lots of Pilot Bread, jam, peanut butter, Trio dried potatoes, oatmeal, tea and Tang. However, it was becoming apparent that, because of the extreme cold, we were eating and drinking more than I planned. I had organized all the food but I neglected to tell Ed I was planning the same thing for breakfast, lunch, and dinner every day for three weeks. I could tell he was a little disappointed but he didn't complain. Ed had his .30-30 along in case there were caribou in the area. I hunted caribou at Norutak Lake in the spring of 1975 and there had also been some caribou groups in the area in the winter of 1976-77 when I was doing caribou work for ADF&G, but the Western Arctic Herd crashed and the range of the herd contracted. There were no caribou wintering there in

Trapping

the winter of 1979-80. In view of the lack of protein in our food supply, we decided we should at least spend some time trying to trap the rabbits that lived in the birch stand and Ed agreed to carry the .30-30 in case he saw any spruce grouse along his 'lines. We figured we could always eat marten too if we got really desperate.

As if on cue, about the time we finished our discussion about meat and I went out of the tent to see if the temperature was really still -55F, I saw a small group of ptarmigan land at the edge of the lake next to the plane. The noise from their wings was really loud in the cold air. Ed grabbed the .30-30, ran to the edge of the lake, and took a bead on one of the birds. At the shot, one bird exploded and five took off. The bird he hit was in three pieces—a gut pile, a gutted body nearby with one leg missing, and the leg about ten feet away in the snow. There were also some small pieces of muscle tissue scattered about. Ed got down on his hands and knees and picked up all the parts and pieces, cleaned them up a bit and threw them into the dinner pot.

Although we got a late start that third day, we still headed out to set up as much as we could on our last 'lines. The difference between -45F and -55F was noticeable. I went as fast as I could, carrying my axe in my hand making pole sets like a mad man, sometimes running between sets while breaking trail. Even at that pace, I was just barely staying warm the way I was dressed. I made a quick lunch fire about 1:00 pm and it felt good but I had to put on my overpants and parka to stay comfortable, despite the fire. After lunch, I left my parka and overpants on and finished up the 'line. I was warm to start but had to be constantly on guard about freezing my nose or cheeks. I didn't have a face mask like Ed did, relying instead on a scarf to keep my nose and cheeks from freezing. It was later than normal when I set out my last trap and concentrated on getting back. I figured I had at least a mile to go when I realized I was starting to cool down, even though I was walking as fast as I could with all the clothing I had on and nothing left in reserve. For about 30 minutes, I hadn't been sure of where I was and got the compass out for a quick direction check. I was headed slightly wrong so I corrected my line of travel, realizing I had probably lengthened the trip back by a good half mile. When I finally came out on the lake, I had about a half mile to go to the tent. I knew I would make it but couldn't help thinking about how much further I could have gone given the temperature and my energy level. I could easily see how dehydration, hypothermia, darkness, and fear of getting lost could cause panic and irrational behavior. More than once that day I thought about the man in *To Build a Fire*.

Ed had been back for a while when I arrived at the tent and he was relieved to see me. We talked about the cold a lot and it took me a couple of hours to get rehydrated and really feeling warm again. He had frostbitten a couple of fingers and was working on getting them going again. I checked the thermometer on the way past the plane and it still said -55F. For the next several days, the thermometer never varied more than a degree or two and that small variation was probably due to the fact it was a coil spring thermometer and I was rapping on it to see if it was stuck. At least we had all our 'lines out and the remaining work would be a piece of cake compared to those first three days, despite the cold. We still had about 20 traps left, mostly Conibears, and planned to use those to beef up parts of the 'lines where sign was best and to replace the Conibears that caught marten. The bulk of the work was over and we celebrated with the ptarmigan and potato dinner. The fresh meat was a welcome addition to the meal. It tasted so good, in fact, that I decided to try to catch a rabbit with a #1 Victor long-spring that I had not yet set for marten. Rabbits found the tops of the birches we cut for firewood and were girdling the bark off the cut branches every night. I placed the trap on a few birch branches next to some freshly cut birch branches and covered it with a piece of waxed paper and a little snow.

We were getting somewhat accustomed to the extreme cold and despite some minor frostbite on fingers, noses and cheeks, we were having a pretty good time. We stopped stoking up the stove before going to bed at night, finding it easier to just let it go out. There was less chance of a tent fire that way. The stovepipe didn't plug up with creosote and we used less wood. Even without the stove going, we were warm at night in our arctic bags on top of caribou skin pads on the snow sleeping bench that was covered with spruce boughs. Getting into and out of the bags, getting comfortable, and getting the drafts under control as the tent cooled down was a bit of an ordeal. Once in bed, we were loath to move before morning. Unfortunately, that was the main problem with the rabbit trapping plan. About 3:00 am, a rabbit started squealing—just like the dying rabbit predator call. I was on the outside, and it was my set, so I got up, slid my mukluks on, grabbed a piece of firewood for a club and went out to deal with the bunny. I didn't want to get my hands bloody by cleaning it so I just brought it into the tent and put it under the foot of my caribou pad on the sleeping bench, where I hoped it wouldn't freeze solid.

We were a little later getting going in the morning. The exertion, dehydration, hypothermia, and frostbite of the previous day had taken its toll, and the interrupted sleep caused by the trapped rabbit didn't help. We anticipated a shorter day anyway and thought the first check would only take about five hours, instead of the nine or ten hours we had been working.

We left the tent just as the sun was peeking over the horizon about 11:00 am. I was better dressed than the day before and planned to go slower and therefore get less dehydrated. I was walking steadily along, calculating the expected catch on my way to the first set. I was confident in my 15 sets on that 'line and I was going to be disappointed if I brought back less than seven or eight marten. The first set was empty with no sign. Nearing the second set, there were fresh marten tracks in the trail and I expected to see a marten hanging from the pole. The tracks went right by, except where the marten broke stride to look up at the wing hanging from the end of the pole. The next set was even more disappointing. A marten had come to the set, obviously interested, and spent a while jumping up and down under the wing attractor. It didn't try to climb the pole and finally went off down the trail. The story at most of the remaining sets was similar. Marten had come by but either acted totally uninterested or interested enough to jump for the wing attractor but not enough to climb the pole. The next to last set had a nice male marten but I spent time on the trip back pondering whether we should remake all the sets.

Trapping

We both got back to the tent at about the same time, with just a little twilight left. Ed was equally disappointed. Like mine, most of his sets had been visited by marten, but they generally wouldn't climb the pole and he only caught a couple. The next day, I headed out to do the 'line north of camp that was on the higher ground with bigger trees. I was hoping the marten that lived in taller trees would be more likely to climb. It was a vain hope. By the time I covered half the 'line, I had caught nothing. At a couple of the sets, it seemed like the marten really wanted the bait or the wing but couldn't figure out that climbing the leaning pole was the way to get there. I shook my head in disbelief at how stupid they were acting. Then I started re-thinking my decision to make pole sets in the first place. Although they are a standard set for marten, I had heard stories about marten that wouldn't climb poles. I guess I only half believed them. The only real reason to use pole sets is to avoid mouse damage to the fur and keep the set working when snow accumulates. The mice were not abundant and in the extreme cold they mostly stayed under the snow.

I began remaking all the pole sets into cubby sets. So much for the hard work being over! After a while, I came up with a quick new set I thought would be pretty effective. While walking along, I grabbed a dead spruce pole that was close to my trail, stuck it in the snow at an angle next to the trail, punched a hole in the snow with my Air Force mitt, and then wired a trap to the pole. It worked with both Conibears and leg-hold traps, with the traps held off the snow with small sticks. Next, I simply threw a piece of bait into the bottom of the hole and tied the wing to the leaning pole right above the trap. Bundled up the way I was at -55F, I was still able to make a set in about five minutes. At some of the original pole sets, I just took down the pole, drove it into the snow with the trap still attached, and punched a hole into the snow next to it.

The following day we completely remade all the sets into cubbies on our third 'lines, so it was a long day. Over the next two days we got most of the other sets reconfigured and we were finally starting to pick up some marten, but then the unexpected happened. I was about an hour from the tent, coming down my north 'line when I heard an airplane in the direction of the tent. It was only the second airplane I heard since Andy came by with our food on the second day. The local Fish and Wildlife Protection officer, Joe Abrams, had flown over us the day after Andy came in, and I thought it might be him. I thought it must be someone looking for us because the plane sounded like it landed and nobody in their right mind would be flying at -55F. I went as fast as I could but arrived at the tent just as the plane took off. Ed was there. He said because of the intense cold and no prospect of it getting warmer any time soon, Audrey and co-workers at ADF&G started to worry about us. Jim Davis agreed to fly his PA-12 up to check on us and convince us to come back to Fairbanks and wait for cold snap to end. He found out from Andy that we were at Norutak Lake. When he landed late in the day, my Piper Cub had about an inch of hoarfrost all over it, the fire was out in the tent and he could barely feel any warmth left, so he wasn't sure if we were OK or not. As he was about to leave, Ed came trudging along. It took a while before they could communicate because Ed's facemask was frozen solid to his beard and mustache and all he could do was mumble. They had to build a fire in the wood stove and thaw out Ed's face before they could talk.

Jim left some extra food with Ed and a couple more gasoline catalytic heaters for getting the plane going and said he would expect us in Bettles the next day or call out the search and rescue. At first, Jim's plan seemed to make a tolerable situation worse, but on further reflection I realized that we would have run out of food before it warmed up and we would eventually have to face the problem of getting the little 90 hp Cub going in the extreme cold. I had never tried to get my plane, or any plane, going at -55F. In those days, portable generators and electric heaters were big, heavy, and expensive, and most people in the Bush used gasoline catalytic heaters, or Coleman one-burner stoves with a length of stovepipe going up into the cowling. Both systems put a lot of moisture into the engine compartment and the cabin. Unless the temperature got high enough, the spark plugs would frost over and not fire. Once that happened it took a lot of dry heat to get the engine going.

Getting the plane preheated the next morning was a long ordeal, despite having the heaters in it overnight. Draining the oil and heating it later on the wood stove would have helped, but I had not done that. I put two gasoline catalytic heaters in the engine compartment, and one in the cabin under the instruments. In the morning we also got a one-burner Coleman going with a stovepipe up into the cowling. Planes have burned up that way, so we watched it closely while we used ropes to get the frost off the wings and lifted up the skis to scrape the frost from the ski bottoms.

About noon, we were finally ready to give it a shot. I had to hand prop that plane because it had no battery or electrical system. Much to my relief, the engine started but would only run as long as I had carburetor heat on. We warmed it up a good, long time while breathing into our coats to prevent the windows from fogging over more than they already had from the catalytic heaters. After about five minutes running, there still was no oil pressure but I assumed it was because the oil was gelled in the line to the gauge. At full power the plane finally began to move toward the runway and gradually picked up speed on the packed surface. We used up the whole packed part of the runway and then went off into the deep snow. At that temperature the surface of the packed snow was like sandpaper although underneath the soft snow it was mostly granular and the skis slid a little better. After a ground run of about 2,500 feet we finally got airborne. The engine would have had about 15% more power if I could have taken the carburetor heat off but it wouldn't run that way. The avgas just wouldn't vaporize sufficiently without the addition of carburetor heat at those temperatures.

About the time we lifted off, the tachometer pegged out on the right side of the dial and started making a horrible screaming noise. I wasn't confident the engine would even keep running so I climbed gradually as I circled the lake. We eventually reached 2,500 feet and the temperature warmed to -10F. The tach stopped screaming, we finally had oil pressure after flying for about 15 minutes, and the heater hose was starting to put out enough heat to defrost the windows. We lined out towards Bettles and I thought the worst was over until I started seeing oil spots on the front windshield. The oil spray didn't really get bad and I had enough altitude that I could have picked a lake to land on if we needed to. We made it to Bettles after losing about a quart of oil and it turned out the crankcase breather was plugged and pressure in the crankcase was forcing oil out of the nose seal. We rendezvoused with Jim, examined the nose seal, and thawed out the breather tube. There was more air movement at Bettles and it was a little warmer there—about -40F. We flew back to Fairbanks together with our big catch of marten— all of about a dozen of them.

I waited out the cold spell in Fairbanks and finally went back up to Norutak Lake with Audrey to pull the 'line in late February. Audrey weighed about 60 pounds less than Ed and I figured I could get everything out in one load with her. The weather remained clear and cold with no appreciable snow in several weeks, but by late February the sun was at least warming things up to above -20F and we were finally able to ski the 'lines. With the longer daylight and skis, we were able to run all six lines in just three days. The catch was better too, and we had about 20 marten and two red foxes in the traps. I was pleasantly surprised that after three weeks of not checking the 'line, there had been little mouse damage and no cannibalism.

The marten were all top quality and we averaged $52 at the March 1980 Seattle Fur Exchange sale. After paying the expenses on the airplane (about $17/hour—or $200) and settling up the food bill, we each pocketed about $750. It wasn't a lot, but close to a month's pay for almost a month's work, so we were both happy.

I also learned a lot about the cold and about marten behavior, and I got in pretty good shape too. The cold was pretty extreme for me but it could have been worse. In 1971 and again in 1989, record lows in the upper Koyukuk basin were around -80F which was more than 20 degrees colder than the -55F we trapped in. I still don't have a good explanation about why the marten wouldn't climb poles, but after that trip I heard more firsthand stories from long-time marten trappers like Gary Bamford on the Hogatza River, and Sydney Huntington, and John Burns. The trip also set a few personal records for me that I have never broken and certainly have no plans to try, including the coldest temperature I have ever tried to get an airplane flying.

And that super abundance of marten on the lower Malamute Fork? No one ever did trap there that winter or the next.

Trapping wolves with the Super Cub

After I stopped regularly running the trapline on Minto Flats in the early 1990s, I continued trapping wolves with my Super Cub, first with Ed Crain as a partner, and then with Dave Kellyhouse after Ed moved to Petersburg. Ed and Dave were both biologists and colleagues at ADF&G and also good and enthusiastic wolf trappers. Our usual method was to fly around and look for kills where we could land within reasonable walking distance. The trapping regulations had been changed and clarified about using moose meat for trap bait. It was now legal to set traps around natural kills made by wolves.

Wolves will return to many of the kills they make, no matter how old they are, especially if kills are on natural travel routes, like rivers and lakes. Some wolves can be very wary of human scent or even tracks in the snow, so it pays to be careful. It is best not to walk on wolf trails, and helps to use clean gloves when making sets. It is also important to set the pan tension on traps to between 10 and 15 pounds, especially where traps are set near kills, otherwise the traps will just catch ravens, foxes, wolverines, or other non-target species. Our normal routine was to go to areas where we knew no other trappers were working and then to fly rivers and creeks, looking for wolf tracks. We would then track the wolves to a kill. On most weekends we would find one or two kills to set up. After we had five or six kills set up, we stopped looking for new kills and just checked and maintained the traps and snares we already had out. On average, we probably caught one wolf for each kill we set. Sometimes the wolves never came back to the kill, or it snowed too much and the traps and snares stopped working, or the wolves just didn't get caught. It was exciting work and good exercise, but considering the expenses of running the plane and the fact that a lot of the wolves in Interior Alaska had lice or *follicular dysplasia*, there was no real profit in it.

On one occasion, what appeared to be a very chancy and likely unproductive set turned out to be the most successful set we ever made. We were looking for wolf tracks along Beaver Creek and just at the mouth of Victoria Creek I saw an old wolf track and then an old piece of moose hide about 50 feet off the river bank. Since we hadn't seen any better prospects and it was getting late, we decided to set it up. Snow conditions were good for landing on the river nearby, so we landed and set eight snares around what turned out to be a very old kill. We checked the set from the air a week later, after some snow and wind, but we could not see any sign that wolves had been around. The following week, there was even more snow and lots more wind, so much so I couldn't really even tell where the set was anymore. On about the fourth or fifth circle I saw one very faint old wolf track so we decided we better check the set from the ground. The problem was that with all the wind and new overflow on the river we had to land a mile upstream. I was sorry we decided to make the set because it was looking like a big investment of time and effort without any likely return. After landing and walking a mile to the set, it took us a while to find it in the wind-blown snow, but we finally found all eight snares, one by one. They held five wolves and a wolverine. Our best set, ever!

Although three of the wolves and the wolverine had decent fur, one of the wolves was very poor and the fifth was a small, brown, mousy-looking female with no fur value. The next problem was getting everything back to the plane. We didn't have a plastic sled or pack frames, so I decided to make a place to land in the willows along a narrow slough nearby. That took us an hour or more of cutting willows, and then I brought the plane up and loaded the three best wolves and the wolverine and took them straight to Fairbanks. I returned for Ed a couple of hours later and we buried the two last wolves in the snow, to be picked up later.

The only animal we caught in our wolf sets, besides wolves and wolverines, was a yearling moose. It was caught by the nose in a wolf snare. We flew back to Fairbanks, picked up some Xylazine at the ADFG&G office, and returned to let the moose go. We gave the moose a very light dose, took the snare off, and headed for the plane. After a hundred yards or so, I looked around. Much to my surprise, the yearling moose was following us. We tried running to get ahead and leave it behind, but it just sped up. It just wouldn't leave us alone and wanted to be within ten feet of us all the time. We took a couple of humorous pictures but then I wanted to get going and take off. The moose now became a problem. I was afraid the moose would walk into the propeller if I started the engine. I told Ed to lead the moose away and I'd start the plane and taxi along and then he could run to the moving plane and dive in as it went by. We managed the maneuver successfully and as soon as Ed was mostly inside, I opened the throttle with the door still open. After we were airborne, I closed the door and circled to look at the moose. It was just standing around looking confused about where we had gone. It was late enough in the spring so that it would have been leaving its mother soon anyway, but I still felt a bit sorry for it nevertheless.

Open Water Beaver Trapping

Open water beaver trapping is not something most trappers associate with Alaska. I wouldn't have thought about it either, but in 2006, Audrey and I started a new wolverine research project at Thomas Bay on the mainland near Petersburg, in Southeast Alaska. We wanted to radio-collar about ten wolverines and to do that we needed bait to catch them. Beavers are like candy to just about any carnivore, so I passed the word in Petersburg that we would buy beaver carcasses for $50 each. The problem was that no one seemed to be trapping beavers that winter.

We then tried buying cheap pork roasts and using them for bait. The wolverines turned them down. It was an indication the local wolverines were not short of food that winter. One pork roast hung at a camera trap for about two weeks without being touched by anything except Steller's jays. One day, while going by the camera trap, I remembered we were low on meat and didn't have anything good for dinner, so I grabbed the pork roast off the bait cable and took it back to the cabin. I cut the slimy outside layer off the roast and cooked up the rest. It was most delicious, and very tender. We had seen wolverines do the same thing with rotten meat (which they don't usually like). They remove the slimy, rotten outside layer, and then eat the inside which is tender, but not nearly so rotten. I also remembered from a mammalogy class taught by professor Dale Guthrie at the University of Alaska that there are no dangerous bacteria or toxins in rotten, uncooked meat, as long as the meat has oxygen available as it rots. Rotten meat that is cooked, or meat that rots in an anaerobic environment, is a completely different story. Meat that rots in plastic bags, for example, is at high risk for botulism.

To solve the bait problem, I decided to trap beaver myself and ordered some different sizes of Conibear-style killing traps. It turned out to be a very fun and rewarding trapping experience and I learned a lot about beavers and land otters in Southeast Alaska in the process. Compared with beavers in Interior Alaska, the Southeast beavers have a tough life. They have a very limited choice of foods and don't get as large as a result. Blueberry (*Vaccinium spp.*) is probably their major food, followed by water lilly roots and spruce bark. Red alder, which is abundant, is seldom eaten. Willow, birch, and aspen that make up the bulk of the diet of beavers in Interior Alaska are either absent or rare in Southeast Alaska. I have seen where beavers eat hemlock bark in Southeast Alaska and on Afognak Island. Beavers occasionally use spruce for building material in Interior Alaska but I have rarely seen them eat it. It is not uncommon for beavers in Southeast Alaska to live in a spot for a few years, eat all the accessible food and then either get killed by wolves when they range too far to find food, or they abandon the place in search of another food source. Once the surrounding blueberry and water lilies recover years later, dispersing beavers find the spot again and set up a colony until the food runs out once more.

On the mainland across from Petersburg, I found several beaver ponds and one dam complex several hundred yards long and four to

During the 1990s, I trapped wolves by finding natural kills in the Alaska Range and the White Mountains. The pelts of wolves were generally very good in the mountains of Interior Alaska through the 1990s. After 2000, many more wolves had poor quality pelts throughout Interior Alaska.

six feet high. These flowages were accessible from old logging roads with either the 4-wheeler or snowmachine. Several of the winters were very snowy and rainy and it was a new experience for me to be driving a snowmachine around in pouring down rain with full rain gear on, looking for places to make beaver sets.

I first started by making some castor mound sets along the shorelines of lakes and ponds in the flowages. Beavers make small mounds of vegetation around lakes and ponds and then mark them with oily, scented secretions from their anal glands to establish the boundaries of their family territory. Putting out the castor of a strange beaver causes the resident beavers to investigate. I quickly discovered that castor mound sets work much better with foot-hold traps than Conibears because the beaver is moving slowly and carefully when approaching the set. I have nothing against foot-hold traps for beavers, but they are more cumbersome to use than kill traps because they require setting up a drowning wire or rod. You also have to be careful to set them at least six inches under water to avoid catching ducks. Because I didn't have foothold traps handy, I stopped using castor mound sets. I also wanted to save most of the beaver castors for attracting wolverines to camera traps and live-traps.

Next, I tried tying bait (blueberry branches, apples, or carrots) to the triggers of Conibears set just under the water. Those sets were largely unsuccessful, even though the traps were sometimes sprung. The beavers didn't seem to really care much for any of that bait. I read that beavers have a reputation for being very easy to trap unless they have an opportunity to learn, but once they get trap-shy they can be virtually impossible to catch. Since I was new at trapping beavers in open water, I needed to experiment with new sets but didn't want to miss too many beavers and thus give them an opportunity to learn to avoid the traps. At Minto, Jim, Rod, and I trapped quite a few beavers but there were so many it didn't matter if some learned to avoid traps. In Southeast it was a different story. There aren't many beavers, so if a few beavers learn to avoid traps, trapping success can really suffer.

Finally, I started setting natural beaver runs in shallow channels connecting ponds, places around the edges of ponds where beavers had to duck under logs, and places where beavers slide over their own dams. These sets proved to be very successful and I seldom had a trap triggered with no beaver in it. One of my favorite sets was a #330 Conibear placed just under the water with a stick anchored on the surface between the opposing side of the trap. The unsuspecting swimming beaver would duck under the stick and pass through the Conibear and trigger it.

One of the traps I decided to try was a Duke #330 magnum (a large Conibear-style killing trap, with a 10x9-inch opening). When it arrived in the mail brand new, I had a devil of a time just trying to set it; the springs were extremely strong. I also realized that if I caught myself in it while I was alone without the right tools to compress the springs, I'd be wearing it all the way back to the cabin, maybe with a broken hand or wrist. I decided then to always carry a six-foot piece of rope with a loop in one end in my raincoat pocket, so that I could always compress the springs of the big Conibears in an emergency, even with just one hand. Because of the smaller size of beavers in Southeast Alaska, #280 Conibears also worked very well and were easier to carry and less dangerous.

All of the traps I used, including the #280 and #330 Conibear-type traps were very effective at catching beavers and I liked using them because the beavers died very quickly. In one case, a beaver died so quickly there was no disturbance to the set at all and I missed finding the beaver the first time I checked it. I walked right by the set, assuming a caught beaver would disturb the appearance of the set enough that I would notice. The second time I came by, I decided to take a closer look and saw a 45-pound beaver dead in the submerged Conibear with not a stick out of place.

I also made sets on slides at the bottom of beaver dams. At first, I really liked these sets because the beavers were going fast down the slide with no time to look for a possible trap. After I caught two otters in those sets, I began to realize these would not be good sets after April 15th, when the otter season closed and otters begin to have their pups. After the first week of April, I switched back to using underwater sets in ponds and lakes, where otters are less likely to travel. I also went back to using Conibears with the bait wired to the trigger. I tried both carrots and potatoes for bait again, but never caught a beaver that way. Water lily roots would probably be worth trying, because beavers eat a lot of those wherever they are available in Southeast Alaska.

In one case I also tried using snares set on the inlet of a small lake. Snares are very effective in Interior Alaska when set under the ice. In open water, snares are much more difficult to use. It is not hard to catch the beaver with a snare in open water, but the snare set has to be designed to drown the beaver too, and that requires rigging a drowning wire to force the beaver into deep water. I did catch one beaver in a snare attached to the top of a red alder tree I cut for a drag. When I checked the set, the drag was gone and the anchor of the drowning wire had come loose. I finally saw an alder bush leaving a wake behind it in the middle of the lake, which was 100 yards long and 50 yards wide. It was the beaver towing the tree around the lake. Every time the beaver saw me it would swim to the opposite side of the lake. When I'd circle the lake, the beaver would swim back to the other side. I finally jumped up and down, yelling on one side of the lake, then quietly backed away and snuck around in a big circle through the woods and came running up to the shore on the opposite side. The beaver saw me and swam as fast as it could, towing the alder behind it, but I ran out into the water, which quickly went over the top of my hip boots, and just managed to grab the end of the alder and pull the beaver in to shore. I was soaking wet from both exertion and going over my hip boots, but being wet most of the time seemed almost normal for outdoor winter life in Southeast Alaska. I had way too many hours invested in that beaver, so I gave up on snaring and relied only on the Conibear-type traps after that episode.

Over the two winters, I trapped 28 beavers and froze most of the carcasses for wolverine bait. I also weighed all of the beavers to compare the weights with Interior beavers and I saved the castors and oil glands for wolverine lure. The heaviest beaver I weighed was 48 pounds. In Interior Alaska, it is not uncommon to get 55-pound beavers. The biggest Jim, Rod, and I weighed from Minto was about 65 pounds. The weight of a beaver seems to be pretty much a function of the quality and quantity of the food they get. I have read about corn-fed beavers in Iowa that have weighed 95 pounds. I skinned all the beavers and had all the skins tanned and gave them away to people who helped us with the wolverine project. I am a slow beaver skinner, partly because I still close-skin them with a curved beaver knife. It takes me about an hour and a half per beaver to skin them, flesh them, and get them stretched round on a piece of plywood, so I had quite a few hours of labor invested in those beaver hides. They were very beautiful though, and they made nice presents for the many people who helped with the project.

We trapped beavers to use as bait during the wolverine study at Thomas Bay in Southeast Alaska. The tanned pelts made great gifts for people who helped with study.

End

Printed in the USA
CPSIA information can be obtained
at www.ICGtesting.com
LVHW020829230124
769607LV00065B/11